She Made Me Laugh

My Friend Nora Ephron

RICHARD COHEN

SIMON & SCHUSTER

New York   London   Toronto   Sydney   New Delhi

Simon & Schuster
1230 Avenue of the Americas
New York, NY 10020

First Simon & Schuster hardcover edition September 2016

SIMON & SCHUSTER and colophon are registered trademarks of Simon & Schuster, Inc.

For information about special discounts for bulk purchases, please contact Simon & Schuster Special Sales at 1-866-506-1949 or business@simonandschuster.com.

The Simon & Schuster Speakers Bureau can bring authors to your live event. For more information or to book an event, contact the Simon & Schuster Speakers Bureau at 1-866-248-3049 or visit our website at www.simonspeakers.com.

Interior design by Ruth Lee-Mui

Manufactured in the United States of America

1   3   5   7   9   10   8   6   4   2

Library of Congress Cataloging-in-Publication Data

Names: Cohen, Richard M. (Richard Martin), 1941– author.
Title: She made me laugh : my friend Nora Ephron / Richard Cohen.
Description: New York : Simon & Schuster, 2016.
Identifiers: LCCN 2016025849 (print) | LCCN 2016029390 (ebook) |
ISBN 9781476796123 (hardback) | ISBN 9781476796130 (paperback) |
ISBN 9781476796147 (ebook)
Subjects: LCSH: Ephron, Nora—Friends and associates. | Women authors—
United States—Biography. | Women journalists—United States—Biography. |
Women motion picture producers and directors—United States—Biography. |
Cohen, Richard M. (Richard Martin), 1941—Friends and associates. | BISAC:
BIOGRAPHY & AUTOBIOGRAPHY / Entertainment & Performing Arts. |
BIOGRAPHY & AUTOBIOGRAPHY / Personal Memoirs. |
PERFORMING ARTS / Film & Video / General.
Classification: LCC PS3555.P5 Z55 2016 (print) | LCC PS3555.P5 (ebook) |
DDC 814/.54 [B] —dc23
LC record available at https://lccn.loc.gov/2016025849

ISBN 978-1-4767-9612-3
ISBN 978-1-4767-9614-7 (ebook)

For Patricia . . .

Introduction

Life is about seat assignments.

You're born in a certain place to certain parents in a certain family, sent to a certain school where you're assigned a certain seat. It was no different on June 17, 1968 when at the age of twenty-seven and with the studied pose of a newspaperman, I was assigned a certain desk in the newsroom of the *Washington Post*. On either side of me were people who I have since forgotten, but directly behind me was the man who was going to get everything rolling. He was Carl Bernstein, who would introduce me to Nora Ephron, who would introduce me to the world that I would inhabit for the next forty years or so. She would become my friend, ultimately my best friend, my mentor as a writer, my counselor when I was troubled, my role model in showing what was possible and the doorman to the rest of the world. With the sweetest of smiles, she would set my table and serve my food and bring me to the theater and to the movies over and over again. She would introduce me to her friends, who were sometimes famous, sometimes not, who were always talented and always smart, who had great humor and who lived immense lives, sometimes with blockbuster movies and sometimes with worthy but obscure novels, finally, to her final and lasting husband, Nick, a writer of classic film-noirish screenplays, a successful author, a former police reporter, a man of the film-noirish street and the literary salon whose great strength was his reserve and whose mission was to make Nora Ephron happy. He succeeded.

She had come at me like a gale. She had come down to Washington, dropping the names of the famous, making exotic references, wearing the clothes of the 1970s but the aura of the 1950s and 1960s—Broadway and Hollywood and, of course, tabloid Manhattan where she had worked. She was a lot of talk, so it took a while to discern that she was all-purpose, straight on, like some sort of sleek torpedo, steaming to a career that had been mapped for her by her parents, particularly her mother. Phoebe Ephron would die before she should have, of drink and dashed hopes, but her life had really been a triumph. She was a woman in an age of girls, a writer for the Broadway stage and the Hollywood film, who had abandoned the steno pad for the writer's tablet and the typewriter—who was doing what few women of the time did, and all the while raising four girls.

She died before I could know her, but nevertheless I know her. She is smart and she is tart and she is warm and she is cold. She writes fast and well and sets a swell table and she will not be confined by any supposed roles for women. She is a writer and she will write until she can write no more. I know her from her daughters, especially Nora, and I respect her for what she did and I am in awe of her for what she was. Nora modeled herself on Dorothy Parker, the writer and wit from the middle of the twentieth century, but Nora did better than that, and the reason she did was because her mother showed her how.

Nora Ephron was not an orthodox feminist. She quibbled and sometimes quarreled with the movement, but she supported it totally and her life was one of full-throated feminism. She loved being a woman—loved it for all its feminine virtues—and loved being one of the girls. She surrounded herself with women, sought out the talented ones, gave them lunch, encouraged their careers, understood their problems as a man could not—and, if she could, made cookies for their children.

Nora wrote about her parents, but not about her own family. There are no cute essays about what her boys did growing up—the usual sitcom calamities of childhood—but her motherhood was fully engaged and enveloping. She was proud of her boys, Jacob and Max—proud of their talents (writing, music), proud of their independence, and proud of their courage. She was never a typical woman, but in many respects she was a typical mother.

For almost forty years, Nora Ephron was a very close friend. But I worked on only one project with her, a script that went nowhere. Aside from her husband, she was probably closest to her sister, Delia. The two collaborated on many projects, movies and plays, while at the same time pursuing independent careers. As sisters and writing partners they had their ups and downs, but never an irrevocable breach. As Nora was dying, Delia sat at her bedside while the two of them worked on a pilot for a television series.

Nick, too, was an occasional writing partner. They worked on a remake of *Love Me or Leave Me*, a Doris Day–James Cagney vehicle about the torch singer Ruth Etting, but as is frequently the case in Hollywood, it never got made. (Movies that don't get made can't bomb.) Informally, however, they collaborated on everything they did. They were both writers, just like Nora's mother and father. Nick was the husband Phoebe never had. Nora was the Phoebe that Phoebe could never quite be.

I found Nora's life to be bigger than I had ever imagined—deeper and even more heroic, too. She was central to the lives of so many people. She gave money to causes she favored—the Public Theater, for one—and time to people who simply asked. She was my peerless tugboat, nudging me this way and that. We went through a lot, often together—usually laughing, sometimes crying, always relishing our dumb luck. I am not sure which is better—to have loved her or to be loved by her. Either way was a blessing. Either way, it began with a seat assignment.

She Made Me Laugh

Room 242

As she went in and out of consciousness, she was typically observing the process. "In out, in out," she said. "So it's happening." The room, 242 of New York Hospital, faced south, so if she raised her head she could see down the East River and, over a bit to the west, the skyline of midtown Manhattan. This was her city. She had come from the West to claim it, to make it her own, to know its writers and actors and politicians, but especially the writers because she was one herself, her fame as a director notwithstanding.

People drifted in and out of the room. Husband. Children. Friends. Relatives. Her dying was taking longer than expected. She had acute myeloid leukemia and it had devolved into the inevitable and unavoidable pneumonia, and so the end was coming, although it was taking its own sweet time. She was awake and then asleep. Sometimes alert. Sometimes not. She lost track of time, once asking in late afternoon to watch an early morning TV show, *Morning Joe*. Outside, the river reversed course as estuaries do, sometimes going north, sometimes going south. It seemed apt.

Calls were being made. The famous, the somewhat less famous; the talented, the brilliant; the immensely rich, the merely rich, the non-rich; the established writers, the young writers; the struggling young actors, the struggling older actors; Hollywood, New York, East Hampton, Paris, London, and the African American neighborhood of distant Riverhead on Long Island where she had put her longtime maid's daughter through college.

A summoning was in process, a call to assemble for a memorial service. There would be no funeral, no imprecations to a god she did not believe existed. (She was mystified that anyone could believe otherwise, and she abhorred the senseless platitude that "everything happens for a reason.") So a call went out to various halls—the Ethical Culture School on Manhattan's Upper West Side and the Council on Foreign Relations on the Upper East Side. Too small. They were all too small. Slowly, it became apparent that a larger hall would have to be secured, something with about a thousand seats. Word of her impending death was spreading, and you could feel a stirring, a deep pain, a tsunami of bereavement that was building and building and which now seems appropriate but at the time was a surprise.

I sat on the bed and talked to her. I told her how much she was loved, about all the love in the room. She raised herself and looked out the window, south to the skyline. She extended her left arm and scooped Manhattan into her. "And out there," she said.

So she could feel it. It didn't surprise her as much as it did the rest of us. Still, she was a writer, and writers do not have the deaths of celebrities—the kitschy mourning of strangers, the sad bodega flowers, TV tears, and then the sign-off from the anchor, "She will be missed." Writers just slip away. They get an obit in the *Times*, maybe, and then a small gathering in some dreary West Side apartment, and then, with any luck or some pull and the proper ethnic bona fides, interment in the weathered cemeteries of the Hamptons. Nora would have scoffed at that, anyway—the last-minute lunge toward religion. It was always dangerous to die while Nora was alive. She had things to say.

Out there, past her outstretched arm, something was happening. There was a movement, a swelling, a something in the zeitgeist—a rolling groan of impending misery. She could feel it and she did not scoff at it because it was real and genuine. She had it coming, she seemed to feel. She had earned it.

But the rest of us were somehow, maybe inexplicably, amazed. Her family, her friends, the doctors chosen by her and thus credentialed as both brilliant and famous—all felt it. And were stunned. Yes, she was sort of famous and she had directed movies, written acclaimed screenplays and best sellers, and even had plays both on and off Broadway and another show in the works. There had been hints. Her books sold really well. And when she made an appearance, throngs materialized. We who knew her, we who had been her friends, we who loved her (not always or all the time), we who still hear her voice on the phone—"Hello, it's Nora."—were too close to see what was happening.

The sorrow came through the window, up off the East River, and it had a power. Afterward, some young person wrote a tribute to her in the *Washington Post*. His name was James McCauley. He had known her. She had made time for him while he was at Harvard and had stayed in touch after he went to work as an intern on the editorial staff of the *Post*. I was her friend. I was a longtime *Washington Post* columnist. I knew nothing about the young man.

There was an item in the newspaper about Nora and the writer Nathan Englander. He had written a short story about Stalin's murder of the Soviet Union's most acclaimed Yiddish writers. It was called "The 27th Man," and it was contained in a collection that Nora had read. The item said that Nora had gotten in touch with Englander and arranged a breakfast at Barney Greengrass, the famous West Side deli. She told him his story could be a play. She told him she would help him. From then on, they met from time to time. The play opened at the Public Theater in December of 2012. Nora had died in June.

I was stunned by the newspaper item. Yiddish writers? Nora could hardly have cared less. A writer on Jewish themes? Not my darling Nora. She once sat through one of my Passover Seders like a traveler marooned in a train station. She abhorred religion. She abhorred my sanctimonious Judaism, erratically and idiosyncratically practiced in delayed homage to the Holocaust. But here she was helping to write a play about Yiddish writers. And she had said nothing to me about the project—me who consumed Jewish history and was, even then, writing a book about Jews and Israel.

I emailed Englander. I confessed mystification. "I know you're busy, but I'd like to meet you and also get to know Nora better," I wrote. "I'd even go to Brooklyn."

We met for lunch. I wanted to know more. I wanted to know the Nora he knew. The Nora the kid at the *Post* knew. The Nora whom others were writing about, notably Lena Dunham. Some of these people turned to me to ask similar questions. I had the answers, they thought. I was her friend, her best friend she had told others, and I knew her better than anyone. Whether that was true I still don't know, but I do know that she knew me better than anyone—including, I'm sure she would add, myself.

I Am Not Now and Never Have Been a Girl

I don't know what I'm doing, writing this book. Nora Ephron was my friend and I knew her well—very well indeed—but I did not know her as well as I thought, or, maybe more important, as well as other people thought. The "other people" were all friends of Nora's and they would often defer to me when it came to knowledge of her, to which I would nod in a combination of amazement and false humility. But I did not know the whole of her life because the whole was so much bigger than I realized—all those friends, so much work, so much written, so many movies made, or written and sometimes not made, so many essays and blogs and mere wisps of articles, some accompanied by recipes, not to mention interviews in which she said the most amazing things—and there is this: I am not a girl.

I state the obvious because it was not, until recently, obvious to me. Of course, I always knew there were gaps in our friendship. We were never lovers, and so I did not know her in that way, but more important—and more germane—was this business of gender, which has nothing to do with sex. On a kind of trivial level, it meant that I never went shopping with her—although she did with me—and we never talked about fashion or purses or cooking or food, and rarely about children, of which she had two and I one. Nora, as countless number of her female friends would tell you, was a girlie girl. Her champagne was pink and her signature cake was called the Pink Cake. She loved being a girl and she was very, very good at it.

Being a woman was extremely important to Nora and, of course, to her readers. She wrote incessantly, not to mention brilliantly, about the problems of being a woman, not just about small breasts and curdled necks and vaginal odor, but about the very essence of being a woman. She raged against beautiful women who complained that their beauty was a handicap—no one took them seriously, they lamented. She, in response, never took them seriously.

Her great fame came from the movies, as a screenwriter first and then a director, then both. In the business—the business is what her parents, screenwriters both, called Hollywood—she was a rarity. The business is not kind to female directors, of which there have been relatively few. A director is kind of a despot, a CEO, a head coach—in other words, a man. Can a woman command? Can she dominate? Can she, if she has to, fire the people who have to go? If challenged, can she push back?

Over the years, Nora proved she could. She fired the kid, the very cute kid, who wasn't working out on *Sleepless in Seattle*—"She fired the kid!" a still disbelieving Tom Hanks exclaimed years later. When the prop man on *Bewitched* contemptuously ignored her instructions about precisely what kind of English muffins to get—the script specified Wolferman's—she fired him, too.

On *Mixed Nuts*, she fired the actor Kadeem Hardison in the first week of shooting. "She didn't think he was delivering," the actor Rita Wilson recalled. "She fired somebody the first week of shooting, which was kind of her tradition to fire somebody the first week of shooting."

At the same time, she oozed thoughtfulness and kindness. While directing *Bewitched*, she not only implored her cast and crew the day before Election Day to vote, but gave them a late call time so that they could. She had a TV monitor placed on the set to get the early East Coast results. On that same movie, she chartered a bus and took everyone down to Langer's, the hallowed Los Angeles delicatessen, so they could have its fabled pastrami sandwiches.

In both New York and L.A., she was forever organizing expeditions to exotic local restaurants and not, as some directors do, eating either by herself or with a select few cast members.

I rarely heard Nora complain about being a woman in Hollywood. She seemed to assume that I understood, which I did in a way. But it was a man's way, which was sympathetic but maybe not empathetic. I was not in her shoes, and those shoes, anyway, seemed to be ballet slippers of some kind. Nora, I thought, could dance above anything (although she, like me, hated to dance). I thought of her as powerful, strong, and immensely capable. I knew she was vulnerable, insecure about matters that for too long I did not take seriously, like her leitmotif about breasts. I read her famous 1972 *Esquire* magazine essay, "A Few Words About Breasts," as a chuckly rant, somewhat exaggerated for comedic effect, not realizing it represented the deep rage of a woman who noticed how a man's eye would drop chest level upon introduction. She had little to stop the eye. She dazzled in other ways. In fact, she dazzled in most ways.

On occasion—maybe on several occasions—I was simply on a different planet, one where men talk to men about women. When Nora was pregnant with Jacob, her firstborn, her gynecologist, Sheldon Cherry, showed her pictures of twins in the womb. Now, this was 1978, and the sonogram was new; pictures of twins had never been taken before. To everyone's surprise, they showed one twin pummeling the other, and since I was a twin myself, Nora summoned me to New York from Washington and I went to see a very nice Dr. Cherry, who showed me the same pictures. Sure enough, one twin—later determined to be the male—was kicking the other, the female. I was stunned by what I saw.

Nora remembered it a bit differently. In a wonderful essay for the *New York Times* titled "Baby," she wrote that one fetus was punching, not kicking, the other. It hardly matters. What does matter is what she wrote about telling me. I was identified as a Washington friend: "I thought he would be interested to know that he probably has genuine cause to resent his brother as much as he does," she wrote. I have a sister, but never mind. "That information, however, is not at all what he responded to," she went on.

" 'Fascinating,' he said. 'I guess it makes you feel different about abortion, doesn't it?' He said this in the triumphant matter of many men I know who believed their opinions on this subject to be morally superior to mine."

I recall nothing of this conversation, but I am willing to concede it happened because I have always been both pro-choice and yet uneasy about abortion. And it strikes me as just possible that I did not grant pro-choice women the same element of confusion-contradiction because abortion was too often stridently presented as a feminist issue.

If so, I had Nora wrong. "I have never believed that there was anything simple about abortion," Nora wrote. She went on to castigate the women's movement for making it seem otherwise—for insisting that abortion has "nothing to do with anything but a woman's need to control her own body."

"Baby" is a long essay of sparking brilliance. It is a kind of Magna Carta of common sense—not only Nora's reprimand to me but also her rejection of trendy feminist dogma, her realization, for instance, that the patronizing authority of the male physician was simply being replaced by the patronizing authority of zealous natural childbirth advocates and their belief that pain and purity were synonymous. One tyranny had been replaced by another and each time the patient, the woman, was being told what to do and not necessarily for her own sake.

There was then and always an air about Nora of great wisdom—not merely, if I may correct myself, of great wisdom, but of *greater* wisdom. She was smart, very smart, and knowledgeable, very knowledgeable, but beyond that she had an inerrant touch for the best of almost anything. She herself was a tastemaker and she did not recommend anything lightly, casually, as if it did not matter. She not only knew what she liked, she knew why she liked it.

Her mentor in matters culinary and such was Lee Bailey, who ran a boutique out of Bendel's on Fifth Avenue and a salon out of his country place in Bridgehampton. Bailey was a renaissance man of style, a champion of simplicity (no hors d'oeuvres), who showed Nora both how to set the table and how to wear her hair. It was undoubtedly he who led her to Bridge Kitchenware, a very upscale housewares store on East 52nd Street. The place was founded by Fred Bridge and had a distinct French flavor. It became a favorite of Craig Claiborne, the longtime restaurant critic for the *New York Times* and an unparalleled foodie. Bridge was where the cognoscenti bought their knives, pans, and, as it turned out, food processors. It is where I bought mine.

The Cuisinart food processor became ubiquitous in the mid-1970s. If the device had one subtle but fatal drawback it was that it was invented by an American and sold by an American company. That, apparently, would not do, and Nora insisted that my wife and I buy a French device from Bridge. So one day in New York, I trudged over there and bought the French food processor. I remember dropping Nora's name, and being warmly greeted—a celebrity by extension.

I was enormously proud of my French food processor, so clearly different and superior to the pedestrian and common Cuisinart that I overlooked its galling shortcomings. After all, it had an unimpeachable and daunting provenance—the Bridge Co., Nora, Lee Bailey, and by extension Craig Claiborne and most of France. It was, in fact, an inferior product—not much good at slicing, as I recall—but it was retained not so much for what it did but what it said. Then one day I noticed that in Nora's own kitchen, the klutzy Gallic device was gone. It had been replaced by the utterly common Cuisinart. I got one myself.

Nora's domain was the kitchen, and she ruled it not just with superior knowledge but with an assurance that simply brooked no questions. At about the time of the Cuisinart silliness, our kitchen in Washington was in dire need of modernization. As luck would have it, Nora had recommended our house for the shooting of *Heartburn*. In exchange for the inconvenience of turning our home into a movie set, we were to get a brand-new kitchen. Into that kitchen would go, besides the fancy French non-slicing food processor, a huge refrigerator-freezer, a Garland restaurant-style stove the size of a modest Bessemer converter, and—quite dear to my heart—a sprayer for the sink. It was, as far I was concerned, the handiest thing to have in the kitchen.

One night I rattled off the things I'd like the studio to provide. At the mention of the sprayer, Nora frowned. "Why would anyone want a sink sprayer?"

she demanded. The question was asked with such contempt that I immediately realized that I had failed to see the utter worthlessness of the thing. I considered that it might be dangerous as well.

In the end, Paramount found that my house did not look like it belonged in Washington. The kitchen remained untouched, but Nora's condemnation of the sink sprayer stayed with me. What did she see that I could not? Indeed, what could she see that so many others could not? When I was in other people's homes, I would sneak into the kitchen and closely examine the sink sprayer. What? What?

Several years later, Nora upgraded her own kitchen. Voilà, a sink sprayer! What had happened? I asked. How come she had changed her mind? She looked at me as if I had gone batty. She had never condemned the eminently utilitarian sink sprayer, she said. Why would she? It was a marvelous device, good for, among other things, spraying. But . . . , I started, but she gave me that look, that *you are a fool but my friend anyway* look. One of us was crazy. But one of us had a sink sprayer and the other didn't. And as Nora would say, so there.

Nora had many audiences. She was a female director. But she was also a female newspaper writer and a female magazine writer and a female magazine editor and a female book writer and screenwriter and blogger and a mother and a wife three times over. She had had all these roles, and in retrospect, she timed them perfectly, working for *Newsweek* when it was at its rambunctious best, and then moving on to the *New York Post* when tabloids were the appropriate vehicle for covering a seemingly deranged city, and then magazines like *Esquire* and *New York* when they were both explosively innovative, and then movies in one capacity or another and the stage, where her parents had begun and where they, too, ended.

She seemed always to be in the right place at the right time, and so her story is also the story of those times and those publications and art forms—their importance and their whoopee fun. Like some peripatetic foreign correspondent, she covered her share of revolutions—the sexual one, the feminist one, the Watergate one (it toppled a president), and the post-Watergate one in which journalism emerged with all its smug righteousness—so important, so very important.

In all her roles she would pause and take stock of what was happening. She hovered above herself, a crane shot in which Nora Ephron could observe Nora Ephron and get the necessary distance to see the humor in her pathos. She wrote about being a girl and then a college student and then a single woman on the make for a career and on the make for men as well. None of these essays were confessions and none of them asked for sympathy. They were reports by a reporter observing herself as material—copy. She was not merely amusing about others. She was amusing about herself.

Nora chronicled what it was like to be a woman in almost every stage of life, including aging. She was direct about it; she didn't like it one bit, not what it did to her neck, her memory, her energy, and even her sex drive. She wrote with a precise and disarming honesty, with a between-us-girls kind of touch. Women found a soul mate, a companion, while for men her stuff was an immense voyeuristic opportunity: Oh, so that's what they think!

Yet she did not write about dying. She did not write about her disease or mention that she had always had a claustrophobic fear of cancer. It seemed to her that it was omnipresent, always lurking, and that the disease that had killed her mother's beloved younger brother, Dickie, at the age of only twenty-eight, was somehow stalking her. Once or twice when she had some procedure done—removal of her thyroid, for instance—I could hear the dread in her voice and would dismiss it with a joke, not appreciating her fear. Yet when it came, she kept it mostly to herself.

She inadvertently dropped hints. There were signs. She and her husband, Nicholas Pileggi, were regulars on the yacht owned by David Geffen, the entertainment mogul. The boat was a 423-foot behemoth. It lacked nothing—not a gym, not salons, not staterooms with drop-down TV screens imbedded in the ceiling—and yet Nora once said she had to get off and see a doctor, and the reason she gave was dehydration. This on a yacht where an outstretched arm would immediately be met by a crew member bearing a bottle of Fiji water. The other guests were puzzled, but they did not catch on.

Neither did The Harpies. This was a luncheon group of women who met irregularly in New York. The name was given to them by Liz Smith, the gossip columnist (an original member of Lee Bailey's set) and a charter member. (The group was formed by Jeanne McCarthy and included Barbara Walters, Lisa Caputo, Peggy Siegal, Cynthia McFadden, Maurie Perl, Beth Kseniak, and Jennifer Maguire Isham—some of the most powerful women in the communications business.) Nora called the last meeting for May 8, 2012, and designated, for its truffles, La Petite Maison as the meeting place. By then, she was only weeks away from going into the hospital. "I'm going under the radar," she told the group. Everyone thought it was a work project, probably a movie.

Kate Capshaw almost caught on. Along with her husband, Steven Spielberg, she had grown close to Nora and relied on her for advice, for wisdom, for validation, but, frustratingly, not for hugs. (Nora was not a hugger.) Nora had lost weight, she noticed. Nora was looking wan. The change in Nora's appearance kept Capshaw up at night, and Nora had told her that if you can't sleep, if something is keeping you up at night, you have to face it, stare it down.

So she called Nora. "I said I am really sorry to bother you, but I am sleepless and you always said that if you're pacing at night, you have to take care of it." And Kate got emotional. "It's me talking and I am just very worried about you and I'm sorry and I'm scared that I'm going to lose you and you're sick and I want to be wherever you need me to be.

"And she said. 'Why would you think that? I've gained eight pounds.'

"Then I was stuck, and I thought, Oh, shit. I know you and I know you like to look good and . . ."

"I gained eight pounds."

Conversation over.

With the notable exception of her sickness, Nora wrote about everything. She not only chronicled her life, she consumed all the best material, leaving nothing but cinders for a biographer to sift through. Several times in the course of writing this book, I would be told some fascinating fact, some charming anecdote, something compelling or dramatic about Nora, and this fact—this whatever it was—would be imparted with appropriate solemnity or drama by whomever I was interviewing: This is something you don't know. Later, though, I would come across it, mentioned nonchalantly by Nora herself in some tossed-off essay or blog. I came to think that Nora's major secret was that she had no secrets.

But, of course, she did. She was less secure than she seemed, more vulnerable, less confident in her abilities than she should have been. She wrote fast, but not effortlessly, and pretty much all the time. She was thinking, thinking, always thinking, always on the hunt for material, gorging on books and somehow reading them before anyone else did. She got the review copies and the bound galleys and the manuscripts and sometimes, because other writers sought her out for advice, the outline.

She read the old stuff, too. She urged me to read *The Moonstone* by Wilkie Collins, a classic from 1868, and when I was working on a script about Lyndon Johnson, she exhumed *The Gay Place*, Billy Lee Brammer's unfortunately named 1961 novel about Texas politics that has nothing whatsoever to do with homosexuality. The book is actually something of a secret, adored by aficionados of politics but unknown to almost everyone else. Nora knew it. She recommended I read it.

Nora was a gifted user of other people's time. She had assistants, most important and for a very long time, J.J. Sacha, a Georgian redeemed by a Brooklyn-born father-in-law. He was a show business veteran by the time he came to Nora in 1998, having worked for both Rosie O'Donnell and David Letterman. Rosie was a demanding boss—not to mention a friend of Nora's—but J.J. was nonetheless unprepared for his interview. It took place in the storied Brill Building, the actual Tin Pan Alley, where Nora was editing *You've Got Mail*. J.J. waited in a conference room. Nora swept in and announced, "You do not want this job. I am a horrible person to work for. I'm demanding and impatient and I will make your life miserable."

J.J. gave her a long beat.

"I'm very serious," Nora said.

"Sounds like just the kind of thing I'm looking for," J.J. said.

"I'm really not kidding," Nora said.

J.J. said he wasn't either.

At first, Nora was as good as her word. It was not that she set out to make J.J.'s life miserable, it was rather that she was preceded by a reputation as a severe taskmaster, whose assistants had the half-life of an infantryman in some hopeless World War I battle. J.J. feared he would make a mistake, get something wrong—"forget to call a car for her or screw up a telephone message or return with Asiago cheese when she wanted Grana Padano," as he himself put it. "I took out a subscription to the *New Yorker* just so I could catch some of her references. I was certain I was going to be fired for the first eighteen months I worked for her." But he lasted until her death, by which time he had become indispensable both to her and to Nick. If Nora's life ticked like a clock, J.J. was the one who wound it.

Nora delegated her research to him—as well as the usual assistant chores such as paying bills; booking flights, restaurants, and the theater; and maintaining the shared Nick and Nora calendar. (On occasion, he even shopped for her, backing up the housekeeper, Linda Diaz.) J.J. was also an astute reader of scripts, both Nora's and others, and was, in some senses, a collaborator.

Later, J.J. was among the very few to know of Nora's illness. He had seen her computer and noticed she was visiting WebMD, a website for medical information. J.J. and another of Nora's assistants, Mary Pat Walsh, called Nora's condition "the blood thing."

As was bound to be the case, Nora noticed that J.J. was noticing, and sometime in the beginning of 2007, she sat him down and said, "I know you know that I've got something going on. I don't want anyone to know about it, so we're not going to tell anyone about it." The conversation took about five minutes. After that, she almost never discussed her condition. She had cancer. She would write movies and plays and blogs and stuff—and she had cancer. It was like that. Movies, plays, cancer, and stuff. Everything in its place.

Nora's productivity was a matter of amazement to people who were themselves amazingly productive. Meryl Streep, who seems to make half a dozen movies a year and appear at countless events in support of one worthy cause or another, marveled at what Nora was able to accomplish. Streep had basic questions: Who did the shopping? (Linda Diaz.) Did Nora sleep late? (Not often.) She must be an extremely well-organized person. (Nora did not think so.) What, then, was the secret? The answer is disheartening: brilliance.

Nora was a non-dawdler. She went at her work with dispatch. For a time, she and Nick rented a house in East Hampton where the kitchen was located directly under the master bedroom. Nick was an early riser, and so sitting in the kitchen, sipping his tea and reading the newspaper, he would hear the alarm go off above his head and Nora's feet hit the floor and soon the pitter-patter of those feet making their way across the hallway to her study. Almost instantly, he would hear her typing—the click-clack of something worthwhile coming.

But it did not always—or maybe even usually—come quickly. As an essayist, she was an inveterate reviser, attacking the subject repeatedly, sometimes rearing back and rushing at the first paragraph all over again, trying to gain momentum for the rest of the piece. She was a former newspaper writer, and she had the journalist's reverence for the lede—the all-important first paragraph—which either captured the reader or did not. She learned early how to do it. When the subways flooded, her story for the *New York Post* did not begin with a recitation of facts—not the standard who-what-where-when and sometimes why—but with Nora looking down and wondering, "Why am I standing in water?" Her lede answered no questions. Instead, it asked one—and the answer to that was the rest of the story. The average reader had no idea that a mold had been broken. Nora's fellow journalists recognized that it had.

In her 1986 essay on how she revised her ledes—"Revision and Life: Take It from the Top Again"—she provides some insight into how hard it is to make writing seem easy. For a fifteen-hundred-word *Esquire* piece, "I often used 300 or 400 pieces of typing paper," which is remarkable in two ways. It shows how hard she worked and it also showed how organized she was. In the pre-computer age, it was not possible to easily cut and paste. The job had to be done by cutting the copy with a scissors or sharp ruler and then pasting it where it should go. Newspaper editors—the copy desk—did it routinely, but that was for a five-hundred-word newspaper story, its format rigorously prescribed by tradition—the all-encompassing lede and then paragraph by paragraph in diminishing importance. The last paragraph could always be cut. Often, it was.

To revise the way Nora did it—to revise and revise and revise and to insert facts where they should be—was a monumental task of organization. (It was often beyond me.) By her own admission, Nora was late moving to the computer. I think she needed it less than ordinary mortals.

In the same essay, Nora allowed that because she paid so much attention to her lede, "the beginnings of my essays are considerably better written than the ends, although I like to think no one ever notices this but me." Alas, it is occasionally very noticeable, and I liken some of Nora's essays to Brahms's Academic Festival Overture with its majestic *Gaudeamus igitur* processional which ends abruptly, as if Brahms suddenly had to bolt to the bathroom.

It may be surprising to some that Nora paid so much attention to rewriting, but it was equally surprising to her friends that she continued to write at all—not just the occasional op-ed columns for the *New York Times* or, of course, the lucrative movie script but blogs for the *Huffington Post* or the odd essay, like the one she did in 2011 for *Newsweek* on a television series based on the old Playboy clubs. As she got older and downright famous, she hardly needed to write at all—not for money, not for fame—and many writers, after a certain age, approach the keyboard a bit as a vampire nearing the cross. Nora, though, never stopped. She wrote furiously and continually.

She blogged for the *Huffington Post* at a time in her life when she hardly needed the exposure—but her friend, Arianna Huffington, needed her. A deal was struck. Nora got stock when *HuffPost* was sold to AOL. That was a nice piece of change, to be sure, but it only made Nora richer, not rich. Surely, her decision to blog was prescient—*Huffington Post* was on its way to becoming a mighty media empire—and it was just another example of Nora knowing when to get off one platform and go to another. (She also helped create *HuffPost*'s "Divorce" blog.) She was extending her brand and she was, for the most part, doing it well.

In some respects, she was merely laying off her bets. For all her fame as a movie director, she remained a writer—a screenwriter, a playwright, an essayist, a feature writer, a newspaper reporter, and a blogger. It was all about writing. It was what she could do, what she could always do. So even when the movies turned sour and directing seemed iffy, she could still write. She could sit down at the keyboard and simply write. No pitch meetings and constant efforts to get things within budget, no worrying about some temperamental actor. Writers didn't have to fret about what the studio was thinking or that the poor box office for some totally unrelated film was going to affect their own prospects. They could just sit down, alone, and write what they wanted. The purity of the exercise is enthralling, cleansing, and makes one wonder, as the sentence comes to an end, "Where did that come from?" How lucky. How lovely.

So she could always be what she always had been. Other directors, when the time came for them to be pronounced too old or dried up, might wait for the project that never comes, the light that never turns green, projects in perpetual development, a ring of hell that never occurred to Dante. Not Nora. She was a writer and writers write. So she always did.

And yet, in retrospect, a hint of desperation is suggested. After all, Nora was blogging and doing other kinds of "light" writing while, in essence, dying. Her time was running out. The disease that would kill her had been identified in 2005, and its course, she was told, was immutable. She would die, one of her several doctors had told her, and nothing she could do would change matters. The prognostication was harsh and delivered in a callous manner—as if the doctor was going to show this celebrity just how little she mattered. The disease, after all, did not give a damn. Neither, it seemed, did the doctor.

A bit after that, Nora and Nick came over for dinner. I was then living with Mona Ackerman, a clinical psychologist who would later be diagnosed with ovarian cancer. (She died five months after Nora did.) Solemnly, Nora told us the news, and told us also not to tell anyone. She had already made up her mind. Her last act was not going to be about dying, but about living. She was not going to let the disease take over her life, make her uninsurable as a movie director, and turn her into an object of pity. She was not going to spend the last years of her life as a dying person. She would spend them as writer. That night, Nora mentioned that she and Nick might go to Seattle for a stem cell transplant. We instantly made plans to accompany them—take a hotel room, rent an apartment, something. Mona was simply not going to let Nora out of her sight.

Nora did not go to Seattle for the transplant. She was sixty-five—a bit old for the procedure—and, besides, as the entire New York literary community knew, Susan Sontag, the public intellectual, had tried a transplant and it had failed miserably and caused her great suffering. Sontag had died in 2004. One of her doctors had been Stephen D. Nimer of Memorial Sloan Kettering Cancer Center in New York. Until he relocated to Miami, he was one of Nora's doctors as well.

The other option was maintenance—prednisone and then later Vidaza, a tolerable chemo, and a slow, barely obvious decline. Nora chose the latter, and with the exception of a brief period when prednisone engorged her face, her condition was not noticeable. She made monthly visits to Memorial Sloan Kettering Cancer Center on New York's Upper East Side for her infusions, often running into the Beverly Hills émigré and breast cancer patient Joyce Ashley there. At Nora's request, Joyce never said a word to anyone—not even her closest friend, Barbara Walters.

After her infusions, Nora would sometimes walk across York Avenue to New York Hospital, where she would visit Mona, whose own cancer was inexorably advancing and whose chemotherapy was causing periodic hospitalizations. Nora would sit on the couch in Mona's room, invariably 242 on the fourteenth floor. Nora would usually bring a gift. They would talk, and I, just to do something, would amble down the hall.

The period is a blur to me, and checking my calendar hardly helps. It is pitted with appointments with doctors and radiation centers—the busy, exhausting schedule of the cancer sufferer. Both Nora and Mona were dying, not in the sense that we all are, but with an approaching imminence. Mona, however, was demonstrably weaker, thinner, and more and more fatigued. I had gone with her to a salon above Columbus Circle where her head was shaved and she was fitted for wigs. We bought odd berets also, and all sorts of goofy caps. Shortly before Nora died, she resorted to chemotherapy even though she had little faith it would work. I went with Nick to the Columbus Circle salon. He bought some caps.

For a time, Nora's numbers, the numbers we all get to know—the reds and the whites and the platelets—teasingly jumped around, up and down, and then, defeated, they leveled off the wrong way. She was moved from the leukemia ward on the seventh floor to the bright, sunlit room Mona had always occupied. She died there, June 26, 2012.

Just Like the Movies

This is the way it began:

I had come to the *Washington Post* on June 17, 1968, and was assigned a desk right in front of Carl Bernstein. He was a District kid, born in Washington and raised mostly in the Maryland suburbs, but he had this New York air about him. We hit it off. It was the Vietnam War era, and Carl, as an alternative to the draft, was heading off to the army, about to do his six months of active duty as a member of the D.C. National Guard. I had already done my stint in the New York National Guard, and so I wrote him a memo on what to expect in basic training and how to game the system. For instance, I told him that rubbing a lead pencil over the rust spots on a rifle will make it look like it had been thoroughly cleaned. Carl was impressed and we became friends, best friends actually.

Carl was married to another *Post* reporter, Carol Honsa. I was married to Barbara Stubbs, whom I had met at the Columbia Graduate School of Journalism and who had become an editor at the *Washington Star*, then still an important afternoon newspaper. We two couples spent a lot of time together.

The Bernstein-Honsa marriage did not last, although the Bernstein-Cohen friendship did. So I was ringside, so to speak, as Carl went from being just another reporter at the *Washington Post* to being a monster celebrity who, with Bob Woodward, was credited with bringing down the Nixon administration. I went along for the ride. By day, I was parked in Annapolis covering the Maryland State House. At night, I was a friend of Woodward's and Bernstein's.

This was 1973. The burglary of the Democratic National Committee's offices had taken place in June of 1972. Within a year, Washington was transformed. The burgeoning scandal—so big it would bring down the president and produce the indictment or jailing of an astounding forty-three government officials—had made Washington into something it had never been: a capital city in the European mode. It was no longer just the seat of government, but a magnet for writers, filmmakers, novelists, playwrights, and itinerant intellectuals from all over the world. They descended on Washington and sooner or later ambled up to the vast newsroom of the *Washington Post*. Always, they sought out Woodward and Bernstein or the paper's editor, the astonishingly cinematic Benjamin C. Bradlee. I was there, attached to Carl and Bob like a barnacle on a ship.

One night at a Washington restaurant I had dinner with the founder and editor of *New York* magazine, Clay Felker, and one of his associate editors, the former *Washington Post* reporter Aaron Latham. Felker wanted to start a new magazine and Latham wanted me to write for it. It would be called *Couples*, and it would cover the new and varied ways men and women—it was only men and women at the time—coupled. Because my wife worked for the competing newspaper, I got assigned to do a story about spouses or partners who competed with each other. One of those couples was the Greenburgs—Dan Greenburg, a famous humorist, and his younger wife, Nora Ephron.

Dan was a hugely successful writer. In 1964, he had published *How to Be a Jewish Mother*, which became a number-one best seller. The book, his magazine articles, and even some plays gave him the kind of fame and income few writers achieve. In 1967 he was among the literary and intellectual elite invited to the Playboy Magazine Writers Conference. It was a stellar collection of writers and intellectuals and those who were both. Normal Mailer was there. Gore

Vidal was there. Gay Talese was there, and so was Arthur Schlesinger and Saul Bellow and Kurt Vonnegut and Calvin Trillin—so many literary celebrities that the magazine got precisely the kind of publicity it sought and Hugh Heffner, its founder and owner, was transformed from a Peeping Tom into a patron of the arts—a regular Maxwell Perkins. Nora was there as well, but she is not mentioned in any of the newspaper stories or present in the group photos. She was—maybe for the last time in her life—a mere spouse.

By 1973, Dan and Nora were beginning to switch places. Nora was obscure no more. In fact, in certain circles—literary and journalist Manhattan—she was famous or fast becoming so. By then, her writing for the *New York Post* had attracted attention. She had transformed a *Post* series on the late-night TV host Johnny Carson into a paperback book, and she was writing extensively, and brilliantly, for a gaggle of magazines before she settled down and made *Esquire* pretty much her home. Early on, she had developed what writers call "a voice"—a characteristic and appealing idiosyncratic style—and while she later wrote about how she had developed it over time, it was in fact discernible in her childhood letters home from Camp Tocaloma in Flagstaff, Arizona. She was a rebuke to writer's schools everywhere. She had clearly learned to write in the womb. But beyond what was an amazing literary output—she compiled her freelance pieces into a collection titled *Wallflower at the Orgy*—Nora had become a personage. She was a slight woman—a foodie but a dinnertime nibbler—but she could throw enormous weight. Something about her attracted the more famous, the equally famous, and the about-to-be famous. She was endowed with heroic chutzpah, a voice that somehow cut through cocktail party clutter, although there was nothing brassy about it.

Nora had what the army calls a command presence. It was somehow picked up by, among others, passing waiters or, it seemed, even cabdrivers who were blocks away. She had immense self-confidence, a ready wit, a capacious hard drive of a mind, and absolute certainty. Some people feared her, a few people hated her, but nobody ignored her. At home, she was setting a table that had not been equaled since the fabled one at the Algonquin Hotel. Hers, too, was round.

Clay and Aaron had wanted Nora, not necessarily Dan, to write a piece for *New York* magazine, but they offered the assignment to them both. Dan accepted. Nora did not. Felker demurred. *New York* magazine was no longer interested, but Felker and Latham were interested in what effect their rejection had on the couple. What did it mean that Nora had titled her 1970 collection *Wallflower at the Orgy* and that Dan had followed two years later with a *Playboy* article "My First Orgy"? "I was playing with the idea of the piece," Latham said later.

Whatever the idea of the piece was, it didn't quite work out. Clay and Aaron gave me a list of couples where the woman not only competed with the man but in some cases eclipsed him. I was to interview the increasingly famous Barbara Walters, whose husband at the time was Lee Guber, a prominent but hardly famous theatrical producer. Also on my list were Barbara Howar, a Southern writer and Washington celebrity, and her lover, Willie Morris, the immensely respected former editor of *Harper's* magazine. I think I had Helen and David Brown. He was both a theatrical and film producer, but she had become the editor of *Cosmopolitan* and had filled its pages with sex and sex and then, just to make sure, more sex.

I was to do other couples as well. One was the combo of Sally Quinn, who had zoomed to spectacular prominence as a writer for the *Washington Post*'s new Style section, and her boyfriend, Warren Hoge, then the city editor of the *New York Post* and on his way to a distinguished career at the *New York Times*. But most of all there were the Greenburgs, Nora and Dan. Their marriage was supposedly in trouble.

I called Nora.

"Oh, Richard, we all wondered who Clay was going to get to do this piece," she said.

"Well . . ."

"You're too good for this."

"Really? You don't even know who I am."

"Yes, I do. And you are too good for this. I mean, I could see cooperating if I was promoting a book, but I'm not. So, why would I do this? Why would I talk about my private life if I'm not getting anything out of it?"

These all seemed like good questions to me. I have put them down as I remember them, but what I clearly remember—no memory fog here—is how precise she seemed, how strong and just so logical. There was nothing evasive about her, nothing about being pressed for time or some other lame excuse. She just didn't want to do it. It made no sense to her. That made plenty of sense to me. I told her so, and we planned to meet about a month later in Washington, when the new journalism magazine *More* was holding a convention and where *Rolling Stone* magazine, even hotter than *More*, was giving a party. We would meet at the party.

The *Rolling Stone* event was held on the mezzanine level of the Mayflower Hotel. It was a boisterous and packed gathering of heroes. Journalism—particularly print journalism—was suddenly triumphant. It was not all that long before that Spiro Agnew, the former Maryland governor and about to be former vice president of the United States (he would plead "no contest" to corruption charges on October 10, 1973), was inveighing against what would later be called the establishment press. He called the members of that press "nattering nabobs of negatism"—a phrase concocted by the White House speech writer William Safire, destined before long to become a nabob himself as an op-ed columnist for the vigorously negative *New York Times*.

Agnew was the point man for an administration that made the press into an enemy. The Nixon people characterized it as elitist and liberal, not sharing the values of ordinary and altogether admirable Americans. Indeed, the Nixon White House was onto something. The press had grown in wealth and importance. The *Washington Post*, not even the most important newspaper in Washington a mere decade earlier, was now vying with the *New York Times* in setting the national news agenda. The television networks were of supreme importance, and what were once regional newspapers—the *Philadelphia Inquirer*, the *Los Angeles Times*, the *Boston Globe*, the *Miami Herald*, and others—were now circulating in Washington and being read carefully. They all tilted left—antiwar and anti-Nixon.

Reporters were becoming famous. They were becoming nationally known, not merely influential in Washington or some state capital, but cheered as tribunes of the people. None were more famous than Woodward and Bernstein, and no newspaper was more acclaimed than the *Washington Post*. It was ousting a president. It had pried a manhole cover off a sewer of presidential abuse—burglaries, wiretaps, the pilfering of personal records, the use of the Internal Revenue Service to punish or harass political enemies—and then a cover-up of all these crimes through the use of the Central Intelligence Agency.

Here, at last, was a story to stop the presses. Here, finally, was the hoary cliché realized—the story to blow the roof off city hall, or the Capitol in this case. In due course (1976), the movie *All the President's Men* was made about Woodward and Bernstein's reporting, but as good as it was—and it was very good, indeed—it seemed oddly redundant. The whole thing had seemed like a movie all along.

In a *New York* magazine piece, Nora honored the great story. "I have been in Washington, off and on, for only the last eight months, but there was no way to be there, in whatever journalistic capacity, and not know it was the best story one had ever covered."

Richard Nixon had just resigned. August 9, 1974 was an emotionally stormy night—rainy and warm, as well—and Carl and I drove around for a while and finally settled on a small party somewhere in the safely liberal Adams Morgan section of Washington. I remember little about it, except that it was dull and non-jubilant, precisely what Carl was seeking. It was important for him not to be seen gloating. He did not gloat.

In her piece, Nora did not gloat either. But she was covering the press, and she knew that for the press there could never be better days. She rued the end of the story, the loss of the Dostoevskyian Nixon as well as his astonishing collection of henchmen, and the plunge into the tepid constancy of the genially conservative Gerald Ford.

The Watergate scandal had seemed a conspiracy buff's concoction, a tale for naïfs. Experienced Washington hands were certain they knew better. Richard Nixon had been on his way to a landslide victory over Senator George McGovern. (Nixon won an astounding forty-nine states.) Why risk it all on what his own press secretary had called a "third-rate burglary"? And why burglarize the headquarters of the Democratic National Committee and not, more logically, McGovern's campaign headquarters, which was much more likely to house secret plans, incriminating or embarrassing memos . . . something!

Nixon had been around forever, entering Congress in 1946, winning a Senate seat in 1950, and becoming Dwight D. Eisenhower's vice president in 1953. He had run for president himself in 1960, losing by a hair's breadth to John F. Kennedy and then losing a California gubernatorial race two years later. He had been a congressman, senator, vice president, and high-powered New York lawyer. He was the most experienced of experienced politicians, and Watergate was dumb—and therefore unlikely.

The naïveté of Nixon's goons was fortunately matched by the naïveté of the *Post*'s Watergate duo. They didn't know enough to know better—or so it seemed. The more experienced reporters at the *Washington Post* tried to get Woodward and Bernstein taken off the story. They were called "the kids." They were inexperienced. They believed what their sources—What sources, anyway?—were telling them. They would embarrass the newspaper.

But Carl came to see the story. He saw it in the same way an artist sees beauty in the prosaic. He had come from a left-wing family that knew Nixon in an almost tactile way. Nixon had been on the red-baiting House Un-American Activities Committee. He had waged one of the dirtiest campaigns in American political history, the California Senate race against Helen Gahagan Douglas, whom he had smeared as a "pinko," a fellow traveler, a naïve lefty in the thrall of the Soviet Union. He had called her "the Pink Lady," pink "right down to her underwear," he added in a smutty aside.

Carl sensed Nixon looming over Watergate. This ability to see over the horizon—which for newspapers is just the next day—was itself seen by Alan Pakula, the director of *All the President's Men*. He was shooting in Washington, and he and I were walking to lunch when he said, "Carl always knew Nixon was behind Watergate." It was a moment of clarity, the sort of thing a film director, like a diamond cutter, extracts from his material. Who is this character? Who is this complex person who has to be explicated in less than a hundred minutes? Pakula had nailed Carl—and Carl had nailed Nixon.

I could not get into the *Rolling Stone* party where I was to meet Nora. It was a boisterous, stuffed affair that spilled out of the hotel meeting room. There was a guest list and I was not important enough to be on it. Woodward was, and he insisted that I be admitted. I entered and I heard someone say something about Nora Ephron. She was pointed out to me, talking to a celebrated investigative journalist. (I think it was James Ridgeway of the *Village Voice*, but he has no memory of this incident.) Her back was toward me. I saw a slight woman; dark hair. I approached and possibly interrupted. I offered my name. The guy from the phone call. I extended my hand.

Nora whirled on me. How dare I write what I had written? I was staggered. My piece had been rewritten by Latham. He had added stuff about Nora and Dan. Nora came out with a book called *Wallflower at the Orgy* and then Dan went to one. "Nora wrote a piece for *Esquire* in which she lamented a life without discernible breasts," I supposedly wrote, and Dan "mentioned with approval that some of his orgy mates were well stacked."

Trouble was, I had written none of that. Aaron had. He had shown me a page proof of my article, but what did I know? I was covering the Washington suburbs. He was in the midst of literary New York. He had the authority that comes from getting a table at Elaine's, the celebrity hangout. I had not protested.

I tried to defend myself, but Nora started quoting from my piece, word for word. Every word. I was under attack, and it was as if she were landing blow after blow. What impressed me most was the recitation of my putative words seemingly flying out of a typewriter and glancing off my forehead. Ping. Ping. This was one smart lady. She characterized my piece as slime and turned to the immensely important journalist who may or may not have been Jim Ridgeway for agreement. I hoped he would disagree, but I was new to Nora and did not yet know that nobody did that. "Right?" she asked.

"Right," he said.

I walked away.

At Christmastime, Carl called from New York. My wife Barbara had gone to see her parents in Ohio. I was working on a book about Spiro T. Agnew and had stayed behind in Washington. Carl had something to tell me. He was in love. He sounded giddy.

And who is this wonderful woman?

Nora Ephron, he said.

"Good-bye, old buddy," I said. "This is the end of our friendship."

Nonsense, he said. They were coming to Washington.

The next day, there was a knock on my door. I opened it. It was Carl, and around him, from the back, came Nora.

"Richard, this will be just like the movies," she said. "We started off hating each other and we'll wind up loving each other."

And we did.

Beverly Hills Writers

*B*efore they moved to Hollywood, Henry and Phoebe Ephron were New York writers, successful playwrights. They went out to the coast for the money and the lifestyle—Nora had home movies of her parents playing tennis in the ridiculous California winter—but not because the conversation was better there or writers more cherished. They arrived credentialed by Broadway. They stayed, temporarily, for twenty-two years, clinging to the lush L.A. life and the studio dole like the houses that threaten to slide off the hills in the rain.

In Hollywood, writers are furniture, rarely cherished, easy to replace, and after a while, sagging. New York writers are a different matter entirely. They matter, or they did. They met at the Algonquin, the Lambs, or the Players. They gathered on the East End of Long Island, the storied and eventually gilded Hamptons, where they drank at Bobby Van's in Bridgehampton and breakfasted at the Candy Kitchen in the same town. There and in Manhattan, writers were not overshadowed by actors' fame and wealth. They were central to the town. They could get good tables at celebrated restaurants, and they were cherished by hostesses for their presumed wit, their expected erudition, and, too often, their amusing inebriation.

In New York, writers were not rewritten by hack producers and ordered to cut a chapter or two to entice a vaguely literate audience. Playwrights were sacrosanct, their words untouchable by producer and director and certainly by performer. Time, custom, and—most important—the Guild said so. This was in contrast to the screenwriter. The term "Hollywood writer" carried the freight of compromise, of selling out, of Nathanael West's *The Day of the Locust*, of William Faulkner gone to rust and F. Scott Fitzgerald gone to drink.

Henry Ephron was an extroverted guy, personable, smart—and probably, like most screenwriters, terrified of the blank page. Husband and wife worked together, but there is the hint in Henry's memoir that Phoebe Ephron was "the closer"—the one who knew how to bring the screenplay home, the one who knew how to fix the problem in the second act, who spied the problem that derailed the script. Henry would pace and dictate, with Phoebe lying on the couch, taking it all down. Phoebe would later type up the notes, not in the least a stenographer's chore. The typist gets the last word.

For a time, Hollywood was good to the Ephrons. They earned $750 a week for starters and $3,000 a week when their contract was renewed. They could afford a maid and a cook. They were writers, making a wonderful living at it, which was not only wonderful but rare. Their friends were mostly New York expats, like themselves.

The dust jacket of Henry Ephron's memoir, *We Thought We Could Do Anything*, is a kind of a Walk of Fame on glossy paper. The names of more than sixty movie stars twinkle from the inside back cover—most of them drive-bys who appeared in one of the Ephrons' pictures. But while the Ephrons were never in the very first rank of Hollywood screenwriters, they did know movie stars and studio heads. They worked at Fox, a major studio with major stars— Cary Grant, for instance, who sat one row ahead of a sixteen-year-old Nora and her mother at a 1957 Fox screening of *An Affair to Remember*. Years later, Nora would incorporate that movie into her *Sleepless in Seattle*—an homage from one picture to another but also to her childhood.

Henry Ephron's book is largely a romp, a version of one of the movies where someone says, "I know, let's put on a play." People then go off and write and become successful on the stage. In that sort of movie, these writers know Florenz "Flo" Ziegfeld, Jr., and George S. Kaufman and then, on the Super Chief, they go out to Hollywood, bumping into movie stars in the narrow, swaying, corridors of the sleeping car.

It was, in fact, just this way. The Ephrons did know George S. Kaufman, and in 1944 they indeed took the Super Chief to L.A. By then, they had two kids—Nora and Delia—and had discovered that Phoebe was not cut out for the domestic life. After a while, she got that cook, that housekeeper, and a nice Beverly Hills house on Linden Drive, the lesser flats for sure, but Beverly Hills nonetheless. With its Spanish courtyard (later torn down) it was the perfect stage set for a perfect life that eventually turned into a perfect horror. The Ephrons became drinkers, matrimonial brawlers with horrendous fights erupting in the middle of the night, sending the younger kids scurrying downstairs into the arms of Evelyn Hall, the housekeeper. They would get into bed with her.

If this were a movie, some studio exec would point a finger to the end of his nose to indicate a predictable cliché. The life of the Ephrons was indeed that—well-paid screenwriters gone to drink. In real life, though, the kids were scared and always on edge. Phoebe would tank up nightly, a bottle of Dewar's an evening, and Henry would match her. They once went to see *Who's Afraid of Virginia Woolf?* and recognized themselves in the brawling George and Martha. They were shocked and vowed to mend their ways. They soon reverted.

For Nora, this was a painful childhood and adolescence. She recounted it in her writing. "My mother became an alcoholic when I was fifteen," she wrote in *I Remember Nothing*. "It was odd. One day she wasn't an alcoholic, and the next day she was a complete lush." Equally odd, if you will, is Nora's flat recitation of what happened. She admits to being terrorized by her mother's late-night banshee behavior, but the record contains very little else. She simply does not dwell on it. Her parents were alcoholics. It was a fact.

It was a fact, too, that over the years Nora mentioned her disruptive and disturbing childhood but seemed undisturbed and hardly disrupted by it. She wrote about her anxiety when her parents came to visit her at college—would they wake the dorm with their shouting?—but it was all material, a combination of the awkward and the absurd. I never heard a confession of pain. A tear never appeared in her eye. She recounted stories of her father's wild behavior—how in a single day he had agreed to buy four houses north of New York for a family compound—but this event was described with a combination of reluctant amusement and smoldering anger, not the stuff of tragedy.

She was fifteen when her parents took to the bottle, maybe past the age of childhood trauma, but the confusion of the time, its hurt and raw empathy for her teetering mother and father, are missing. By then, she had put emotional distance between herself and her father, and talked about him in an antiseptically flat way, although sometimes with rising anger: He did this. He did that. It is too easy to repeat the words of her mother when Nora saw her in the hospital, dying: "It's all copy." But it seemed that way. She rarely wept. Her friends wondered about that, but then they considered her fearless, too. Not so. Among her fears, I think, was crying. She was afraid to cry.

One story stands out. It is the one she wrote about the famous *New Yorker* writer Lillian Ross, who came to her parents' house for a party. Ross was a last-minute addition, brought along by St. Clair McKelway, a former newspaper reporter who had joined the *New Yorker* staff, where he became a mainstay. Ross was young and already dangerous. She had done the famous takedown of Ernest Hemingway in which he blathered silliness and she recorded it in tight notes. Ross asked to see the house. Phoebe took her around, and they came upon pictures of the Ephron children—Nora and her three sisters.

"Are those your children?" Ross asked.

Yes.

"Do you ever see them?" Ross asked by way of rebuke.

Phoebe responded with the bum's rush. She asked Ross to leave.

The story became Ephron family legend. It was about their mother, the chic hostess in the Galanos dress, erupting into the indignant momma, furious that she could be asked whether she could be both a writer and a mother. It makes for a good story, but Phoebe's was an odd reaction. A humorous or self-deprecating rejoinder was in order, or maybe flat-out honesty: *Yes, I know what you mean. I have two full-time jobs.* Something like that.

Anyway, Nora herself doubted the story. It wasn't until years later, when she had moved to New York, that she again saw Ross. They met at a party given by Lorne Michaels, the producer of *Saturday Night Live.* The two women shook hands, meeting like fighters touching gloves before the first bell, asking each other innocuously barbed questions, Nora all the time circling and circling so she could get in the punch about her mother: Had it actually happened?

"I went to your house once," Ross finally said.

"Really?"

"I didn't see much of you, though."

The story is called "The Legend" and it is a very nice piece of work. It ends with Nora now convinced that her mother had indeed given Ross the ol' heave-ho. Ross's confirmation redeemed Phoebe in Nora's eyes. The drunk of her later years reverted to the steely-eyed writer-housewife-mother she had once been, a capacious woman who, much like Nora, could do so much and do it simultaneously,

"I got her back; I got back the mother I'd idolized before it had all gone to hell," Nora wrote.

But Ross had confirmed nothing, only that she had been to the home. Hers was a one-shoe recitation of the fact. The other never drops—nothing about the getting the boot, no fist-slapping ending, and the story's emotional content is disproportionate to the facts. Nora wanted so much to redeem her mother, to restore her to the remarkable woman she had once been, that she took this reed and tried to weave a basket from it. In this sense, it fails as a story, but not as an expression of yearning for what was lost. The pain, it seems, endured.

Back in New York, Henry Ephron had worked for George S. Kaufman as his stage manager. Along with his frequent partner Moss Hart, Kaufman was responsible for one hit after another. He was a sought after play doctor as well, but his importance to this tale is that he was a celebrated wit who personified Hollywood's idea of New York theater. Kaufman was an acerbic man, formidably talented, who had been born in Pittsburgh and had a convert's zeal for New York. He also had a seat at the Round Table.

The Algonquin Hotel was—and is—located on West 44th Street in the Theater District. The *New York Times* and the *New York Herald Tribune* were then located nearby, as was the *New Yorker* magazine and various publishing houses. The place had the three virtues real estate people cherish—location, location, location—and so it was there that in 1919 a Broadway press agent named John Peter Toohey gave a lunch for Alexander Woollcott, the drama critic of the *Times*. Such a good time was had by all, that the next day they had another lunch—and then another and another. In 1929, it all ended. The famous Round Table was no more.

In the intervening years, the Round Table became celebrated. Two of the attendees were newspaper columnists—Franklin Pierce Adams and Heywood Broun—and they were probably neither loath to nor ethically proscribed from mentioning their friends in their columns, almost certainly improving their witticisms. Kaufman was no slouch as a humorist, but the one who is best remembered for both the Round Table and her wit is the lone woman writer among them: Dorothy Parker. She is widely considered Nora's antecedent. Early on, Nora considered her to be a role model.

The similarities are obvious. They were both women—indeed, Parker was the only female at the Table who was not there as a wife. She was a theater critic, an essayist, an accomplished short story writer, an occasional radio performer, and for a time, a highly successful screenwriter. Her trademark was lacerating, acerbic wit—one-liners that have zinged through the ages.

As Parker got older, she became increasingly involved in left-wing politics. Nora, too, was left of center, and she might have moved even harder left had she lived in Parker's era—the Depression, the Holocaust, and the McCarthyism of the 1950s. Parker wound up being blacklisted, and for a while she could not work in Hollywood. Nora's politics were never that intense, and unlike the boozing, disconsolate Parker, she had a sunny personal life. Early on, though,

Nora wanted only to be Dorothy Parker. She once wrote that she was raised on Parker's lines—and, of course, by a mother who more resembled Parker than her daughter did, the drinking above all. That, though, came later.

"All I wanted in this world was to come to New York and be Dorothy Parker," Nora wrote.

The connection between the table at the Ephrons' Linden Drive home and the round one at the storied Algonquin were both aspirational and real. New York, the Algonquin, and the Broadway stage were the Jerusalem to which this staunchly secular household would someday return. In the meantime, the Round Table was re-created at dinner. The Ephrons were writers. Moreover, they wrote dialogue. They got paid for wit, for sparkling words, for a way with a story. Their kids not only grew up in a talkie environment, but were expected to do some of the talking. They discussed world affairs and politics. They worshiped FDR and his New Deal, thought Adlai Stevenson should have triumphed over Dwight Eisenhower, and knew the names of obscure nineteenth-century feminists such as Lucy Stone, nowhere near as famous as Susan B. Anthony or Elizabeth Cady Stanton. Nora's characteristic way of talking, a manner that swiftly commanded the table, was surely developed at these dinners. Her lingua franca was theatrical, the language and speech patterns of the stage. Sentences were packed with meaning, and when they ended, it was not because she was out of breath, but because a point had been made (a little applause, please). If Henry and Phoebe Ephron hit all the marks in a wonderful career, it nevertheless meant writing not for oneself or for people like oneself, but for studio bosses who wanted to make money—movies, not cinema. The Ephrons were what Jack Warner had in mind when he supposedly exclaimed, "Writers! Schmucks with Underwoods!" Julius Epstein, an Ephron family friend and cowriter of one of Hollywood's most revered pictures, put it this way: "There wasn't one moment of reality in *Casablanca*. We weren't making art. We were making a living."

The idea was to take the money and run—to leave Hollywood at the top of your game. But the Ephrons, like many, stayed too long. The jobs were drying up. The absurd salaries were going to others. The half-life of the screenwriter was closing in on them. Henry was philandering, and Phoebe, like her mother before her, was drowning in a maddening deafness. The clever response that meant so much to her was no longer possible if she could not hear the initiating remark. Someone had corked the round table. The sounds were muffled. The quips evaporated in midair.

In 1963, after completing the script of *Captain Newman, M.D.*, the Ephrons sold the Linden Drive house and moved back to New York and the Broadway stage. New York is where Phoebe died in 1971 at an East Side hospital where, to the last, she begged for a drink and Henry, out of mercy, gave her an overdose of Demerol. Phoebe's last words to Nora have become legendary, if not famous. Nora repeated them all her life, cited them, invoked them in her eulogy, and many years later her son Jacob Bernstein used them as the title of the documentary film he made about his mother. They were, it seems, her mother's last tutorial to her daughter, showing her once again how things were done—even dying. Phoebe was physically diminished, wracked by her cirrhosis and a terminus for countless life-sustaining tubes. Nora gasped when she entered her mother's hospital room. "You're a reporter, Nora. Take notes," Phoebe said.

In his memoir, Henry Ephron had it somewhat different. "Take notes, Nora. Take notes. Everything is copy."

Phoebe Ephron was fifty-seven when she spoke those words. By then, she was a sour alcoholic, her wit curdled into spite and cocooned by an engulfing deafness. She was dying a very early death. She must have been angry and scared, all the usual emotions, but what we get is this sort of George S. Kaufman quip, something from the Marx Brothers, nothing to suggest a career hollowed out, a woman who had thrived in a man's world and then, what with four children and a husband who had his own troubles with the bottle, could write no more. She lacked the flint to make the spark that would burst into a play or a screenplay.

Phoebe Ephron's final project was a play called *Howie*. Significantly, it was a solo effort, Henry apparently relegated to kibitzer. *Howie* was about a Long Island family and the twenty-one-year-old daughter was played by Patricia Bosworth, who would go one to become a journalist and biographer. One of her books was about her father, the celebrated lawyer Bartley Crum, who, among other things, represented the so-called Hollywood Ten, the screenwriters who went to prison for refusing to cooperate with the House Un-American Activities Committee. Bosworth had much in common with Nora—not just a background in the leftist politics of the Hollywood writing community, but also parents who were alcoholics. In his latter days, Bart Crum was a pathetic drunk.

Howie tried out in Boston. The play was Phoebe's alone, but Henry attended the rehearsals, offering unsolicited and unwelcome advice as the script went through the usual revisions. The cast was one day told to expect some more revisions, and so they assembled on the stage of the Colonial Theater. Suddenly, Phoebe came running down the aisle with Henry in pursuit until, blocked by the stage she could go no farther. Henry grabbed her from behind, whirled her around, and socked her in the jaw.

Phoebe left. She returned to the theater with her jaw wired.

Howie opened on September 17, 1958, suffered poor reviews, and closed three days later. On opening night, both the Ephrons and Bart Crum were drunk. Nora went backstage. She had a question for Bosworth: Why was she wearing falsies? Bosworth, who like Nora was hardly busty, replied that Phoebe had insisted on it. Nora was flabbergasted. Her mother didn't even wear a bra until after her fourth child was born, she told Bosworth.

It was many years before Bosworth told Nora the story of her parents' brawl. Nora's reaction was nonchalant. Sounds right, she more or less said. In his later years, Henry Ephron was often violent and subject to rages. He became a feared, unpredictable presence, sometimes on the periphery of Nora's life, sometimes commanding immediate attention. Phoebe died in 1971 and Henry in 1992. In 1978, he married June Gale, the widow of Oscar Levant, famous for his musical genius and his mental instability. Gale is not mentioned in Henry's *New York Times* obituary, which, judging by her quotes, was approved by Nora.

In the telling of her daughters, Phoebe Ephron took to drink suddenly—one day not a drinker, the next day a lush. Nora, as the eldest of the four girls, got if not the best of her mother, then the best years. Phoebe was Nora before Nora could become Nora. She was a writer, which is a statement not just of occupation but of lifestyle and fervent commitment and a commensurate determination to rid herself of the ghetto, the shtetl, which was just down the hallway in her own home. Phoebe Ephron spoke Yiddish to her mother.

Kate Lotkin, was born in 1891 in Bobruisk, Belarus (then Russia). The town was a provincial capital with a sizable number of Jews. It had all the trappings of Eastern European Jewish life, a theater and numerous synagogues. In 1904 or thereabouts—the records are sometimes in conflict—Kate joined the mass exodus of Jews from the Russian Empire to America. She apparently traveled by herself, following her brother, Louis, who had emigrated two years earlier. For whatever reason, Kate did not live with him but boarded with a family on Manhattan's East 103rd Street. The 1910 census had her working at a factory—probably a sweatshop. That same year she married Louis Wolkind, who had arrived from Russia in 1899. Phoebe was born four years later.

There would be three Wolkind children—Harold, the eldest; Phoebe; and then Richard, born when Kate was around thirty-five. Dickie, as he became known, was fourteen years younger than Phoebe and, in effect, became her ward. It was apparently Henry and Phoebe who paid for his college education. He became an artist, and when the entire family followed Henry and Phoebe to California, he went to work for Disney.

For Kate Wolkind, her son's death was the first of several tragedies in a life that was both fortunate and accursed. She had avoided the Holocaust and the mass murder of the Jews of Bobruisk. She had worked and married her way out of the sweatshops and the tenements of East Harlem. She married a businessman, had three children, and died in sunny California. It was, on the face of it, a good life.

But her husband had cheated on her—maybe frequently. A son had died young and a daughter at fifty-seven. Her husband had repeatedly gone broke, and he wound up living a faux retirement in Los Angles, existing not on his savings, as he pretended, but on the Ephron dole. Kate herself had preceded her daughter into deafness—"Bacon and eggs, as usual," Nora's sister Delia wrote her grandmother replied when she asked, "How are you?" To her daughter, she was an object lesson in a housecoat: This is how not to conduct your life.

Phoebe Ephron would never be a housewife. It was not only that domesticity bored her but also that she was a woman who didn't just want to be a writer, she *was* a writer. And additionally, she had witnessed her mother's faithfulness to her unfaithful husband, and if it was not a lesson to her, then it was to her daughter Nora. The imperative to control her environment—to, in effect, direct—had to stem at least in part from the way her father and her grandfather treated their wives. If one was making an old-fashioned movie of Nora's life, one would isolate the day Henry Ephron insisted on driving Nora to her new elementary school. He got lost.

To see these patterns repeated generation after generation—the strong woman, the wayward husband—suggests the futility of therapy or behavior modification and a surrender to the power of genes. Nora would no doubt argue with that, and I, finding the thought merely interesting, would indifferently move on. But the indomitability of Kate and Phoebe, their resoluteness and concern for others, surely wended their way into Nora's character.

Nora was, really, the kindest of persons. She could be stern and withering and all of that, but if you needed someone at your side in the hospital, if you needed companionship, if your child needed a surrogate mother or an internship or, really, anything at all, Nora was the one to turn to. She not only was the occasional godmother but she was the patient ear for the children of her friends who had come to a parenting dead end. She remembered birthdays; she celebrated weddings. Talk to my kids, her friends would plead. She was a vast mother to a brood of kids who had their own parents but looked to her as somehow wiser, maybe because their parents did as well.

In 1989, Nora's college roommate, Marcia Burick, lost her son, Ken. He had been a student at Bates College in Lewiston, Maine, and in a fit of depression he went to a local gun shop, bought a weapon—and killed himself. Nora, who had been in England at the time, hopped a plane for the funeral, and a few years later was the inaugural speaker at the Ken Goldstein Memorial Lecture. Afterward, Marcia insisted that the two of them drive to the gun shop where

Ken had bought his weapon. Marcia wanted to confront the storekeeper. Nora would not permit it.

"She said, 'You just go across the street and wait for me.'" Nora entered the shop and came out some minutes later.

"I said to her, 'What did you say?' She said, 'We're not to talk about it.'"

Years earlier, Nora had shown Burick just how cheeky she could be. Not long after leaving Wellesley, the two women were rooming in New York when Nora took a call for Marcia. The caller was Clayton Fritchey, the press aide for Adlai Stevenson, who was John F. Kennedy's ambassador at the United Nations. Marcia had applied there for a job and was at that moment wandering the streets of New York, unemployed, broke, and down in the dumps. Fritchey was reporting that Marcia was still under consideration for a spot in the press office.

"I came back at Friday at five o'clock or something, and Nora said, 'I didn't know where to find you, you have the job at the U.S. Mission.'

"And I said, 'How did that happen?' She said, 'Mr. Fritchey called and said tell Marcia to come in next week, we want to have another interview with her.' And Nora said, 'Well, she can't possibly come in next week, Mr. Fritchey. She's been offered a very high-level job at the Ford Foundation and she has to let them know on Monday. So you need to tell me now that she does or doesn't have the job.'

"And he said, 'All right, tell her she's got the job and to be here at eight thirty Monday morning.'"

Did Nora confront the storekeeper? Did Nora really bluff out Clayton Fritchey? Hard to say, but my guess is yes. In the first place, she was no liar. And in the second place, both these stories are consonant with everything I ever saw of Nora. She was not physically brave, not some sort of reckless skier or mad spelunker, but she had no trouble confronting people. She once told off the Secret Service when some agents were clearing a space for the vice president's limousine. Nora and I were in a cab, which was waved away by the Secret Service as we were on our way to some event. Deferring, as usual, to authority, I told the cabdriver to move on, but Nora leaped out to give the Secret Service agents a piece of her mind. Unimpressed, they sternly ordered her back into the cab and on her way.

Far more dangerously, she one night effectively challenged about a dozen Neapolitan waiters to a fight. We had arrived late in Naples and dashed to a famous pizzeria located on the picturesque but ominous waterfront. We got to the place just as it was emptying and, to the fury of the waiters, simply took a table. A reluctant waiter arrived and we ordered a special pizza, a Neapolitan favorite. He returned with the sorriest pizza any of us had ever seen—payback for keeping the place open. Nora took one bite, rose, and faced the waiters who were lined up against the far wall. There were about a dozen of them, a sinister lot, some of them I histrionically recall picking their teeth with stilettos.

"Napoli!" Nora cried out.

The waiters snapped to attention.

Nora inserted her right hand into the crook of her elbow—the universally known gesture for *Fuck you!*

I gulped. What, was she out of her mind?

The waiters didn't stir. None of them made a move. We were alone in the restaurant, surely about to die, I thought.

Nora gave the waiters a triumphant look. She sat down, pleased. We dutifully nibbled at our awful pizza and somehow got back to our hotel, a grandiloquent dump with played-out air conditioning. Nora never said a word about it. I never forgot it.

Line Up Naked

Mahatma Gandhi, the revered founder of the Indian state, and Jawaharlal Nehru, the country's first prime minister, were lovers. This stunning, unsupported, and hugely ridiculous item of gossip was imparted to the touchingly innocent women of the Wellesley entering class of 1958 by the incoming freshman from California, Nora Ephron. She had come from Hollywood, and she knew things that no one else did; and when she conveyed them they were not couched as rumor or speculation—never preceded by the modifier "I have heard"—but imparted as truisms. Not to believe them was a sure sign of denseness, of naïveté, of not knowing how the world, the real world, worked. Nora Ephron, recently from Beverly Hills, knew how the world worked.

Nora was not the only person from Beverly Hills in that class. There was at least one other, and her name—at least the name Nora gave her in an essay for *McCall's* magazine—was Bonnie. Bonnie Sloan, as it turned out, although "Sloan" was some Anglicized version of an Eastern European name. Bonnie's father was not in the movie business but in the paper cup business, and her mother did not write or, for that matter, do anything much at all. Nora reported that her mom's days were devoted to playing canasta or gin rummy.

Nora and Bonnie were best friends, and at the age of thirteen they decided they would both go to Wellesley. But by the time she arrived on campus, Bonnie had had a nose job, which she had attributed to an auto accident, had collected a huge amount of "Chanel suits and Dior dresses," some twenty jars of face creams, a copy of the New York Social Register, and a smattering of an English accent which she had acquired the previous summer on a trip to Europe. By then, Bonnie was in the process of becoming a gentile, which for her was a matter of wardrobe and speech inflection and possibly an indifference to food, and so she arrived at Wellesley that late summer of 1958 in a Chanel, while Nora, by her own description, wore "a plain little red plaid dress and red hat." It is not however how she is remembered.

She is instead recalled as breezing in as a bold Californian—no pleated skirts for her. She wore Capri slacks and a Hawaiian shirt and she soon planted her flag: an eleven-by-fourteen framed black-and-white photo of her mother "draped in furs and getting out of her car going to a premiere in Hollywood," recalled her close college friend, Jennifer Carden. "It was just so exotic."

The fur, as it happened, was symbolically important. It was a mink that Phoebe had bought around 1954 from a Beverly Hills furrier who had run into a spot of trouble with the IRS. "It was an enormous mink," Nora wrote in a 1975 essay called "The Mink Coat," but what set it off was not its size or its color but its astounding provenance: It was not a gift.

Minks flowed by the acre off the women of Beverly Hills. But they were gifts from their husbands. Phoebe's mink was nothing of the kind. It came not from Henry but from the partnership of Phoebe and Henry. Phoebe was "defiant" about that—about not being like other mothers, "the other mothers who played canasta all day and went to P.T.A. meetings and wore perfume and talked of hemlines . . ." Phoebe was different.

For that era, Phoebe Ephron was exotic. She did not merely work—odd enough for the time—but she had a genuine career. Her letters to Nora at Wellesley were not handwritten on some sort of girlie stationery, fibrous and parchment-like to the touch, but were typed. This announced a backstory, possibly a job—and not the usual Wellesley route of school, pinned, engaged, married, and then life as a homemaker Junior Leaguer. Phoebe's letters were businesslike, briskly written, and tart. To at least some of the Wellesley girls, her letters came not just from Hollywood but from the future—from a place women would someday go.

Nora would read the letters out loud to her college friends. Who had a mother like this? Whose mother could write like that? In fact, who had a mother who worked, who earned money, who eschewed housework and domesticity, the way Phoebe Ephron did? When Phoebe was asked what a particular woman did, she would dismissively say, "her nails."

Henry Ephron used the phone. He would call Nora at Wellesley, frequent and lengthy phone calls in an era when a long distance call was a great luxury, reserved for whispered family tragedies. He would pour out his heart to her. As far as her parents were concerned, Nora had gone straight from high school to adulthood. In a family of careening emotions, the eldest daughter became wife and mother.

The troubles of the Ephron family were not evident to the women of Wellesley. Instead, they saw in Phoebe nothing but glamor. One recalled spotting her at the intermission of a play she and Henry had written. It was called *Take Her, She's Mine*, and it was based on the lives of two teenage girls, a lightly disguised Nora and Delia. It opened on Broadway at the end of 1961 and had previewed in New Haven earlier that year. Nora and some friends came down to Connecticut from Wellesley for the show. Not only was it a signal event for the young women—how many of them had seen a Broadway-bound production?—but there, in an alley at intermission, was Phoebe, catching a moment alone. She was smoking a cigarette and wearing that voluminous mink coat—confirmation of all that her letters had intimated.

Predictably, Nora became a college journalist. She had been on her high school newspaper, and so it was just a matter of time until her name would appear on the masthead of the *Wellesley College News*. It was, however, a snoozy time on America's college campuses. The storm of student disruptions was not even on the horizon.

Still, being on the newspaper was both fun and exhilarating. Lynn Sherr, also at Wellesley and bound for a great career as a print and television journalist and the author of several books, recalled the sense of excitement and importance that every journalist experiences—at least at first—but hardly ever acknowledges. That feeling of being special that comes with review tickets to local plays, with review copies of books from publishers, with being the first in so many ways—but mostly from writing something that everybody reads. The paper sets an agenda that is widely discussed, debated, or merely noted. For the journalist, this is thrilling—or, sometimes, frightening—but the feel of it is mighty like the one described by entertainers when they first hear the narcotic of applause: Me? Yes, you.

But with the thrill comes accountability. This Nora faced head-on when, in her junior year, she and Jennifer Carden reviewed a novel by May Sarton, a Wellesley faculty member. Sarton was not one of those college teachers who tosses off the occasional book infected with footnotes. She was an important novelist who would later, daringly, reveal herself as a lesbian and become a feminist icon.

Sarton was not yet out of the closet when she published *The Small Room*, but it contained hints aplenty—same-sex relationships between college teacher and student, teacher and teacher, and so on. (It is set at a school much like Wellesley.) One of these relationships the Wellesley reviewers—Nora and Jennifer—called "abnormal." Maybe that's what set Sarton off.

For both reviewers Sarton's sexuality was not the issue at all. Their gripe was with her condescending treatment of both students and student government. This was too much for both Nora and Jennifer, who concluded that *The Small Room* was too small in its outlook. They panned it. Sarton, furious, ordered them to appear in her office.

As it happened, Nora at the time was in Massachusetts General Hospital, in nearby Boston, having a pilonidal cyst removed. The cyst is located at the base of the spinal column, making sitting painful. So for the showdown with the imperious, intimidating, and indignant Sarton, Carden went alone.

The prospect of facing Sarton without Nora at her side terrified Carden. But as she was approaching Sarton's campus office, a taxi pulled up and Nora popped out. She was holding a rubber ring that served as a cushion. They went to face the formidable Sarton together.

For the next thirty minutes, Sarton upbraided them as nonentities who wrote for a student newspaper that no one read anyway. A terrified Carden said little. But a resolute Nora, gripping her rubber cushion, stood her ground. They were journalists, she said. They had offered an opinion—and that was what they were supposed to do. Nora offered no apologies. She was right and that's was all there was to it. Nora was Nora even before she became Nora.

When the writer L. P. Hartley said, "The past is a foreign country: they do things differently there," he might have had in mind college life in the 1950s and early 1960s. This was not a place where young people merely dressed somewhat differently or listened to a different kind of music. It was a place of stifling convention and conformity. The rules were rigid, in loco parentis regulations of all sorts, so bizarre in our rearview mirror they seem not just quaint but insane. College was in some senses merely kindergarten for big kids.

As if to show just how conformist college life of the early 1960s could be, the young women of Wellesley were asked to join students across the county to be photographed in the nude. This shockingly dopey program lasted from the late 1940s through the 1970s. It was developed to examine the rate and severity of several diseases. One of the diseases was rickets, usually caused by malnutrition and not likely to be found in Wellesley students or the students of other elite institutions. Nevertheless, without a murmur of protest, thousands of students over the years lined up naked to have their pictures taken. Such was the docility of the times. Such, in a snapshot, or many, was the 1950s and early 1960s. In those days, students did what they were told.

That culture—compliant and conformist—would crash in a frenzy of demonstrations and protests in the later 1960s. But at the moment, all was quiet. Vietnam was still called Indochina, and France was fighting to retain it as a colony. The Reverend Martin Luther King, Jr., was at Boston University earning his doctorate in theology; Jews were still being excluded from prestigious law firms; and women were expected to marry, have a brief career, and then stay home with their two or more children, one boy and one girl if at all possible.

It is tempting to see the Nora of Wellesley as always ahead of her time, which in a sense she was. She was aiming for a career. She also had her eye on a marriage and a family, but like her mother before her she saw no reason why she could not have it all—after all, men did. She wanted a career, but she also wanted to get married—and at the time she almost did. She described her intended as "a humorless young man," who doubtless saw no humor in that description. He was finishing up at Harvard Law School and moving to New York, and she was going to transfer to Barnard College in New York to be with him.

Nora went to see the class dean about arranging the transfer and was given a bit of advice that she wrote about later: "You have worked hard at Wellesley. When you marry, take a year off. Devote yourself to your husband and your marriage."

Roy Furman was at the Shubert Theater in New Haven the night of the mink. He was Nora's boyfriend at the time, a Harvard Law School student who went on to establish a hugely successful investment firm, become an important New York–based philanthropist, vice chairman of Lincoln Center, and—most pertinently—a Broadway producer. In fact, he became a lead producer of Nora's final work, the play *Lucky Guy*, but never conferred with her about it—maybe because he wondered if Nora would object to his participation. Their college romance had not ended well.

Furman was a typical Nora boyfriend. As a Wellesley student, her social life revolved around the elite New England schools. From Harvard Law School alone, she dated Mortimer Zuckerman, the real estate magnate who at one time or another owned the *Atlantic* magazine, *U.S. News & World Report*, and the New York *Daily News*, and Stephen G. Breyer, an eventual Supreme Court justice. Years later, Nora and Zuckerman resumed a relationship. It was brief and deteriorated into a lasting friendship.

Furman's recollection of that night at the Shubert varies from those of others who were there. He remembers a glamorous Phoebe Ephron all right, but he also remembers her as being drunk. He recalls both Henry and Phoebe as being witty and garrulous company, but he was more than awed by them. He was intimidated. He found them loud and overbearing, throwing off cultural references the way a wet dog shakes off water. He was a kid from Brooklyn, a graduate of the proletariat Brooklyn College, a self-described provincial, and here were these people, the slightly tipsy Ephrons, Outer Borough Jews once themselves, who had somehow managed to vault the rivers (East, Hudson) to command Beverly Hills and Manhattan. They were not New York Jews at all. They were not wedded to a neighborhood or tribe but to wit, repartee. They were always sitting down to dinner.

As for their oldest daughter, Nora was already what she would become. She was as voluble as them, as witty, as well-read, as exuberant. Furman's friends were charmed by her and sought her company. Furman, while dazzled and in awe, was not in love. Nora was extraordinary, and Furman knew he was not likely to meet someone like her again. She was rare—a star shooting by. Should he catch her?

His answer was no. If he wanted a wife—and that prospect hung over their yearlong relationship—then it would have to be a woman who cooked, who made his breakfast, raised his children, and did little else. Nora could cook and raise children, but she wanted to do more—plenty more. Her prefix of choice for wife was working, not house. That much was clear and all Wellesley knew it. Nora was going to New York. Nora was going to write.

Furman backed out of the relationship. Later, when he became a financier, they sometimes met—at this or that cocktail party, at this or that event, in Manhattan, in the Hamptons. The encounters were cordial, not warm. At home, discussion of Nora's latest book or essay or pronouncement was not tolerated by Furman's then wife. The past lingered. It threatened.

Roy Furman runs a billion-dollar investment fund. He has been a passive or active producer of more than fifty Broadway plays. He's been vice chairman of Lincoln Center and a past chairman of the Film Society of Lincoln Center. He is an active alumnus of both Brooklyn College and Harvard Law

School and was finance chairman of the Democratic National Committee. Roy Furman is a man of immense accomplishment, power, and prestige. Yet one reason—an important reason—he ended his relationship with Nora Ephron is that when she was twenty-one and he twenty-two, she overwhelmed him with her Hollywood background as well as her personality, brains, and ambition. He felt mismatched.

"I was scared," he said.

Furman was hardly alone. The word "scared" or "scary" is a leitmotif when classmates of Nora's are asked to recall their time with Nora back in her Wellesley days. Sometimes the word is offered as a synonym for awe or respect—as in she always seemed to know more than anyone else and was always absolutely certain about what she knew.

"She was scary in that she always knew she was right. You didn't want to cross her," said Lynn Sherr.

All Wellesley knew Nora would have a career and a marriage—but simultaneously or, if not, in what order probably even she did not know. She not only told everyone she would be a writer, she was quite specific about where she would write. It would be for the *New Yorker*. (She and Jennifer even papered their dorm room with *New Yorker* covers.) For once, Nora was wrong—or premature. Eventually, she would write for the *New Yorker*. First, though, she'd clip newspapers for *Newsweek*.

The Mail Girl Delivers

On graduation day 1962, Nora got into a rented car and drove to New York. She had already leased an apartment at 110 Sullivan Street, down in the coffeehouse, folk-scene part of Greenwich Village, and she had already been to an employment agency where she said she wanted to be a writer. She was sent to *Newsweek*.

At $55 a week, Nora would be a "mail girl." That was the title, the job description, and the limitation. Women, she was quickly told, did not write at *Newsweek*—although in actual fact, one of them did, but Liz Peer was in the faraway Paris bureau, where she could be overlooked as much as possible.

Right off the bat, Nora got a lucky break. She was made the personal mail girl of the magazine's editor, Osborn Elliott, and became what was known as an "Elliott girl." She sat right outside the big man's office and watched as he transformed *Newsweek* from a traditional news magazine—more or less a wrap-up of that week's events—to a journal that didn't wait for the news to happen but set out to make some itself. By the end of the decade, *Newsweek* had pitched itself into the civil rights struggle, devoting three covers written by Peter Goldman to the movement, and had also come out against the Vietnam War.

Newsweek was about to become what Madison Avenue called a hot book. Just a year before Nora's arrival, the magazine had been bought by the Washington Post Company. The deal was the work of Philip L. Graham, an extremely bright but extremely troubled Floridian who had married Katharine Meyer, whose father, Eugene, in 1933 had bought the *Washington Post* at a bankruptcy auction. Graham was an energetic and ambitious owner, and *Newsweek* soon became an energetic and ambitious reflection of himself. It was a fun place to work.

Newsweek was on the make, attempting to catch up to the older and more established—not to mention politically conservative—*Time* magazine. It never succeeded—not in circulation or ad revenue, but attention was a different matter entirely. In 1957, the magazine had hired the adventurous Ben Bradlee as its Washington bureau chief. Bradlee, who later became the editor of the *Washington Post*, had helped arrange *Newsweek*'s sale to Graham. In 1961, his Georgetown neighbor and friend, John F. Kennedy, had become president. The magazine was very well situated.

Being an Elliott girl had its advantages—proximity to power, and therefore to office skinny, most of all. In the days before email there was just mail, and it had to be delivered and picked up at each desk or department. The mail girl got to circulate, to get an overview, to meet everyone, and, no small matter, to make an impression. Someone who was as smart and personable as Nora was bound to be liked and, in due course, consulted: What was going on? Is this a story? What do young people think? And, much more important, what was going on within the bureau? Who was sleeping with whom? Who was drinking too much? Who was being transferred to London and who in London was coming home? Has so-and-so been fired and is so-and-so pregnant? Mail girls knew so much.

This particular mail girl was more than well informed. She was already well connected. She had already dated Victor Navasky, soon becoming the first degree of separation for so many New York writers. While at Yale Law School in 1960, the polymorphic Navasky had founded a satirical magazine called *Monocle*, which he promised to publish more or less regularly. (He called it a leisurely monthly.) After law school, he went out to Michigan to work for the progressive governor, G. Mennen Williams, and then returned to New York, bringing *Monocle* with him. He soon collected a coterie of young writers, Nora among them. They met weekly for drinks, in totally self-aware homage, at the storied Algonquin Hotel. Calvin "Bud" Trillin, already a *Time* magazine writer, called it the "square table."

Through Navasky and his soon-to-be wife, Anne, Nora connected with other writers. It would be natural to label her a networker or a social climber, but as much as she sought out interesting people, so interesting people sought out her.

From the telling, it seems that she did not so much move from Wellesley to New York as simply take her proper place in the city. She was the child of screenwriters and playwrights. She knew her way around the Algonquin dining room because her parents stayed in the hotel when they were in New York. She effortlessly dropped names, and it was impossible to tell—at least I never could—if the relationship was close or merely passing. She could excite a gathering with a single question—at a stiff Scarsdale dinner party, she shocked Anne Navasky by asking the women at the table if they had vaginal or clitoral orgasms. She was young and something more than attractive; she was magical. She not only made things happen, but things happened to her. She trailed buzz like a cartoon character does fairy dust.

Through the Navaskys she met young literary New York. She became a fixture at Elaine's, the saloony restaurant established by Elaine Kaufman in 1963, which soon became a writers' hangout. The Navaskys introduced Nora to her first husband, Dan Greenburg, an already established writer, and through him she met her eventual best friend, Judy Corman.

Victor Navasky connected her with Lynn Nesbit, who would ultimately become her agent. And Lynn would later hire Amanda Urban. Binky, as she was better known, became Nora's lifelong literary agent and her very close friend.

Nora dated Tom Wolfe. She dated Ward Just. She dated Charles Portis. They were all newspapermen making the long turn into magazine work or novels. Wolfe and Portis were at the *New York Herald Tribune*; Just had been at *Newsweek* before following Ben Bradlee to the *Washington Post*. They were all big names at the time—and, with the exception of Just, would go on to phenomenal success as novelists. (Just's success was more d'estime than commercial.) Nora dated *Esquire* and *Playboy* editors. She dated her *Newsweek* colleagues. She dated a lot. Mastheads spilled from her lips.

It was a phenomenal period. Sex had not only awakened from its 1950s dormancy but become a political statement. Blacks were being liberated. The Vietnam War was being protested. Students were duking it out with the faculty. Drugs were everywhere. Abortion was demanded as a civil right. Turmoil, turmoil, turmoil.

The Pill, the contraceptive, had been approved by the government in 1960, and although it was legally unavailable to single women in some places, Manhattan was hardly one of those places. Now women, too, were being liberated. They were not just demanding equal rights and being called by their own names—not the "Mrs." before their husband's—but they were having sex and were only slightly more likely to get pregnant than men.

Nora was hardly an exception. By her own testimony, she had an abortion—although she might have said that as a political statement, an affirmation of sisterhood, rather than because it was an actual fact. At first, she went to Planned Parenthood for the Pill, and then only if she was in a relationship. Later, it became a matter of routine. She used drugs—marijuana, of course, but also cocaine on occasion. She had the best of all alibies: She was young. It was the sixties.

For a kid just out of college, *Newsweek* in the 1960s was a feast. Like many journalistic enterprises it had a very high estimation of its own importance. Yet it was true that if not the whole world then key parts of it—New York, Washington, and some European capitals—read it avidly and wondered along with more than about two million readers what would be on its cover.

After a slow start, *Newsweek* became the chronicler of the 1960s. The magazine's cover stories from that era were the usual stuff of politics and war, but there, too, was a naked Jane Fonda (shot from the back) who had starred in the movie *Barbarella*, and more substantial and consequential subjects such as "The Negro in America" and separate issues on "Marijuana" and "LSD." For the marijuana cover, the magazine allowed its reporter to buy dope—and use it.

But before *Newsweek* plunged into the chaotic 1960s, it held fast to the 1950s. Its covers were mostly a march of political or government figures—New York governor Nelson Rockefeller, House of Representatives speaker John Mc-Cormack, Attorney General Robert Kennedy, Secretary of Defense Robert Mc-Namara, Arizona senator Barry Goldwater, and a stark profile of John Fitzgerald Kennedy dated December 2, 1963, a bit more than a week after he was assassinated in Dallas. That was followed a week later by one of Lyndon Johnson.

With the exception of Jomo Kenyatta, the leader of newly independent Kenya, all the covers were of white men—or of themes such as "The Mighty U.S. Consumer." There was nary a hint of the looming cultural unrest that would mark and mar the 1960s, and indeed the magazine itself featured a last-page column by Raymond Moley, a onetime New Dealer who had turned hard right. In the March 4, 1963, issue, he praised J. Edgar Hoover's stewardship of the FBI in language so effusive Hoover himself might have scoffed: "As long as Hoover or the Hoover tradition is on guard, Americans need not fear the perils of a police state."

Even as the sixties took hold, though, there was one tradition that *Newsweek* would not break: A woman's place was in the mail room. Or the library. Or on the research desk. But not as a correspondent, writer, or editor. When, in 1970, the women of *Newsweek* filed a sex discrimination lawsuit, Elliott owned up not only to the truth but to the provenance of the practice: "The fact that most researchers at *Newsweek* are women and that virtually all writers are men stems from a newsmagazine tradition going back almost fifty years," he said in a statement. In other words, don't blame *Newsweek*. *Time* magazine had been doing it even longer.

Nora was long gone from *Newsweek* by then, but she was so upset by Elliott's statement that she wrote to Katharine Graham, who had succeeded her late husband as the CEO of the Washington Post Company. Nora wanted to know if Graham was aware of the situation. It turns out, she wasn't.

According to Lynn Povich, a former *Newsweek* writer and the author of "The Good Girls Revolt," an account of the sex discrimination lawsuit, Nora wrote something like "I don't know what you've been told, but this is the situation. . . ." Graham, who was slowly and somewhat tardily coming to terms with the women's movement—she wound up being personally tutored by Gloria Steinem—sent Nora a courteous non-reply reply by return mail. She found Nora's letter to be very interesting, she wrote, and invited her stop by to discuss it. The two later became friendly, and possibly the *Newsweek* situation was discussed, but by then such overt sex discrimination was in the past.

Back in Nora's day, the bright young women the magazine hired from the very best colleges were there to deliver mail, clip stories from newspapers for the library, known as "the morgue," and work as researchers, which meant fact-checking and doing original reporting. They had one other function. They comprised an ever-refreshed sexual buffet—gentlemen, help yourselves. It wasn't just that men—married or single—had affairs with the always-younger mail girls and researchers, it was that they sometimes even had sex in the office. In fact, one room—ostensibly an infirmary—was definitely not for the infirm.

Newsweek, like *Time*, kept an odd schedule. It started the workweek on Tuesday and ended it on Saturday night—often very late indeed. Nora was a researcher for the Nation section, where, on Tuesday morning, the editors met to discuss the week's likely news. (Obviously, this could change daily and almost always did.) The most senior editors were called the Wallendas, after the Flying Wallendas, a circus high-wire act that defied both gravity and death but cheated by doing it sober. *Newsweek*'s editors, in contrast, pulled off their weekly high-wire act with an occasional snort.

Within three months, Nora was promoted to "clipper," meaning she ripped out articles from the newspaper for filing in the library, and a short while later she was made a researcher. Ordinarily, that was as far as a woman could go, but before Nora in fact went, she left behind the kind of work that is remembered to this day. The magazine had scheduled a cover story on Mc-George Bundy, who was President Kennedy's special assistant for national security affairs. Nora was dispatched to Yale, where Bundy had been an undergraduate, to see what she could find. The result "was not just good, it was magical," recalled Peter Goldman. (Alas, the file has been lost.)

The bulk of the story concerned Bundy's Washington responsibilities, which, according to *Newsweek*, he discharged with breathtaking aplomb. (The piece itself is a virtual parody of the sort of star-struck journalism that Kennedy engendered—"In the Kennedy inner circle, Bundy shares a place with a handful of advisers, all of whom—like the man they advise—are tough, brainy and energetic.") In news magazine fashion, the article was mostly reported by one person in Washington and written by another in New York. Almost all of what Nora contributed was, as she and everyone else expected, not used. It was, though, noticed.

"Word got around the shop that the kid had done something amazing," Goldman continued. "Pretty soon, ditto copies of her file were being passed from cubicle to cubicle, like samizdats in the late Soviet Union. Jaws dropped. Eyes popped. It was Nora's first big hit in the pro game, and nobody in the world beyond the walls of 444 Madison [*Newsweek*'s headquarters] got to see it." In fact, by the time the Bundy cover came out, March 4, 1963, Nora had moved downtown.

Get Your Ass Out
of My Chair

"I'm Nora Ephron and what should I do?"

"Well, first you can get your ass out of my chair."

Thus began Nora's first day at the venerated but down-at-the-heels *New York Post*. She had come into the city room and casually taken the seat of the city editor, Edward Kosner.

In his telling, Kosner remembers that Nora got her job because her parents knew the paper's owner, Dorothy Schiff. In her biography of Schiff, *The Lady Upstairs*, Marilyn Nissenson says that actually the Ephrons knew Schiff's daughter who lived in Los Angeles, but she gives more credence to the story Nora herself told, which is not only the better one but has the virtue of being true.

On December 8, 1962, the unions at four of New York's major newspapers—the *Daily News*, the *Journal-American*, the *World-Telegram and Sun*, and the *Times*—went on strike. In solidarity, the remainder of the city's papers—the *Daily Mirror*, the *Herald Tribune*, the *Post*, and both the *Long Island Star Journal* and the *Long Island Daily Press*—closed down. For most of those newspapers, it was the beginning of the beginning of the end.

But for Nora it was just the beginning. Not surprisingly, Nora's stint at the *Post* was the work of the ubiquitous Navasky. He came up with the idea of *Monocle* filling the newspaper void with parodies of the stricken publications. They were to do the *Times*, the *News*, the *Tribune*, and the *Post*.

Dan Wakefield, soon to be a famous magazine writer and novelist, parodied the *Post*'s pompous columnist Max Lerner. Sidney Zion, a Yale classmate of Navasky's and at that time an assistant U.S. attorney in New Jersey, went after Murray Kempton, the most exalted of the *Post* columnists. Both Lerner and Kempton had distinctive writing styles that lent themselves to parody. Not so Leonard Lyons, who it can be fairly said hardly had any writing style at all. His forte was the harmless, often unctuous, usually pointless anecdote that sometimes did not end but merely trailed off with three dots . . .

"When President John F. Kennedy was inaugurated President, his entire family attended," Nora wrote in Lyons's inimitable non-style style. "They include Rose and Joseph P. Kennedy, Eunice and Sargent Shriver, Ethel and Bobby Kennedy, Jean and Steve Smith, Jean and Teddy Kennedy and many others. My wife, Sylvia, who met Kennedy when he was only Senator, remarked to me, 'He's older, isn't he?' . . . I told the President that story at the party for former Ambassador Earl E. T. Smith at the Waldorf-Astoria. . . . He had a good laugh."

Lyons did not.

Neither did some of the *Post*'s editors. The managing editor, Al Davis, wanted to sue—although on what grounds is not clear. A bemused Dorothy Schiff suggested a different tack. "Don't be idiots," she supposedly said. "If they can parody us, they can write for us. Hire them!"

This account—which was Nora's account—sounds apocryphal. The *Post*, after all, was shuttered and was officially hiring no one. This might account for why it was widely believed that Nora got her job through family connections. Yet Zion told the same story. He got hired on the basis of his Kempton parody—the beginning of a raucous career as a writer and agitator that took him from the *Post* to the *Times* to the *Daily News*.

In due course, Nora moved on. But the newsroom stayed with her, as it does with most people. Newspapering is a job, of course. And after a while it can be like any other—repetitive, boring, predictable. But for a time—and for some that time never comes—it can be a true moveable feast, a term Hemingway misapplied to Paris.

Every day as a journalist you seek the new, the bizarre, the different, the exotic, and of course, the salacious. Every day you seek the stories that other people want to read. You barge into the lives of others, you demand the truth from them, you nod in ersatz sympathy, you pretend—you lie and lie in the proclaimed cause of the truth. You accumulate a lifetime of experiences in a year—maybe a month. You go where most people never do—and where you never will again. There is nothing like it, and no one who has done newspapering ever forgets it or, when life dulls down, doesn't miss it just a bit.

Paul Sann, who had taken over from the erudite Columbia graduate James Wechsler as editor (Wechsler remained editorial page editor), was apparently one of those newspapermen who considered a college education an affectation if not a downright hindrance. Sann was a Brooklyn kid and inordinately proud of it. He did not much care for Nora, although she later wrote how much she respected him. Still, within a week of walking in the door at 75 West Street, she went from being a provisional reporter to being a full-fledged one.

The *Post* was a dump. It occupied two floors of a sagging building built in 1926 and, in a symbolic repudiation of its origins, later converted into a fancy apartment house. It was located in a remote part of the city, up against the Hudson River, which in the winter did its level best to approximate the Bering Sea. The area was frigid. The *Post* was in Gotham's gulag.

It was also losing money or, depending on the year, not making much. It wasn't spending much, either, so that for instance it was a big deal to take a cab to an assignment. Pete Hamill, who started at the paper at the age of sixteen with a degree from nowhere but with the proper attitude, remembered how he'd hope to find a photographer going his way so he could get to an assignment before some building superintendent had hosed the blood off the sidewalk. Photographers had cars. Reporters had the subway.

New York in the 1960s was not so much a city as a collection of tribes. Rather than have markings, the tribes had newspapers. You were what you read, and in the afternoon, if you were middle class and Jewish, you read the *New York Post*. If you were Catholic and conservative, you read the *Journal-American*, and if you were Protestant, you read the *World-Telegram and Sun*. (Protestants were rumored, but never seen.) This peculiar Balkanization suited the publishers of the afternoon papers. "You have the Jews, we have the Protestants, and the *Journal-American* has the Catholics," Roy Howard of the *World-Telegram and Sun* told Schiff, according to a Gail Sheehy profile of her. "Let's keep it that way."

The *Post* was avowedly liberal, pro-union, had swooned for Roosevelt and his New Deal, was staunchly Zionist, and had been enthusiastically opposed to the anti-Communist antics of Joe McCarthy. The paper carried the editorial page cartoon of the *Washington Post*'s Herbert Block—he signed his drawings "Herblock" and claimed to have coined the term "McCarthyism" in a 1950 cartoon—but few noticed or cared that he was not a *New York Post* employee. The out-of-towner Herblock became the face of the *Post*.

But its soul was its owner. The paper had been founded by Alexander Hamilton in 1801 and bought in 1939 by Schiff, the granddaughter of Jacob Schiff, a German-Jewish financier of immeasurable wealth and well-known philanthropic endeavors. Dorothy, known as Dolly, was different from her parents and grandparents in one enormously important respect: She was a liberal Democrat. In all but her social class, she mirrored both the ethnicity and the politics of her readers. She was one of them—if they happened to be filthy rich, something of a snob, and four times married.

The newspaper that Dorothy Schiff put out and that Nora joined in 1963 was liberal in an era when it was often convenient to make no distinction between liberalism and communism. (Among other things, the *Post* was the first big city daily to hire an African American reporter—the grandiloquently named but abundantly talented Theodore Roosevelt Poston.) The Jewish community was by far the *Post*'s most important constituency, but the African American one mattered as well. It was, in fact, the two communities that Calvin Trillin had in mind when he wrote the mock headline, "Cold Snap Hits Our Town. Jews, Negroes Suffer Most." It was intended for Navasky's parody of the *Post*, but it was never used.

Years after leaving the *Post*, Nora wrote a biting essay about Dorothy Schiff, but there was much to admire in the grande dame. She was, of course, everything Nora said she was: entitled, very rich, and cavalier about the obligation of a newspaper to actually publish news.

On the other hand, Schiff was working with her own money, which had been a bequest to her from her fabulously rich grandparents. Her business was heiress. All she really knew how to do was economize—so much so that her newsroom was a dirty, unsanitary, and fetid mess, the hallway redolent with the smell of urine wafting from the men's room. "Philthy," was etched into the dust on the city room's glass door. It was, though, not nearly as "philthy" as the bathrooms.

A year could go by before anyone in the *Post*'s newsroom would see Dolly Schiff, but Nora did. She was one of the select few occasionally invited up to lunch with the publisher—sandwiches from the cafeteria—and once she confronted Schiff with a memo she had written as a union rep about the *Post*'s grubby and decrepit working conditions, particularly the smelly lavatories. Schiff responded that her employees were the sort who could make a mess out of anything.

The *Post* was unionized, and so Nora's job was protected. Still, a publisher could make her feelings known—a memo here, a frown there, a remark dropped, and soon the editors got the drift: Keep Ephron out of the paper. Send her to cover cops. At night. That did not happen, of course, because Nora was too valuable and too liked by Schiff, but here again is a display of Nora's astounding confidence, a conviction not just that she belonged and could not be removed but that she was right. Who could argue? Schiff did not even bother. Mostly, she just ignored Nora's complaints.

Later, however, Schiff came to rue both her hiring of Nora and her patience with her. She told the *Post*'s one-time managing editor Robert Spitzler that she rued giving Nora a pass for what was, really, a grave journalistic sin. Nora, it turned out, had written for the *New York Times* at the same time she was writing for the *New York Post*. Journalism has few rules, but one of them is that you never write for a competitor.

If Nora did not quite see the *Times* as a competitor—or, to put it the other way—if she did not quite see the *Post* as a *Times* competitor, who could blame her? The *Post* was an afternoon paper. The *Times* was morning. One was a racy tab; the other was a broadsheet and proclaimed itself the newspaper of record. Nonetheless, the papers competed and so Nora, faced with a severe prohibition but very much wanting to write for the *Times*, compromised. On June 11, 1967, an essay appeared in the book review section. It was headlined "Eating and Sleeping with Arthur Frommer." It was about the man who conceived and published the many books that enabled Americans of modest means to travel almost anywhere in the world on a modest $5 a day. The piece was written by someone named Nora Greenburg. She was identified thusly: "Mrs. Greenburg made her first trip to Europe and the Caribbean guided by '$5-a-Day' guides."

This Mrs. Greenburg was a dandy writer. Her piece is charming and zippy, humorous, too, but it is also unexpectedly indignant. It turns out that the surprise about "surprising Amsterdam" is that Frommer had a deal with KLM, Royal Dutch Airlines, which is why he kept promoting the surprisingly charming Dutch city. Mrs. Greenburg did not approve and she says so.

How Nora expected to get away with writing for the *Times* while still at the *Post* is impossible to say. I think she used her married name just to spare Schiff and her editors any embarrassment, but the article is pure Nora and was bound to be noticed. By then, though, she was on her way out of the *Post* anyway, heading for a freelance career that would make her a star. She needed that *New York Times* piece more than she needed the *New York Post*. In any event, Schiff essentially looked the other way. Nora was retained, but it was seen as proof to some at the *Post* that she was just passing through on her way to bigger, better, and when it came to the lavatories, less smelly things.

The taciturn and phlegmatic Schiff withdrew the *New York Post* from the publisher's association and resumed printing on March 8, 1963. Almost instantly, Nora's first story appeared. It involved the fruitless attempt of the New York Aquarium at Coney Island to mate two hooded seals. Nora wrote it funny. She knew she had succeeded when, after submitting her copy, she heard chuckles from the city desk.

Her second article was a sprightly written piece on Tippi Hedren, the star of Alfred Hitchcock's movie *The Birds*. In true *Post* style, the article was brief and pointless, but it wasn't supposed to do more than mention the movie and the star, which it did.

No one can recall Nora's first days at the *Post* and what exactly compelled her editors to compress the tryout period to a mere and unheard of one week. But she remembered why. She simply went on a rip. She had a fast typewriter, the gift of wit, the eye of a born reporter, and, not the least, a voice. She wrote like she talked—and when she talked, everyone listened.

Nora skipped whole eras of a writer's life—no awkward beginner's stuff, no gross mistake of fact, no crazy juvenile error, and no crash-and-burn tryout at some provincial paper. She went straight to the *New York Post*, which, say what you will about it, was a New York newspaper and the voice of New York liberalism. The paper was read. The paper mattered.

Astoundingly, she was already giving advice to other novices on how to how to handle themselves in the big time. "She told me never admit you don't know something," Lynn Sherr said. Pretend you do. Walk out of the building and go right to a phone booth and then call someone and ask where you go."

And how do you get to where you have to go? The subway. Beverly Hills raised, yes, Wellesley educated, again yes. But Nora became a master of the subways, which daunted her not one bit. Many years later, when she was a rich movie director and screenwriter, she'd still hop on the subway to swiftly get to where she had to go. She called it "magical."

At the *Post*, Nora was used mostly as a feature writer and she frequently wrote a staple called "Woman in the News." The profiles were usually tied to some sort of manufactured event—the publication of a book, the opening of a movie—and they were not intended to be either biting or particularly candid. It was sometimes hard to tell if Nora had even laid eyes on the subject, never mind interviewed her.

For instance, she wrote a profile of Sybil Burton, the ex-wife of the actor Richard Burton, who had absconded with Elizabeth Taylor. The ex–Mrs. Burton had founded a New York discotheque named Arthur, but the peg for the story was not her former marriage or her current nightclub, but her marriage a week earlier to Jordan Christopher, who was, Nora tells us in the very first paragraph, a mere twenty-four while his bride was thirty-six. She quotes from various sources but never, it seems, directly from Burton. The piece was mostly, maybe entirely, a clip job.

The term "clip job" is almost always used pejoratively since it entails a lack of reporting—journalistic laziness, in other words. But all the articles in *Newsweek* and *Time* were versions of clip jobs, since one person did the reporting and another did the writing. The ability to take some old newspaper clippings and turn them into a vivid story was a valued talent at afternoon newspapers. Nora was a master of that art.

This is Nora doing Doris Day: "That little twinkle in the eyeball and crinkle 'round the eye, and blue, pink, yellow, Easter egg colors with sunshine, smiles and freckles." That week, the actress of almost pornographic wholesomeness had "for the umpteenth time [been] named the biggest box office draw on Earth." Nora went on to paint a portrait of an emotionally tangled woman, more attached to animals than people, somewhat reclusive, who converted to Christian Science via Catholicism and Unitarianism and who was "close to a nervous breakdown because she thought she had breast cancer or tuberculosis" but who finally saw a doctor at the insistence of her husband, himself a convert to Christian Science via Judaism.

It is all there. A jumble of religions, a train wreck of contradictory facts—cancer or TB, a Christian Science husband who calls in the doctor. The article was accompanied by a photo of the gleaming Ms. Day, looking off into the proverbial middle distance and appearing, at the same time, a bit more frantic than happy. Nora, it seems, was nowhere near her. The closest she got was an apparent telephone interview. It was so brief and so anodyne that almost none of it is quoted, but Nora noted what Day herself called her personal gem: her recipe for ice cream and pretzels.

"We take very thin, crispy pretzels and have a big dish of chocolate and vanilla ice cream. Oh, it's great."

Nora did the comedian and civil rights activist Dick Gregory and the TV personality George Gobel and the actor Kirk Douglas. She wrote about teenage drinking and female drug addiction and over and over again about the

Beatles. (Their arrival in New York is something she talked about for the rest of her life.) "Well, friends," she wrote on one occasion, "guess what happened Friday night at the Beatles concert in Forest Hills? About 26,000 Beatle fans—most of them young girls who are willing to spend their allowance—came and did The Shriek."

She wrote a piece on *Monocle* magazine and somehow suppressed the urge to disclose that she had once dated its publisher and creator, Victor Navasky. She went to Washington for the visit of Britain's Princess Margaret and her husband, the photographer Antony Armstrong-Jones, and then returned for the wedding of President Johnson's daughter, Lynda Bird, to Charles Robb, a Marine destined to become a U.S. senator. For that one, she got "the wood," a page one headline so huge the mold for it had to be made out of wood.

Most of what Nora wrote was routine, tabloid boilerplate. Afternoon newspapers were always written on the run. Stories were sometimes dictated over the phone to rewritemen (or women) who were required to keep a cigarette in their mouth and a flask in the drawer. (One of mine at the *Washington Post* even quoted the words of a bank robber—"Stick 'em up," he had him say. I had him take it out.) Bit by bit, though, peeks of the real Nora can be glimpsed glowing under the punchy modifiers. In a story about a discharged high school teacher, Nora noticed the kids hanging around the school. They "smoked cigarettes rather badly," she observed.

She posed as a rich man's wife and pretended to be interested in renting a $5,000-a-month apartment in the Carlyle Hotel. After that, she wrote that she went home to her own $135-a-month apartment, where she kept "the golf clubs in the hall." Since I never knew Nora to play golf, the hallway is where her clubs must have remained.

Yet again she pretended to be on the hunt for a home and went to see the one being sold by the hugely popular TV comedian Jackie Gleason. The place was anything but conventional. Again she played ordinary housewife. "How would I dust a television set suspended from the ceiling over the round bed with the round sheets and the round blanket?" she asked.

Nora was emerging as a name, a recognized byline. News stories are conveyed by the material, the facts, the data—the what-where-when-and-how of them. Bylines are extraneous and were once awarded sparingly, the conceit being that it didn't matter who wrote the story. What mattered was the story.

With feature stories it was a different matter. They required good writing, and so good writers got noticed. They brought an eye to what they did. They demanded attention: Look at it my way. Nora made you look. Nora made you look at it her way.

Nora learned quite a bit at the *Post*. She learned to write fast and she learned how to report and she learned how to conduct herself in a newsroom mostly populated by men, although she was far from the only woman on the staff. Most of her colleagues liked her and some of the women felt she was special. One of them was Helen Dudar, who had started at the *Post* way back in 1956 and had married Peter Goldman, the *Newsweek* writer. When she died, Goldman asked Nora to write a commemorative essay for *The Attentive Eye*, a book of Dudar's writings he had compiled. A man might have written about Dudar's writing skills. And Nora did. A man might have written how fast Dudar was on the typewriter—"She was, in a city room full of world-class rewritemen, the greatest rewriteman of all."

It might seem that Nora made a man out of Dudar, when, in fact, she had simply shattered the sexist categories, and anyway she quickly moved on to other things she admired about Dudar, and they included her fish soup with rouille, her copper pots, and her love for the South of France. The rewrite man was a girl after all.

Nora's years at the *Post* taught her that she was special—that she had the gift. She discovered that she could write fluidly and fast, teasing the deadline like a matador does the bull. Beyond that, though, she had an unmistakable voice, that ineffable quality that's so difficult to explicate and so impossible to miss.

She was present in every story, talking to the reader in a direct and engaging way. The stories were always about something—a crime, an accident, an opening, a closing—but always in some way about her. A Nora Ephron piece was like a Hemingway short story: distinct.

Nora was twenty-one when she skewered Leonard Lyons. She was just starting out in journalism. What you want—at least what I wanted—was to be welcomed into the circle of journalists, to be recognized as one of the boys by the boys themselves. Nora had no need for that—and no apparent fear, either, that she could make enemies that would block her career path. The Leonard Lyons piece was an example of Nora's bristling self-confidence, as if she knew that the world would judge her on the basis of her writing and not on who her writing happened to hurt. By hiring her, Dorothy Schiff, of all people, proved her right.

In January 1967, Nora wrote a series for the *Post* on Johnny Carson, host of NBC's late-night show. This was both a coup and a triumph, hardly an assignment to be given to just anyone. Carson, by then the most popular figure on television, was also the most enigmatic, and a series about him was bound to be well read. Nora did not disappoint.

The writing was staccato. You can almost hear the typewriter keys hitting the paper, the return of the carriage, and a new sentence beginning. The writing is fast, simple, the details slipped in like dolphins curving into the water.

To Nora, Carson himself is cocooned, unknowable, and renowned for being a blank. Politicians come on his show, but he avoids talking politics. He eschews complexity, possibly thought itself. He hates interviews. "He submits to them, sitting in his newly upholstered gold couch in his newly decorated office paneled in wood-patterned Formica," she wrote. Johnny Carson was then making $1 million a year, with thirteen weeks off so he could play Las Vegas, where he made $40,000 a week. He could have had any kind of office he wanted. Do you want to know about Johnny Carson? Nora asked her *New York Post* readers. Come into his office and notice the "wood-patterned Formica."

A year later she expanded her series into a book titled *and now . . . Here's Johnny!* In her acknowledgments, she mentioned some of her *Post* colleagues as well as her friend Anne Navasky, "for wanting to be acknowledged." Finally, she acknowledged the famous author Dan Greenburg. He was about to become her husband.

How to Be a Jewish Housewife

*N*ora was a throwback, not just to the Algonquin Round Table, but farther back and across the ocean. She was a latter-day salonnière, an updated version of the well-off Jewish women of nineteenth-century Berlin and Vienna who advanced science and medicine, as well as gossip, until most of them assimilated by converting to Christianity and faded into history. The most famous of them was probably Rahel Varnhagen, so dazzling a personality that the German émigré and New York intellectual Hannah Arendt one hundred years later considered the dead woman her best friend. (Arendt's real best friend was Mary McCarthy, the American writer whose feud with Lillian Hellman Nora chronicled in her play *Imaginary Friends*.)

Nora's purpose, unlike Varnhagen's, was not to effect assimilation or discuss the scientific or medical advances of the day—although no topic was off the table—but just to have a bang-up conversation and a rollicking good time. The laughs, though, had to be underpinned by a wry sophistication, a tart knowledge of "the business," a familiarity with politics and foreign affairs, a preferred—but not required—liberalism, and a gift for performance. A good story had to be well told, otherwise why tell it?

In 1967, Nora made two significant moves. She left the *Post* and she got married. Dan Greenburg was a Chicago-born former advertising man who in his spare time had written his Jewish mother best seller. The book was excerpted in *Playboy*, of all places, tucked in among the fabulous breasts and ribald humor. Greenburg was, in fact, a *Playboy* writer, published there frequently.

Nora and Dan were fixed up by the omnipresent Navaskys. The four had dinner, and Nora and Dan hit it off and started to date. First it was a Friday night–Saturday night sort of affair, then one more day was added and then another, and then, Dan recalled, "there were no days left, so we moved in to-gether"—or, to be a more accurate, Nora moved into Dan's place, a cozy duplex at 67th Street and Fifth Avenue.

On April 9, 1967, Nora and Dan were married in Rockefeller Center's famous Rainbow Room, where Dan, from his old advertising days, had connections. Rabbi Ira Eisenstein, a founder of the Reconstructionist branch of Judaism, presided. It was, as far as I can tell, Nora's last brush with a rabbi. Neither her marriage nor the rabbi went the distance.

The Ephron-Greenburg marriage was perfect . . . on paper. They were both smart and witty and both writers. Dan was famous, Nora less so, but she was the impresario of the many dinner parties they gave. "Nora was somebody who had an incredible gift," Dan recalled. "She could walk up to a celebrity and say, 'Hi, my name is Nora Ephron and I'm a reporter for the *New York Post*. Would you like to come to dinner?' Hardly anyone said no because she was so appealing."

Dan, on the other hand, was somewhat shy and unskilled in the art of entertainment. "I would not know how to give a dinner party. I have all the social finesse of somebody who was raised by wolverines."

Dan was possibly the first to notice Nora's gift for collapsing the vaunted six degrees of separation, the notion that one can reach anyone in the world through an introduction to six people. Nora had it down to one—herself—and in later years anyone who knew her knew that she knew anyone you wanted to reach. I exaggerate just a bit by saying that if I wanted to get in touch with the Pope, I would first call Nora. She'd know how.

Nora's early dinner parties, the ones she threw with Dan, established her presence in New York. She went through literary-journalistic-showbiz Gotham like a kid on monkey bars, swinging from one person to another to another. At someone else's party, she and Dan met the director Frank Perry, whose first film, *David and Lisa*, had been a low-budget hit. Perry had since become a big-time director and was casting his western *Doc*, which was to star Stacy Keach and Faye Dunaway, with a script by Pete Hamill. It was to shoot in Spain. Perry needed someone for the part of a character named Clum. He took one look at Greenburg and said, "That face, that face. I have to have that face in my movie." Perry promised to send the script the next day.

Nothing arrived.

Nora responded with a dinner party. She invited Perry; and he was, as intended, suitably impressed by the other guests: Mike Nichols, the screenwriter Buck Henry, and the as-famous writers Joan Didion and John Gregory Dunne. Perry, who spoke a Hollywood-hipster patois, said to Greenburg, "This is peers-ville, man. This is peers-ville, man. In other words, you're on my level and it's safe to send you a script." He did. And after a trip to Spain and some makeup, Greenburg became "Clum."

What's My Line? Redux

To those who knew her name, Nora Ephron was a movie director and a writer—or maybe the other way around. To those who knew her, Nora Ephron was a hostess—an impresario of the round table, whose invitations were cherished and, in some respects, feared. She learned early the value of home cooking and celebrity. The combo had gotten Dan his part in a Frank Perry western. All it took was some dazzling guests and some really good food.

Nora had been giving dinner parties since leaving Wellesley. She had made a study of what worked and what did not. Early on, she had leased an apartment on University Place in Greenwich Village because it was above a restaurant that offered takeout. Lack of money was no reason not to have dinner parties, she felt.

But after a while, no takeout was used. Nora did the cooking. She did the cooking because she liked to cook, and she was good at it, but also because her food was an offering, a gift—an expression of her affection for her guests. For Nora, food was an embrace, and the hugs she offered so parsimoniously were placed on the table.

The Nora Ephron dinner party soon took on outsized meaning and importance. It was calculated. She had studied the art of hospitality. Famously, she insisted on a round table for dinner, not in mimicry of the Algonquin's but upon instruction from the cookbook author and entrepreneur of home entertaining Lee Bailey. He told her—he showed her—that it facilitated conversation.

Interesting people were invited and required—or so they thought—to say interesting things. Nora often announced the subject with a sharp tinkle of the wineglass. If there were more than eight guests, then there had to be two tables, each one weighted, like an airplane's luggage compartment, with celebrities or personalities. No good loading one table with loudmouths and the other with listeners. This thing had to be calibrated. I was often seated to Nora's right, why I do not know, since we had probably talked earlier that day, certainly that week, and we had nothing to say to each other. Still, I was pleased.

For many of her friends, Nora was a one-person admissions committee. If she was interested or intrigued, she would extend an invitation to lunch. Some people got invited once and then never again. Others were asked back— dinner, poker, or other games. Many of them felt not just complimented by her friendship but honored. Her acceptance of them testified not just to their fame—lots of others were even more famous—but to their wit, their intellect, their personality.

By the time Steven Spielberg met Nora, he was fabulously rich, not to mention famous and incredibly powerful and influential. Probably no movie director has ever been as successful, and the success came at a remarkably young age. Before he had turned thirty, he had made *Jaws*. He soon was a producer, owned a studio, and was turning out hit after hit. Steven Spielberg had become the wealthiest, most powerful, and possibly the most creative figure Hollywood had ever produced—and yet, somewhere in his own mind, he remained a kid from various suburbs while Nora was an urbane figure taken right off the tiny black-and-white screen of his boyhood TV set.

"I felt like I had met the original panel of *What's My Line?* all wrapped up in one person," Spielberg said.

Steve Martin felt no differently. He, too, had had huge success—writer, comic, musician, novelist, and playwright, and, not incidentally, an art collector with a keen eye. It nevertheless took Nora's acceptance and friendship for him to feel recognition as something more than a comic.

"I had made it in a kind of stand-up and . . . I didn't feel I belonged in that [her] company," he told me.

Nora's dinners were happy, jolly occasions, but the guests were not there just to eat. These were participatory events. Guests were obliged to perform, to make the party better—sometimes to ask a question of the table.

"She would come over to me and she would pull me over to the side and say, 'Do you have a question?'" Tom Hanks recalled. "Meaning that you had to come up with the question that would start off the single conversation. Nora would let the dinner party go for a while and then she would tap the glass and she would say, 'Okay, now, here's the question.'"

Hanks remembered one night when the guests were given slips of paper and asked to write a brief description of their first job. The slips were then deposited in a pan and picked at random. The idea was to guess which guest had had which job.

Another time, she asked who was to blame for the Monica Lewinsky scandal. Hanks, a frequent guest, was there for that one, too. "We went around the entire table. And everybody said something different. Some people blamed Lewinsky, the White House intern whose affair with Bill Clinton resulted in his impeachment. Some people blamed Linda Tripp, the Lewinsky pal who betrayed her. Some people blamed Ken Starr, the special prosecutor. And it went around the table until it got to Nora and she said, 'Well I just can't believe that none of you said Bill Clinton.' And we all said, 'Well, yeah, of course it's that.'"

Nora sometimes asked her guests what they would want named for them. Some said a building or a monument, but Nora—or maybe it was me—suggested a dance step, and I—or maybe it was Nora—suggested a sex act. "Are you up to doing a Cohen? (or an Ephron?)" one could ask, either on the dance floor or in bed. At moments like this, the ones of utter confusion and the melding of memories, we would look at each other and laugh. I had once been me. She had once been her. Somewhere along the line, we had become each other's anecdotes.

No, No, No

I was once asked by *Vanity Fair* magazine what Nora might have been had she not become a movie director. I paused just to make it seem that I was thinking, and then I said, "Dictator of Argentina." I thought the line was both funny and apt, but Nora thought it was neither. When the magazine came out, I got a call from her.

"Y'know, Richard, not everything you say is funny."

Spoken as a true dictator.

In the years afterward, I had no reason to reassess. Nora was no Eva Peron and she was not one for firing squads, but she had an irrepressible need to run the lives of other people. She did this not because she was a busybody and not because she needed to interfere, but because it was clear to her that some if not all of the people she loved were inexplicably incompetent at everything they did, with the possible exception of what they did for a living. That is why, for instance, she seized control of my son's bar mitzvah, transforming it from a High Anglican ritual held at a proper hotel on Washington's very proper Massachusetts Avenue to a raucous, joyous affair of ethnic exuberance held at a New York–type place run by guys named Mo and Joe. *L'chaim!*

Nora was not content merely to direct her own dinner parties; she took over those of others as well. At one, she commandeered the table and asked the guests to describe the house they grew up in. What followed was not something out of *House and Garden*, but intimate stories of childhood.

Twice a year—summer and winter—she would take control of David Geffen's yacht as surely as if she had boarded with cutlass and blunderbuss. The boat, an astonishing 453 feet long, gave Nora the chance to be her own maître d'. To Geffen's delight, she chose the menu, organized the seating at dinner, and suggested the game to be played, the movies to be shown, and the sights to see in port. She organized shore expeditions—once to a shop in Sicily that made the world's best flat bread, or so she maintained. That entailed an hour-and-a-half car ride followed by a hike up a hill and, finally, the shop itself. As promised, the bread was terrific.

The actress Candice Bergen and her husband the real estate developer Marshall Rose were once guests on the Geffen boat at the same time as Nora and Nick. In her book *A Fine Romance*, Bergen described a week at sea with Nora: "She was an authority on, it seemed, everything. In St. Barths, she came back to the boat with six-packs of some juice no one had ever heard of and then drank all afternoon. She decided the menus on the boat, she did the seating at every meal, she chose the games after dinner and the movies we would watch. She knew everything and the best of everything."

Just about everyone surrendered to Nora, turning things over to her. Running the Geffen boat—I'm not sure she had it gassed, but I bet she checked the oil—was small potatoes compared to what she did with the super-lawyer David Boies's sixty-fifth birthday party. His wife, Mary, had planned a weekend of festivities at the Las Vegas hotel they then (2006) favored, the Venetian. She sent an invitation to Nora and Nick. It prompted an immediate phone call.

"No, no, no," Nora said. "Not the Venetian."

"But . . ."

"The Bellagio," Nora ordered. "Call Elaine Wynn," who along with her then husband, Steve, owned the place.

Mary did not know Elaine Wynn. Mary, an accomplished lawyer and usually fearless, was hesitant to call.

"Fine," Nora said.

Elaine Wynn called Mary. Soon, she was in New York, and samples of tablecloths, napkins, and other stuff were spread out for Mary to see. Elaine wanted to know what public rooms of the hotel Mary wanted and what colors she favored and what her themes might be.

Mary's mouth is still agape.

Nora was not yet through with Mary and David Boies. In 2012, they wanted to celebrate the fiftieth wedding anniversary of Meredith and Tom Brokaw. Again, invitations went out, this time for Blue Hill at Stone Barns, a dandy, bucolic place north of New York City, with impeccable foodie credentials.

"No, no, no," Nora said.

"But . . ."

"You're doing it at your place and I'm doing the cooking," Nora commanded.

Mary pointed out that her apartment could not possibly accommodate sixty people.

Move out the furniture, Nora said.

Move in ten round tables, Nora said.

The party was held on September 7, 2012. The guests ate meat loaf, mashed potatoes, fried chicken—the kind of comfort food Nora had always adored and often served herself. The party was joyous and intimate—but also sad. Nora had died in June.

I know, I know. The Boieses are rich and famous, and the Brokaws are rich and even more famous, and Nora herself was both. But she was not offering to throw a party for them and then bask in a cloud of puffy air kisses. She was yearning instead to make a good time even better. One of her many gifts was the urge to give, to make life better for the people she cared about. She had not, after all, offered Mary Boies the phone number of her caterer. She had offered to do the cooking. It goes without saying that she knew how to cook. It needs saying that she knew how to love.

Another Opening, Another Show

For Nora every dinner party was a little movie. We all had our parts to play. She would do the set, which was her apartment, and she had already done the casting and, often, some of the script. But it was up to the "actors" to act. The telling of a story was as important as its content—there was little use in having the latter without the former.

As for me, I was one of Nora's frequent non-famous guests. She collected many of them, mostly writers, and often women, whose names were recognizable to other writers but not the general public. Nora was not starstruck, although some of her guests surely were. Some nights it seemed that her round table was where the red carpet ended.

It was possible to flunk dinner party—as if it were a college course. I can't supply the names of those who did, who were never invited back, but I am sure it happened. I myself felt I had flunked many times. Since I was not famous, I felt I had to be funny or interesting, but this was a grievous misjudgment of what Nora expected. Her guests might be famous, but while that may have been an admissions ticket, they were also expected to be entertaining in some way. Above all, they had to be both likable and to like the other guests. Nora over time assembled a core cadre of dinner guests. Some were actors and some were directors and some were writers—but what they all had in common was obvious affection for one another.

At a Nora Ephron dinner party, it was often not enough to come up with a topic for discussion; guests were also required to play a game afterward. One of Nora's favorites was called Running Charades. Guests were divided into two teams, an umpire or judge supervised, and each team was given the same list of items or phrases that comprised a theme. The writer John Leo remembers that an item might be the book title *House of Seven Gables*, and another might be the Muhammad Ali phrase "Float like a butterfly, sting like a bee."

Each contestant would have to act at least one of these out, and after several more had been performed, some very smart person might connect Clark Gable with Butterfly McQueen and realize that the theme was the movie *Gone with the Wind*. The team that guessed it in the least amount of time was the winner. It was that simple.

It was also that terrifying. Among Nora's guests were entertainers like Bob Balaban and his wife, Lynn Grossman, a writer and one-time pianist who had put herself through college accompanying drag queens in piano bars (also conducting tours of Lincoln Center). These were performers. Even so, some performers got stage fright. Diane Keaton one night simply refused to play.

I loved being asked to Nora's for dinner. Who would be there? What stars? What interesting people? What would she cook? But along with anticipation came anxiety. The invitation was similar to being asked to make a toast: How nice. How flattering. But how nerve-wracking. The desire for applause, for acknowledgment as a wit, was more than offset by the fear of failure. I had seen the funniest men of my day flame out at some event or other. Being a dinner party guest of Nora's was not quite the same, of course, but one was expected to sparkle at dinner and then, afterward, to act out some nonsense word or phrase in a game of Running Charades. It was beyond me.

I would meet the challenge of, say, acting out "Clark Gable" by exploding into a sweat. The entire effort was an exercise in post-traumatic stress disorder,

reliving moments from high school when the teacher called me to the black-
board to solve a geometry problem. I would stare at the triangles and rect-
angles much as Napoleon's troops much have stared at the hieroglyphics of
the Rosetta stone, and no meaning would announce itself. "Clark Gable" was
a geometry problem with a mustache and dimples.

The "teacher," in this case Nora, took the games very seriously. Everyone
knew that and was appropriately intimidated. Once, a flummoxed player, frus-
trated to the point of criminal insanity, inadvertently blurted out the word she
was supposed to be acting out. It was a reckless, virtually suicidal thing to do,
and Nora exploded. She stopped the game and said, "We do not play this way.
That's cheating."

The "cheater" looked stricken.

Holy shit! a guest exclaimed.

Once—just once—I cheated. It was more of a prank than an actual cheat,
but, anyway, I got my entire team to go along and we ran away with the game.

Nora was dismayed that she had lost—or, maybe, that I had won. I felt
regret, remorse, as if I had made her lose confidence in herself. Out of pity,
I owned up. I cheated, I announced, thinking that getting away with cheating was more of a triumph than winning the game. She was dumbfounded,
stunned, uncomprehending. *I had cheated?* What kind of person would do
such a thing? What kind of person would treat a game as if it was, well, a game?
I felt as if I had burst some kind of bubble, like telling a kid that there is no
Santa Claus. For a painful moment, I feared our friendship would not survive,
as if I had cheated on *her*.

The essence of Nora was her work—her writing. No, that's not right. The essence for me was Nora herself. And I could say, too, that the essence of Nora
was those games. She had a severity that could frighten people, frighten the
very same people who loved her. She had a strange power that compelled people to play games they did not enjoy—as if they understood, in some Marxian
way, that they had to do this bit for the greater good of the party.

Nora knew her power. She knew how much she meant to people. Those people were not always aware of her insecurities and how much she sometimes needed them. But with very few exceptions—Mike Nichols, Bob Gottlieb (her editor at Knopf), Amanda Urban, and possibly (but not always) me—she was the dominant one in every relationship. (Her marriage to Nick was in a different category.)

It wasn't that Nora was one of those characters with multiple personalities. The overall personality, the character trait, was love, affection, caring solicitude. When her friends were in trouble, they turned to Nora. They didn't even have to turn. When the wife of the performer Martin Short died, Nora and Nick just arrived at the house with food. She brought food the next night and the next and "on the fourth night, she arrived with a giant platter of fried chicken."

"I said, 'Nora, it's just the kids and me,'" Short said. "'We have so much food already.' She handed me the platter and said, 'And now you have more food.'"

When Nancy Dolman Short died in 2010, Marty Short was already famous and successful and a charter member, if there could be such a thing, of a clique of the celebrated who cruised the Mediterranean in the summer and the Caribbean in the winter on David Geffen's boat. So Nora's solicitousness could be seen as either the attention due a friend or the attention due a star. But the attention and sympathy she gave Short in those days—and many after—were hardly any different from the way she reacted when a somewhat less famous writer named Deborah Copaken Kogan, whose book *Shutterbabe* Nora had admired, called her in East Hampton in something of a panic: She was thinking of leaving her husband.

While they were on the phone, Nora checked the bus schedule and had Kogan come out from Manhattan. She served her lunch, temporarily resolved the marital situation—and put her on the next bus back to the city. Nora gave that writer more than a quickie meal and some wise words. She gave her an afternoon—time. In the short run, she had no more of that than anyone else. In the long run, she had less.

By the time Nora met Kogan, Nora was already a famous person. But this ability of Nora's to engender trust was not dependent on celebrity or popularity, but was, for want of a better word, innate. Back in her high school days she became the confessor to Barry Diller, a Beverly Hills kid himself who lived about two blocks from her and who was a frequent companion as they walked to and from school. Diller was to become a media magnate, a billionaire, but, more to the point, an occasionally irascible and coldly methodical tycoon. He opened up to Nora. They were two years apart in age, Nora the older one, and she was in some ways the worldlier one. His feelings for her, always complicated, came out in verbal spasms of contradictions:

"It was not hard to know why I talked to her. Not that she was wise. But I trusted her, I trusted her. I don't know if trusted her. I talked to her, I did talk to her."

Tough Knows Tough

As far as I was concerned, that "Holy shit!" was way overdue. I knew of Nora's penchant for overreacting to some perceived slight—something she would take very personally but that was meant innocently. Years before, she had come to my house in Washington for dinner and another of the guests was Patrick Caddell, then a very big deal as President Jimmy Carter's in-house pollster and political adviser. Caddell brought a date, a young woman—a very young woman—whose contribution to the conversation—was it about the Soviet invasion of Afghanistan?—was to refer to Communists as "reds." I flinched. Such a retrograde word! So 1950s. So . . .

Nora hit the roof.

"Reds? she demanded. "Reds!" she repeated. Her voice was loud. She was indignant. "Who says reds anymore?"

The young woman instantly recoiled. She clearly meant nothing by the word. She clearly was unaware of its McCarthyite provenance or that Nora's parents had lived through the Hollywood blacklist, the Red Scare, and were themselves liberals, as, for that matter, was their daughter. She knew none of that. "Reds!" The word had somehow come tripping lightly off her tongue. It had hit the floor like a sack of rocks.

The very young woman instantly deflated. Explanations aborted in her throat. She gagged on second thoughts. She could say nothing. The verbal blows rained down on her. "Reds!" My God, she had said "Reds."

She was just a kid. It didn't matter what she'd said. This was child abuse. I was appalled.

Holy shit! I thought.

Nora was tough. She was tough in her writing, sending laser-like sentences from her keyboard to the printed page or the Internet, and she was tough in her personal life. Everyone who knew her—everyone who loved her—knew that, recognized that, and either felt her wrath or feared her wrath. She could turn suddenly dismissive, not in so many words—although the words would be there—but in body language, in a look, and then she would somehow inhale room temperature air and exhale frost. Almost anything could trigger such a reaction—a business dispute, an act of disloyalty, mistreatment of a friend, lack of respect, or something else entirely. It was the last category that was the most frightening because it was so ill defined, so impossible to anticipate. All the victim knew was that one day his or her relationship with Nora went from animated to inert. The loss—the loss of such a cherished friend—was incalculable, but what made it worse was the realization that she was not just a pal but the nexus of your social life. You had not merely lost a friend. You had lost a social set.

"She sort of ran the city," Scott Rudin, the theatrical and film producer, said.

"You didn't want to be on the wrong side of her. You know what I mean. She could be cutting, as you know, tough. You cross her selectively."

And yet the same people who feared Nora loved her. Of course, the people who feared her admired her, but love is an emotional metric beyond that, and love is what they felt. It's hard to explain how someone could be both feared and loved—maybe parents have that quality, and military leaders and coaches of football and other sports—but in Nora's case some of the fear had to do with losing her love. She was so charming, so smart, so witty, and so sweet that if she turned cold, it was more than an emotional rebuff, it was a failure: You had flunked Nora.

I luxuriated in Nora. I loved the life she offered me—the food I ate, the plays, the screenings, the people I met, the conversations we had—the fun, the laughs, and after a while, the shared history. We were like an old married couple. No one—with the exception of her sisters, especially Delia—knew her as long as I did, and possibly none knew her as well.

Maybe more important—at least to me—is that no one knew *me* as well. We had been through so much together—the breakup of her marriage and two of mine, her comically misguided relationship with a guy who took her to shoot birds in Georgia, the affair with Joe Fox and then the lasting one with Nick, the hurt over the *Heartburn* reviews, the distressing period of movie flops, the challenge of raising two sons in a Manhattan where the subway to anywhere was right downstairs, the upheavals of her father, and the times I came to her with a bruised heart and chaotic plans and she calmly talked me into a soft landing. Once she gave me permission to marry. Once she gave me permission to divorce. Both times it was the same woman.

I felt romantic toward Nora, which means I loved her, which means I loved walking next to her, sitting next to her, watching her cook. I loved shopping with her, which meant I was shopping for a gift and she was helping me. I loved her smile, loved to make her laugh—loved that above all—loved the sense that we shared so much but sometimes not our political views. I supported the war in Iraq, the one that led to the American occupation, and she did not. I assured her it would not lead to an increase in terrorism but might extinguish the threat. I was wrong, of course, and she was right, and only once did she ever acknowledge that. It happened one night at dinner when I confessed that I was wrong and she, nodding, said something like "I'll say"—and, mercifully, left it at that.

I loved her when she was irrational or emotional or whatever you might call it. I loved her when she told off the Secret Service agents who had the audacity to forbid our cab from pulling over to the curb at some Washington event just because the vice president was about to arrive. I loved her when she flipped off those waiters in Naples and when, right after her wedding with Carl, she told off the limo driver who had taken Third Avenue uptown and not the FDR Drive.

I loved her the many times I stayed with her—the apartment at the Apthorp on Broadway and the houses in the Hamptons. The first was called Trees. It was located in Bridgehampton and was named for the huge elms on the property. The house was an attempt at a Victorian. Nora and Carl spiffed it up and put in a pool with a telephone jack nearby. That enabled Carl to call me in tropical Washington—he on a rubber raft in the pool, I encased in industrial air conditioning. I felt painfully deprived.

Over time, I became the Nora interpreter. I supposedly knew her well enough to explain her, but it took a while. She got less complicated as she got older, warmer and less guarded. After a while, I could see beneath the jokes, and sometimes, as when a person gets hit the wrong way by an unflattering light, I could see the cracks of insecurity and notice when the touch was less than sure. That came with time, an accretion of cuts, the occasional calamity, and then I wanted to engulf her, but I rarely did. We exchanged vows—"I love you," "I love you"—and left it at that. I sometimes had to recall her words, those words, when she turned distant, and then I had to remember that she was scared of something.

I loved her even when I did not love her. I loved her when the phone went dead or I felt a chill and resigned myself to the fact that our friendship had inexplicably gone cool. I resolved not to care and every day I did. She frightened me, God only knows how she did it, and I would question our relationship and what I was getting out of it. Yes, it was wonderful to be her friend. Yes, it was flattering to be included in her guest list. Yes, I basked a bit in reflected fame and the celebrity swoosh of entering a many-starred restaurant, our table, always the best table, materializing with a proper grovel. But none of that came close to explaining why she meant so much to me. I still don't know the answer—but, surely, one of the reasons that I loved her is that, just as surely, she did.

Mouseburgers, Mush, and Breasts

*H*elen Gurley Brown was one of the most celebrated magazine editors of her time. Remarkably, when she took over *Cosmopolitan* magazine in 1965, as a female editor she was a rarity, and she immediately changed both the style and the content of the magazine. No longer was it targeted at the suburban housewife. The "single girl" took her place. If the suburban housewife was obsessed with her husband and her kids, the single girl had but one thing on her mind: sex. *Cosmo* told her when to do it, how to do it, and to do it as often as she pleased. The formula worked, and the magazine, either sexist or liberated depending on your point of view, took off. Circulation and advertising rocketed. Helene Gurley Brown became both controversial and famous. She was something new under the sun. So was Nora. She profiled Brown for *Esquire*.

By the late 1960s, Nora was one of the more successful freelance writers in New York. Magazines in the 1970s were not only influential but prosperous. They paid well—well enough so that it was the goal of many a newspaper reporter to become a freelance magazine writer. Nora had achieved just that. She wrote for *New York*, *Cosmopolitan*, *McCall's*, *Ms.*, and *Esquire*, as well as frequently for the *New York Times*. In fact, it was Nora's *Esquire* profile of Helen Gurley Brown that caught the eye of Lee Eisenberg, a young editor at the magazine. Just a year earlier, he had been a senior at the University of Pennsylvania and had entered a contest devised by Harold Hayes, the editor of *Esquire*, to rewrite a single issue's captions and headlines. By September, he was a junior editor at *Esquire* and under enormous pressure to come up with story ideas.

Eisenberg submitted so many ideas for articles that he feared he had emptied his mind. Then he recalled the Penn campus and the books that were selling there: *Love Story* by Erich Segal and anything by Rod McKuen.

Segal was an English professor at Yale, and McKuen was a songwriter, poet, and entertainer who, along with countless millions of others, had fallen in love with himself.

"And I said maybe there's a story here, sort of a dual profile of these two guys who are ridiculously mawkish and sentimental," he remembered. "But they must be selling tons of books even on an urban, radical college campus—was that an idea?"

Hayes said yes.

So Eisenberg took his idea to Don Erickson, who was the managing editor, and Erickson asked him who he thought should get the assignment.

"What about the woman who wrote the mouseburger story?" he suggested.

"Nora Ephron?"

"I said, 'Yeah, yeah, that's the one.'"

The "mouseburger" story was Nora's February 1970 profile of Brown, and in it Brown had referred to her readers—many of them timid and quite lost as to how to conduct themselves in a world that had turned threateningly sexual—as "mouseburgers."

"If you're a little mouseburger, come with me," Brown had said. "I am a mouseburger and I will help you. You're so much more wonderful than you think." And so on.

Nora turned him down.

Dismayed, Eisenberg reported the rebuff to Hayes, who suggested another try. This time, Eisenberg mailed Nora a reworked version of the memo he had originally written to Hayes—and it worked. She would do the article. It was called "Mush."

The piece was pure Nora. It was chatty, with a between-you-and me tone to it. It combined standard third-person journalism—the eye of the writer focused on the twin subjects and their phenomenal overnight success—and then the sudden switch to the first person: "It's not entirely easy to interview McKuen, you see."

Suddenly, the reader was in her shoes, seeing McKuen her way, which was as loquacious, meandering, maudlin, self-venerating, and entirely genuine—a mediocrity writing at the top of his game.

It was the same with Segal. He, too, was not the phony New York critics took him for, his professorship at Yale notwithstanding. He, too, had done his best. *Love Story*, the much-scorned and parodied movie and book—the movie came before the book—was really the best he could do. Its lachrymose ending was not the product of a highly educated man playing the indifferently educated reader for a sucker. It was what he felt. He, too, was moved by the death scene ending.

"When I got to the end of the book, it really hit me. I said, 'Omigod,' and I came and sat in that very chair and I cried and cried and cried." The last time he had cried, he told Nora, was at his father's funeral.

The demolition job was complete. Both men had failed to meet Nora's standards. It would have been all right with her, I think, if she had discovered them both to be phonies, really good writers who had mastered the art of turning out the literary equivalents of Margaret Keane's big-eyes paintings. That would have been something. But these guys were on the up-and-up, totally legit, and, once unmasked, unforgivably boring. If their readers believed in them, it was understandable. So did they.

The piece got Nora a perch at *Esquire*—a regular column about women—which she soon used to publish an article that is still remembered for its shocking honesty, its deadpan humor, its timing (*it was about time someone said that*), and its craft. It was a tour de force in the art of the essay. "A Few Words

About Breasts" is still remembered, it still resonates. It made Nora both famous and infamous and has been widely misread since 1972 as a self-deprecating trifle—shocking, yes, and coruscatingly honest, yes, but, all in all, funny. But as in *Heartburn*, her novel that was to follow, the humor camouflaged considerable anger. "Breasts" was a deeply felt howl against a world that cherished big bosoms and the women who had them.

The essay was published in May, which was a month before a collection of misfits in the pay of the Nixon White House burglarized the office of the Democratic National Committee at the Watergate office building in Washington. Watergate drew Nora to Washington for *New York* magazine, but unbeknownst to her, it was at the same time drawing Carl Bernstein to the *Washington Post*'s city desk, where he was hanging around, finagling the chance to get in on what he thought would be a great story. He got the assignment and, in due course, Nora.

By the time she came down to Washington to write some Watergate stuff, she was already famous—not nationally famous, not as famous as she was to become, not movie star famous, but well known, especially in journalist circles. I had read her. I knew who she was and I knew, too, about her breasts piece. It had given her that fame. The article was bold in its subject matter, light in its touch, but it was not seen as the rant of a hurt woman but rather as the biting observations of a gifted writer. That, at least, was the way I read the article, until one night at dinner in a Japanese restaurant in the Washington suburbs, when Nora proved me wrong.

Nora, Carl, Barbara, and I were joined by another couple. The man was Michael Levett. The woman was Patti Sterne. Levett had run George McGovern's presidential campaign in Maryland and was a rising political operative. It was Sterne, however, who mattered that night. Nora took one look at her bust and exploded.

"Tits!" she exclaimed. "What is it with you guys and tits?"

This is my recollection, and it is traumatically clear. Patti's recollection is different. In hers, she and Nora got into a heated argument over Dolly Parton's use of her voluminous breasts to advance her career. Parton had been a country-western singer who was going mainstream—and helping her go was an astounding figure. Patti was sympathetic. What was the poor woman to do? Nora was contemptuous. She was just flaunting the damn things.

Much later, there was a similar incident. This time the locale was the Hamptons and Nora was giving a dinner party, and Levett showed up accompanied by another buxom woman, an entertainment lawyer. Nora took one look and exploded again. "Tits! What is it with you men and tits? You haven't changed at all."

It's possible that Patti has it right. It's possible I've transposed the incidents. It's not possible, though, that Nora did not at one point have that explosion, and it's not possible, either, that she was not as formed by her teenage looks as Freud insisted we all are by our infancy. Her body and her brain were out of synch. The former was nondescript and unremarkable. The latter was extraordinary, effervescent, and sparkling, and it took her places where the ticket of admission was frequently a C cup or better.

Nora went where the pretty girls went. She did not have their advantage, and while she did not necessarily resent them for it, she most certainly resented women who rued their good looks, who pretended—it had to be pretense, didn't it?—that a big bust or drop-dead prettiness was a problem. No one took them seriously for their brains, they complained. Nora begged to differ. She wrote, in fact, that they were "full of shit."

Nora came by her indignation honestly. She had had the misfortune of being a teenage non-looker, afflicted with a 1950s deformity—small breasts in the sweater girl era. Sex was repressed, but not breasts. They came flying at you like the intimidating bumpers of 1950s cars, torpedoes lashed to the front of high school girls, the first thing you saw, the last thing you remembered. Even the title of Nora's first collection of essays, *Wallflower at the Orgy*, reflected not just the journalist's anomie—that necessary detachment—but her insistence that if she did indeed go to an orgy and lie naked on the floor, she would be stepped over by men on the way to someone else.

"Nora was not pretty," Barry Diller remembers from their high school days. Diller's recollection is not entirely borne out by pictures from that time, but never mind. He was there and I was not, and his recollection is so clear that when later he and Nora maintained a distant relationship he attributed it to his special knowledge.

"It was almost as if Nora felt in a little way that I knew her in her ugly period," Diller said.

Nora made her physique into one rollicking joke, a shtick—a façade. She managed to turn being flat chested into the functional equivalent of being stacked.

Whatever Nora was back at Beverly Hills High, she had left it far behind by the time I met her. As she aged, she got prettier and prettier. By her fifties, she had become very attractive. In a clutch of middle-aged women, she was the good-looking one. She watched her weight, ate sparingly, drank little and never to the point of tipsiness, and had learned how to dress. Gone were some of the more outré outfits, for example a black jumpsuit apparently of Martian provenance which she wore one night and made the mistake of asking me my opinion. "You look like a Japanese policeman," I jokingly said. I had no idea what that meant, but it stung. Her face fell. Years later, she brought it up. I should have called the outfit "memorable."

The "Breasts" piece—explosive and unforgettable—was not assigned to Nora by one of her *Esquire* editors. She wrote it as a regular columnist writing under the heading "Women" with the intention of getting more women to read what had once been a men's magazine. But *Esquire*, while occasionally randy, was in fact excessively literary. It had published Hemingway in its first issue (1933) and numerous times thereafter. It also published John Dos Passos and F. Scott Fitzgerald frequently and a woman who could have been a Nora role model, Helen Lawrenson. (Like Nora, she wrote effortlessly and candidly about sex. Her "Latins Are Lousy Lovers" got *Esquire* banned in Cuba and her "A Few Words on Fellatio" has an echo in Nora's "A Few Words About Breasts.")

By the 1960s, *Esquire* was publishing Norman Mailer, Tom Wolfe, James Baldwin, and Gay Talese. A compilation of *Esquire* articles published in the sixties, *Smiling Through the Apocalypse*, billboarded twenty-four writers on the cover—not one a woman. *Esquire* still fashioned itself a men's magazine, and it still featured the hopelessly innocent drawings of fantasy women by Alberto Vargas. He used as his model a fifteen-year-old girl.

Along came Nora. She was not only a woman, but she was writing for women. Best of all, she was no doctrinaire feminist, which did not mean that she didn't believe in what was then called "women's lib," but that she did not swallow it all whole. She had a hard time with any movement or person, for that matter, that did not have a sense of humor. Feminism was hopelessly humorless.

At the same time, there could be no doubt about where Nora stood on the feminist issues of the day. Everything she did was in keeping with its tenets. It was how she was leading her life and how she was writing. Many of the major female writers of the time adamantly refused to write as women. Their aim, in effect, was to be one of the boys, and since most of them had overcome the rigorous doctrinaire sexism of previous decades—and, moreover, strongly felt they had done it on their own—they not only would not deal with women's issues such as the blossoming feminist movement but shied from it. You can scan the writings of the relatively few female newspaper columnists of the early 1970s, when the women's movement was at its most rambunctious and persuasive, and find almost no mention of it.

This was not Nora. In fact, at the 1972 Democratic National Convention in Miami Beach, she crossed the line from journalist-observer to activist. To the befuddlement of many (male) observers, the women's movement played an important and contentious role at the convention. The Democratic Party's rules had been changed to require the participation of women, and challenges were being brought to the seating of delegations that had too few women. The party's eventual nominee, Senator George McGovern of South Dakota, was not only an ally of the women's movement, but it was under his aegis that the party's rules had been changed.

Into that maelstrom jumped a woman named Shirley Chisholm, a member of Congress from Brooklyn. Chisholm would later become the first black woman to run for president, but in 1972 she was willing to settle for vice president—second spot on the McGovern ticket. Many women supported her. A meeting was called—a secret meeting, of course—to come up with a way to submit a petition to the McGovern forces. Lynn Sherr, then with the Associated Press but freelancing for *Saturday Review* magazine, attended the meeting. She went as a reporter. So did Nora.

The meetings soon dissolved into chaos. It was one thing to want a petition demanding a seat on the ticket for Chisholm, but it was quite another thing to properly draw it up and have it delivered. It was then that Nora spoke up—a characteristically Nora performance. Somehow she knew enough about the rules and the process to tell the meeting how these things should be done. She was thirty-one at the time, not all that young by the standards of the Democratic Party's insurgency (McGovern's campaign manager, Gary Hart, was only five years older), but she was hardly a party activist. Nonetheless, she had the confidence, the inexplicable assurance, to command the meeting and impress the women in the room. Lynn, though, was appalled. They were journalists, not activists. She told Nora she had crossed the line.

Without naming Nora, Lynn wrote the following in her *Saturday Review* article: "I tell her that I think she is losing her objectivity. . . . She sort of agrees."

Later, Nora was outed by, of course, herself. She wrote about what she had done and confessed regret. She had gotten "a little carried away," is how she put it. Lynn, who recounted the incident in her memoir, deadpanned "I don't think her [Nora's] offer of help hurt her career one bit." As all *Esquire* was soon to find out, Nora wrote her own rules.

Esquire's editors pronounced Nora's breast piece a winner. There was, however, one problem. Arnold Gingrich, who had been one of the magazine's two founding editors and was by 1972 its exalted publisher, had a rule about four-letter words. They were forbidden. Nora was told to excise "they are all full of shit." She refused to do so. If that was taken out, she would not allow *Esquire* to use the piece.

Nora's kicker ended the piece with a pow! And it is impossible now to read the article and imagine it without that—a bit like *The 1812 Overture* ending with the tweet of a piccolo and not cannon fire. But killing the kicker would not have gutted the piece. It would not in the slightest have changed its meaning or have protected a guilty individual by sparing him or her some embarrassment. These are the usual reasons for a writer to put her foot down. None of these reasons are present in the "Breasts" article—no reason to risk a sinecure at the magazine that had published Hemingway and Fitzgerald, and in the 1960s had published, among many others, Saul Bellow. Nora's foot went down anyway. Gingrich, to the dismay of the staff, folded.

Other *Esquire* writers complained. Why did Nora get to use a four-letter word when they not only were told not to but had them snipped from their articles? Gingrich had no answer. He could not say that ordinary rules did not apply to the extraordinary Ms. Ephron. For the next issue, he reinstated the rule.

Later, when Nora was commuting between New York and Washington, I got a call from a woman who was having a hard time at work because she was so beautiful. Women resented her and men hit on her—and no one of either sex took her seriously because, as she kept telling me on the phone, she was so beautiful.

So, sensing a grave injustice, I went to interview her. She lived out in the Washington suburbs, in a high-rise where each apartment had a green steel door with the buzzer in the center. When this particular one opened, I saw a woman who was not a stunner, but pretty nonetheless, which I suppose could be a problem in certain workplaces. But the bigger problem for me was that she was dressed in a tight sweater and high, insolent black boots. This was beauty looking for a beast.

Still, the poor thing was having a tough time of it at work. No one ever took the problems of beautiful women seriously. Everyone thought they were a joke, and I, as a columnist for the *Washington Post*, could rectify matters by adding beautiful women to an ever growing list of victims—you know, albinos, paraplegics, dwarfs, and beautiful women.

Later that night, I told Nora the sad story of the beautiful woman, which represented, as far as I was concerned, not merely the plight of one particular woman but of beautiful women everywhere. Their story was a sad one and something had to be done. I, as it happened, was just the person to do something. Let me at the typewriter.

Nora scoffed. It was a roaring scoff, the scoff of the MGM lion. The jungle shook. Contempt rained down on me. I don't remember her words, but I do her scorn, her derision. There was an oomph to it, the torque of ridicule, and I could see after a while how wrong I was.

Now, though, I was stuck. I could not write what I had set out to write. Nora had seen to that. Nora was smarter than I was. Nora saw things I didn't. Nora saw around corners and beyond the horizon, and besides, she was a woman and knew things I did not about female beauty.

So the next morning, up against a deadline and with nothing else to write, I wrote about the complaining beautiful woman. Imagine! Look who thinks she's a victim. And while I did not use quite those words, I dismissed the woman and her complaints.

She was, in so many words, full of shit.

Of course so was I.

Arnold Gingrich Was a Slow Learner

Four years later Nora again butted heads with Gingrich. This time the issue was not a question of questionable words, but a matter of journalistic principle. Nora had assigned a novice writer named Bo Burlingham to write a piece about Richard N. Goodwin. Better known as Dick, Goodwin had been a White House aide under both John F. Kennedy and Lyndon Johnson and before that had worked as a congressional assistant.

Along the Boston–New York–Washington corridor, the adjective most often assigned to Goodwin was "brilliant." A second adjective might have been "controversial." As it happened, an article about Goodwin had been published in the *New York Times* the very morning that Burlingham had come to see Nora at *Esquire*. The *Times* piece was about a publishing dispute involving both Goodwin and his future wife, Doris Kearns. The two of them might as well have been tabloid concoctions. They were connected to just about everyone.

Kearns had worked for Lyndon Johnson in the White House and followed him to the LBJ Ranch in his Texas retirement. Goodwin had even better White House connections, plus an enduring relationship with the Kennedys—John, then Robert, and then Edward M., the senator from Massachusetts. It seemed that there was no one of any importance in Cambridge, Manhattan, or George-town that Kearns and Goodwin did not know. Burlingham's article, over ten thousand words, was gaudy with famous names. It was also critical.

Goodwin and Kearns were not happy with it. Even before the piece appeared, they implored *Esquire* not to publish it. Their pleas reached such a level that Gingrich, still the publisher but almost literally on his deathbed, was brought into the negotiations. Through it all Burlingham was kept in the dark, protected by his editor, Nora Ephron.

Publication did not settle the matter. Goodwin went to war. He was represented by the same lawyer Richard Nixon had used to defend his presidency, James St. Clair. Goodwin threated to sue and then, as is routine in these matters, decided to accept a settlement of $12,500, which was precisely $11,000 more than Burlingham had been paid to write the piece. *Esquire* was then up for sale, and the settlement may have been an attempt to clear the books of suits. Still, it was bad form to buy off the irate subject of an article. What made it worse was the publisher's column that was drafted in Gingrich's name and published in the next issue.

Gingrich essentially retracted Burlingham's article. He wrote that after reading about Goodwin in his own magazine, he met the man and was surprised to find him a genuine gentleman and a total charmer. Burlingham's portrait was "sufficiently at odds with the man himself that an appraisal is in order," the publisher decreed. Gingrich then offered that appraisal himself: a takedown of Burlingham's piece. Now it was Nora's turn to go to war.

For her next column, Nora repudiated Gingrich's repudiation, insisting that Burlingham's article had been true in fact and true in tone. She called Gingrich's column "a bad moment for this magazine," adding that *Esquire*'s owner, Abe Blinder, was wrong when he had told her that the settlement with Goodwin was fine because "there is no principle involved."

"I would like to state the principle involved," Nora wrote. "It's very simple. A magazine has an obligation to writers and readers to stand by what it prints."

Nora recounted something else Blinder had told her. Since Gingrich had by this time died and could not defend himself, he would not permit *Esquire* to run Nora's piece. She wrote that in the piece itself—and then had it published by *More*, a magazine for the news business that was then widely read. It was tantamount to a letter of resignation and it was proffered, in the sense that it was proffered at all, on behalf of a writer whom no one had ever heard of. Burlingham could have been unceremoniously dumped without much fuss—after all, he had almost no reputation to either assert or defend. What's more, his integrity could have easily been impugned. He was a recovered radical, a former member of the Weather Underground, a group known for inchoate violence and ideology. But Nora stood by him.

No resignation was demanded of Nora. *Esquire*'s other editors completely supported her. She had done the right thing. Burlingham was in awe of this editor who had gone to bat for him. "I was amazed and incredibly grateful," he said. "I would have done anything for Nora."

Already, Nora had established an enviable rep. She had gotten the "Mush" assignment on the strength of the earlier profile of Helen Gurley Brown. That profile quoted Brown directly, accurately, and at great length—Brown certainly got her say—but Nora surely realized she was taking on a very powerful figure. Brown was a mercurial and potent magazine editor, married to David Brown, a former journalist turned Hollywood and Broadway producer. The Browns combined the worlds of New York and Los Angeles. They were rich and very influential, and they lived, appropriately enough, in a tower atop the Beresford Apartments on Central Park West, from which they could see nearly all of Manhattan. It was their town.

Nora's approach in the Brown article was both classic and instructive. The piece is incredibly detailed, intensely reported, so that there could be no complaint afterward of shoddy or superficial reporting. The article is also humorous—not with jokes or put-downs, but with the juxtaposition of facts—and it is chatty. It starts, for instance, with a memo Brown wrote to her staff in which she proposed an article "on how men should treat women's breasts in love making." It got leaked to the press.

"Perhaps you remember it," Nora wrote.

Another writer might have made reference to the memo, sayings something like "Brown was referring to a memo she wrote on July 6. . . ." But no. Nora imparts the information as something she is sharing with the reader, a reader so much like her that she (or he) is likely to already know of it. Pull up a chair, reader. You have been invited over for dinner.

In Nora's telling, Brown is a faintly ridiculous figure, which she was in real life. At the same time, in Nora's telling, she is a deeply sympathetic figure who is also deeply authentic. She is not some male magazine editor of the type who once edited women's magazines and who wonders what *they* must want and what *they* must need—and what *they* can tell male advertisers who wonder all the same things.

No, that's not Brown. She is constantly at war with her corporate bosses who think of sex as an erotic silliness and not as an immense problem. *Cosmopolitan* was then being compared—likened, actually—to *Playboy*. But *Playboy* was a fantasy journal about fantasy sex—the Playboy Mansion was the Versailles of casual sex, in which naked women roamed as courtiers once did—while *Cosmo* was about problems, about everything that could go wrong in sex and love and career and even merely in how to dress for a cocktail party. The magazine was fraught with failure. *Playboy* was fraught with success. The latter was for the seducer. The former was for the seduced—and, too often, the abandoned.

Brown was that woman—once and for a long time a single girl and always, just like her readers, a work in progress. The piece ends the way Brown must have wanted it to end—sympathetically. She is exposed as authentic. A smile vaults off the page.

"Helen Gurley Brown Only Wants to Help" has an additional virtue. It's a great story. It is a great story told well but, above all, honestly. For Nora, the story came first. It was paramount. Telling it was her job, her duty. She rarely let sentiment get in the way. That was admirable, occasional troubling. It cost her some friendships. It's not clear, though, if it ever cost her a night's sleep.

An example, almost a trivial one, is Nora's account of attending her tenth college reunion in 1972. Titled "Reunion," it pretty much set out what Nora thought of her elite women's school: not much. It was at variance with what her classmates recall of Nora's college days, but that was almost beside the point: She tattled. She reeked of condescension. She had made it as a writer. The rest of her class—many of them, anyway—were still symbolically wearing the white gloves of 1950s housewives. They had taken their husbands' names. She had taken the world by storm. It took years for the Wellesley class of 1962 to forgive Nora for that *Esquire* piece—and it's probably fair to say that some members of the class never did.

"It had an amazing effect on a lot of people," her college classmate and later New York roommate Marcia Burick said. At one later reunion, Nora and Marcia joined three former classmates at a breakfast table. "One of the classmates said, 'Are you on assignment now, Nora, or are you sitting here?'

"Nora said, 'Well, you never know.'"

With that, three of the women got up and walked away.

Nora was stung by the rejection. Burick could sense it, although, of course, Nora never admitted it.

Oddly enough, Nora frequently mentioned what to her was the paradox of classmates who had become traditional housewives and found satisfaction in charitable or volunteer work as opposed to those who had chosen a career and had bumped up against a glass ceiling—either their own limitations or sexism. The former seemed a lot happier than the latter.

In the name of honesty, in 1975 Nora wrote her piece on the woman who had, in effect, made her career: Dorothy Schiff. Her *Esquire* essay was shockingly uncharitable, and Schiff was grievously hurt by it. In characteristic style, it began with a charming disclaimer—"I feel bad about what I am going to do here"—and proceeded to flatten Schiff. Nora ended the article by referring to one done for *New York* magazine by Gail Sheehy in which she "quite cleverly compared" Schiff to Scheherazade. Nora had a slight improvement: "It would be more apt, I think, to compare her to Marie Antoinette. As in let them read schlock."

Again, a powerful person. Again, a tough piece. Again, faultless in its honesty. Again, a fragging, a typed grenade flipped over the shoulder with Nora sort of gleefully skipping away—and moving on to that most august of American political writers, the extremely august Theodore H. White.

White was ripe for parody and criticism. He had written the groundbreaking *Making of the President 1960*, focusing on the dazzling John F. Kennedy. The book had transformed political journalism. All of a sudden, the errant meaningless detail seemed to matter so much. Who was in the room and what was the outside temperature and were there flowers on the table? The media-savvy Kennedy had given White unheard of access, and the onetime *Time* magazine correspondent had reciprocated by falling in love. No matter. Teddy White was Teddy White. He could be imitated, but never mocked.

"He was alone as always," she began. "A man who finishes a book is always alone when he finishes it, and Theodore H. White was alone. It was a hot muggy day in New York when he finished. Or perhaps it was a cold, windy night; there is no way to be certain, although it is certain that Theodore H. White was certain of what the weather was like that day, or that night, because when Theodore H. White writes about things, he notices the weather, and he usually manages to get it into the first paragraph or first pages of whatever he writes."

For Theodore H. White it was a stormy night when he picked up the August 1975 *Esquire*.

BeeBee Fenstermaker Goes to War

In 1973, Nora traveled to Israel to cover the Yom Kippur War for *New York* magazine. Upon rereading, the three articles she wrote not only hold up but are surprisingly prescient. She sensed right at the outset that the Jewish state was involved in a never-ending war, and war, she reported with what I'd like to think was regret, was what the Israelis did best. "The Israelis wage war better than they do anything else," she wrote in the December 3, 1973, issue.

She had arrived in Israel on the thirteenth day of the war, which had famously begun on the Jewish holiday of Yom Kippur with surprise attacks by Egypt and Syria. She wrote on how the American press was covering the war and on the role of women ("Women in Israel: The Myth of Liberation") and on the outsized role of religious authorities. She visited the Egyptian battlefield, a piece which, in case you were expecting what might be called a Nora Ephron touch, is appropriately grim: "At one point the bus stopped about five kilometers from the Suez where two tanks had been blown off the road. Three Egyptian soldiers lay in the sun, black and swollen, filling the desert air with the smell of death."

Nora saw no action—no bang-bang in the TV locution of that era—but neither did any of the other American journalists. (Only Israeli reporters got to go to the front.) But she caught the machismo—the ersatz Hemingway writing, the staccato burst of quick, tight sentences, that many male correspondents were wont to adopt. She understood their need to prove themselves both to their readers (and editors) but especially to themselves. "Working as a war correspondent is almost the only classic masculine endeavor left that provides physical danger and personal risk without public disapproval," she wrote.

What's remarkable about Nora's reportage is the absolute sureness with which she wrote. Her observations are keen and not in the least buried in layers of irrelevant data. Here she was, the inexperienced girl reporter for a magazine best known for snarky writing and bargain hunting, and she says straight out what she thinks. And what she thinks is tough, sinewy, critical and condemnatory. She cannot abide what she considers Israeli racism, and its warrior culture repels her. She is a product of the Vietnam War era—a war, she writes, "which if it accomplished anything at all, managed to give war a thoroughly bad name. In any case, that is true for me."

Understand: Israel had been sucker punched. On October 6, 1973, the armies of Syria and Egypt invaded and for a while did very well indeed. The Egyptians even managed to cross the Suez Canal and punch deep into the Sinai Peninsula. For a time, Israel was on the ropes. The Soviet Union was backing the Arab states. The good guys were on one side and the bad guys on the other, and there was no doubt which was which. That was especially the case in New York City, which was more Jewish than even Tel Aviv, and yet Nora never wrote down to her presumed audience and instead must have brought many of them up short.

When Nora worked at the *New York Post*, she had a nickname. It was Bee-Bee Fenstermaker, taken from the play *The Days and Nights of BeeBee Fenstermaker* by William Snyder, which had opened in the Village in 1962. It was about a young woman who graduates from college and comes to New

York where she takes an apartment to become a writer. Only in the broadest sense did the description fit Nora. BeeBee had not come from California but from the South. She did not go into journalism, but attempted to write a novel. Maybe more to the point, BeeBee was not Jewish—not that it mattered any to the wise guys at the *Post*. Fenstermaker sounded Jewish, and Nora, no doubt about it, looked the part.

But Nora's Jewishness was, literally, skin deep. She had come from a family that was orthodox only in its atheism. Her sister Hallie characterized their parents as "culinary Jews" only. Their religious devotion was limited to visits to the deli for lox, bagels, and such.

The Ephrons celebrated Christmas with gifts and the requisite Christmas tree. In the 1940s, they probably had the common enough desire to distinguish themselves from the Jews of the ugly stereotype—newly rich, loud, garish, tasteless—so much so that their own daughter Hallie considered them to be borderline anti-Semites. They did not hate Jews; they just didn't want to be any.

Nora had the Pale of Settlement plastered on her face. She simply looked Jewish, although political correctness insists there is no such thing. She owned up to it, never pretending to be anything other than the product of a Jewish household and reveling in the culture. She was not content, for instance, to merely yank my son's bar mitzvah from a sedate hotel to a New York–style restaurant, we also had to engage a klezmer band, and at the proper time Nora shouted for a hora to begin. Soon after, Nora plopped my son in a chair and had it hoisted into the air—the traditional airborne seat of honor. High above the dancers, Alex bobbed back and forth, a trifle terrified (as was his father), until Nora decided it was time to resume the real business of the day—eating. She had the makings of a tummler, the Yiddish term once applied to the recreation directors at Catskill resorts.

Nora's writings are replete with mentions of her Jewishness and that of others. She exhibited some disdain for Bonnie Sloan, the other Wellesley girl from Beverly Hills. The name Sloan itself came in for some contempt, and Bonnie's affectations—including her adopted English accent—were not merely reported as social climbing but as an effort to pass as a gentile. Nora did not approve.

It was at Wellesley, in fact, that Nora was compelled to identify with her Jewish classmates. The school had sent her a form to be used for student housing, and it asked her religion. Nora did not respond, and so the school wrote her back: "Please, what are you?" She responded "atheist," but by way of acquiescence said she had been born a Jew. (Surely, the school knew that.)

As she and Lynn Sherr discovered when they looked into the matter as reporters for the *Wellesley News*, the college made sure that roommates had at least one thing in common: religion. Protestants were paired with Protestants, Catholics with Catholics, Jews with Jews, and atheists, presumably, with someone of their ancestral religion. The *Wellesley News* broke the story that everyone already knew—and the policy was changed.

Nora may not have been much of a Jew, but she was proud of her heritage and on the alert always for the errant anti-Semitic remark. She found it once in something William F. Buckley, Jr., had written. Buckley, the ultra-urbane founder of the *National Review* magazine and an important intellectual mentor to Ronald Reagan, had in fact largely purged American conservatism of its fusty anti-Semitism. Buckley had the look and the manner of a sniffy Jew hater, but not the convictions of one. Still, Nora, reviewing his book *Overdrive*, for the *New York Times*, found it "appalling that Mr. Buckley should mention Shylock when discussing the *National Review*'s landlord." What she meant by "appalling" was anti-Semitic—we had discussed the matter—but more interesting to me than Buckley's klutzy insensitivity was Nora's sensitivity.

In her *New York* magazine articles from Israel, Nora does all the expected things—the tough things. She visits the burn ward of a military hospital, which is tough, tough work—hard to read, harder still to have seen. "There was room after room of soldiers wounded in tank battles, some using breathing machines because their lungs had been so badly burned, others wrapped from top to bottom in gauze that a yellow iodine compound showed through, others who were in better shape physically but were almost unbearable to see—their faces and limbs alternately raw red and then covered with huge black scabs."

She ends, as she must, with a visit to the cemetery. Here she notes the stoicism of the Western or Ashkenazic Jews as contrasted with the raw, emotionalism of the Jews who had come from Arab lands, whom she calls "Oriental." She also notes the difference between young mourners and older ones. The young show little emotion; they are tough Israelis and their fight is a long one. The older ones show no such restraint. "*Lama? Lama?*"—"Why? Why?"—wails an old woman as she hugs her son's headstone—and the article, Nora's last from Israel, might have ended there, because here was a Jewish mother asking the age-old question of Jewish mothers from time immemorial: Why? Why?

But on the way out of the cemetery, Nora runs into an Israeli woman she knows, a lieutenant colonel in the army. "We embraced," she wrote. " 'It is only the beginning,' she said. The remark seemed cold and hard compared with the reactions of the older people; what was most depressing is that it also seemed to the point."

Nora's Israel coverage—cool to the touch—did not in the least affect her latter-day standing as an adored Jewish celebrity. She did not think of herself as a Jewish writer—she shunned labels—but she nevertheless later became a darling of the Jewish lecture circuit. For Jewish groups, she was a major draw. Middle-aged Jewish women considered her one of their own. Most likely they were unaware of her reports from Israel, or since she was not primarily a political or foreign affairs writer, they considered it an insignificant part of her oeuvre—not that they used the word "oeuvre," Nora might have added.

But in an interview with the writer Abigail Pogrebin for her book *Stars of David*, Nora was hardly coy. She was the child of atheists. Her parents celebrated Christmas, and Nora celebrated it in a big way. In religious terms, she was not in the least Jewish—nor did she know anything much about the religion—but, on occasion, she embraced the *label* of Jewish. She ended a 2003 *New York Times* essay about yet another John F. Kennedy tryst—this one with a White House intern—by puckishly wondering why the president never hit on her. (She had been a summer intern in the White House press section.) She ran down the possible reasons—"my permanent wave," "my wardrobe"—and ended with the astounding, and possibly irrelevant, suggestion that in sex, although in nothing else, Kennedy may have been an anti-Semite.

"Don't laugh," she cautions. "Think about it. Think about that long, long list of women JFK slept with. Were any Jewish? I don't think so."

By 1973, I was beginning to know Nora. I might have read her reportage from Israel at the time, but more than forty years later, it reads fresh and new to me. I have no memory of it. If Nora and I ever discussed it, I have no memory of that, either—which is noteworthy. Reporters—writers and such—who have been to war or who have seen its hideous aftermath—"Three Egyptian soldiers lay in the sun, black and swollen . . ."—invariably bring it up. It is a credential, like the storied, soiled trench coat of so many battles and even more bistros.

Nora never mentioned her Israel reporting to me. She did mention being there, and what I take it was a dalliance with a (presumably) dashing British war correspondent, but she never told war stories, as men are wont to do. She did, however, evince a barely concealed antipathy toward Israel. In this she was a typical leftie—many of her friends held the same opinions—but the subject became taboo between us after I began living with a woman who had been born in Israel and whose emotional commitment to the country was passionate. Mona would often bring up Israel in conversation—she could hardly contain herself—and Nora, out of love and fervent consideration, would say nothing. Not that she had once been there. Not that she had covered a piece of the war. Nothing. I was grateful. She may not have loved Israel, but she loved Mona.

An Ailanthus Grows in Brooklyn

"Marlon Brando's gay, everybody knows that."

Nora said that one night in my house in Washington. I can't remember how Brando's name came up, but there it was, this startling (at the time) piece of information, so inside, so unknown to the general public, who considered him—fools that they were—a womanizer of great repute. I can remember exactly where I was at the time. In the living room. Standing in front of the sofa and to the right. The remark hit with the force of a dumdum bullet. Marlon Brando's gay? Who knew?

Everybody, it turned out. Everybody knew. And whether they did or they didn't, whether it was true or not, was totally beside the point. When Nora said one of these things—and she said them quite often—she did not do so with any sort of tentativeness, with hesitation, with the suggestion that this might be the rawest gossip and possibly wrong, but with a firmness and robust confidence that transformed the gossamer of hearsay into something chiseled into the frieze of a Greek temple. It was beyond dispute. Behold what she knew and behold what you didn't. You knew some things. She knew *everything*.

One time she slipped in the Latin name of the tree Betty Smith had used in her best-selling novel, later a movie, *A Tree Grows in Brooklyn*. Ailanthus. She said it, and then she translated it, "Which is the tree that grows in Brooklyn." Ailanthus. Who knew? All my life I had been looking at those trees and not only never knew their name but never thought to know it. It had never even occurred to me that they had a name or, for that matter, that there was an actual tree that actually grew in Brooklyn.

Nora knew. She recognized the tree for what it was, assigned it its proper name, and recalled it just at the right moment. I don't have any idea what we were talking about, but her reference to the tree is as fresh as if I just walked into one.

When Nora did something like that, I usually pretended nonchalance. Ailanthus. No reaction. Let's move on. The same with Brando. Nothing from me. Of course, Brando. Gay. Very gay. Extremely gay. No one knows. I did not exclaim, What, Marlon Brando's gay? I was determined not to seem nonplussed, to earn Nora's respect: Of course. Marlon, gay? Who doesn't know that? She was Hollywood, after all—a graduate of Beverly Hills High. She was a New York magazine writer and, before that, a reporter for the *New York Post*.

I had worked a bit in New York journalism myself, as a reporter for United Press International. Reporters knew things back then. They knew what had been withheld from the papers—the sex stuff, the dirty stuff, the potentially libelous stuff in what was a far more dainty age. There was no Internet, no blogging—none of that. Reporters had access to information no one else had. They had exotic phone directories so they could look up someone by the address or the phone number, not only the name. You could walk your fingers up and down the hallways of apartment houses, even the fancy ones on Park or Fifth, and know who lived behind every door. One telephone directory was called the crisscross and you could look up a person by his telephone number as well as her name.

We had files and libraries, ominously called "the morgue," but best of all we had old-timers who knew everything, forgot nothing, and in stunning rebuke to medical science, had their memories honed by regular snorts. They not only knew the cops, they were like cops themselves and could have been cops had they not gone astray and taken a night school course or two. The cops, of course, knew everything, stuff not even the newspaper people knew.

Scandal itself has since been diluted. Homosexuality is no longer considered outré. Premarital sex is now passé, as are open extramarital affairs. Ingrid Bergman's affair with the director Roberto Rossellini—they were both married to others at the time—all but had her banned from America. Ed Sullivan would not have her on his popular and influential TV show. Nowadays, she would be a sought-after guest.

I was privy to some of the secrets, but I was working for the *Washington Post*, covering the Maryland State House, while Nora had been a reporter on a genuine New York tabloid. I knew the skinny on certain Maryland figures, but who cared? Nora, on the other hand, knew New York stuff and, often more sensational, Hollywood stuff. There is absolutely nobody who knew Nora in her early days—from college onward—who did not make an immediate Hollywood association. That's because she did. She wore the town's considerable aura like a tiara: She knew the secrets.

The names that dropped from Nora's lips were never drumrolled—not even preceded with a modest cough. They were simply stated. They were inserted here and there in sentences or used, with appropriate understatement, to clinch an argument. As far as I could tell, Nora never met someone famous for the first time. They had somehow always been present in her life. I can be excused for thinking that Mike Nichols was her childhood friend, that they had met at camp or even earlier, in Berlin, where she had never been— something like that. His name, when rarely invoked, was never accompanied by the unheard rumble of an organ, a trumpet voluntary of a buildup, but by the same matter-of-factness that made Marlon Brando gay and rendered the forlorn tree of Brooklyn a dendrologist's delight.

When she got older—after her Washington period, for sure—Nora became protective of her famous friends. I suspect the reason for that was that they really were her friends then and not just marquee names to drop. She rarely mentioned Tom Hanks, for instance—or Steven Spielberg or Steve Martin—and she never gossiped about them. At the same time, she did not venerate them either, did not invoke them or their presumed authority to, say, clinch an argument. They were rarely cited, and in fact, when she and Nick returned from the Geffen boat—a nautical red carpet, as far as I was concerned—she would never offer the names of the other guests. I'd have to ask and then, sometimes, ask again. She was a reformed name dropper.

Mike Nichols was in a singular category. Nora had a special relationship with him that was rarely mentioned. If she went to the Fifth Avenue apartment he shared with Diane Sawyer, she never talked about it. If they had lunch, she said nothing. If he warned her off a project under consideration, she was mum. If he did like a script, loved a script, improved a script—whatever—I knew nothing about it. Nora and Mike were celibate lovers.

Back when Nora had first approached Nichols and asked him to dinner, he had not yet reached cult status. That would come at the end of the decade when he directed *Who's Afraid of Virginia Woolf?* and, more important and creatively, *The Graduate*, for which he earned an Academy Award. For both Mike and Nora, their meeting was something like love at first sight. Mike "got" Nora the way he had gotten Elaine May. "I instantly recognized a kindred soul," Nichols said.

They had their own language, I think—a matter of nods and frowns and common cultural references. They knew whose marriage was a sham and who could not act and who had a bad drug problem. They knew the business—the business of movies and the business of theater and, because they were hyperventilating readers, the business of books and magazines. They had words, a torrent of them, but they talked also in shadows and in knowing they were both smart—but neither smarter than the other. They learned from the ricochet.

Nichols had been selected to direct the film version of Joseph Heller's absurdist antiwar novel *Catch-22*, and Nora was assigned by the *New York Times Magazine* to write an article about the making of the movie. In 1969, she and Dan flew down to Mexico to join Nichols for the shoot.

At that point in Nora's career, Nichols loomed large. He was no mere film person, no Beverly Hills–Brentwood person, but someone who while recognizing the pleasures of Los Angeles preferred the stimulating abrasiveness of New York—just as she did. He was a figure of the theater—just as her parents had been before and after their movie careers. He had been a performer, an actor, an entertainer, and he had about him the air of the worldly German-Jewish intellectual, a man familiar with all the Marxes—Karl and Groucho and the boys—and someone who appreciated depravity. He had come to America from Nazi Germany on a boat that delayed its departure for a broadcast by Hitler.

If Nichols had a precursor it was Billy Wilder (1906–2002), who had won numerous Academy Awards as director, writer, and producer. The similarities are obvious. Both Wilder and Nichols were émigré Jews. Both were astoundingly fecund. Wilder directed comedies, dramas, farces—and he directed or wrote in both his native German and, astoundingly, his adopted English. But the key to Wilder is the epitaph on his gravestone: "I'm a writer, but then nobody's perfect."

The last part of that is the final line from *Some Like It Hot*, and it's sort of impish. But the proclaimed reverence for the word, for an appreciation of film as an extension of what is written—not just structure but dialogue as well—this and not merely a Mitteleuropa heritage, is what links Wilder to Nichols and Nichols in a way to Nora. They all had baseline occupations, and just as Nichols always returned to the theater so, too, Nora always returned to writing.

Nichols's instant infatuation with Nora had a precedent: Elaine May. Here, also, was a very smart, dark-haired Jewish girl who not only could make a joke but get one, too. Nichols and May had created a pioneering and astoundingly successful comedy act and had had a brief romantic involvement. But the essence of their relationship—and of their act, which had originated in improvisation—was a kind of cerebral chemistry that had become apparent shortly after they bumped into each other in a Chicago train station. May, whom Nichols had met just once before, was sitting on a bench.

"May I sit down?" Nichols asked, affecting a Russian accent.

"If you veesh," May replied, and the rest, as the cliché goes, is show business history.

Mike Nichols had been an immigrant kid (Mikhail Igor Peschkowsky), son of a Russian-Jewish father and German-Jewish mother, affluent in the Germany to which his father first emigrated, then comfortable in the New York to which they fled in 1939, and then outright poor after his father died. The Nichols family, his mother and a brother, then lived in a drab apartment on the Upper West Side. Nichols had lost all his body hair at the age of four—the result of a reaction to a whooping cough vaccine—and arrived in New York a bald child who could not speak the language.

"I was a zero," Nichols told the *New Yorker* writer John Lahr.

Nora was never so marked. But she was plain, with a drooping eyelid that seemed to half draw a curtain over her face. (It was later surgically corrected.) Like Nichols she wound up observing herself, choosing journalism, as she once wrote, because you were officially deputized not to join in. You could observe. Take notes. Be at the orgy, but not participate.

Among the many mysteries of life, there is this one: No one ever romantically linked Nora and Mike. I was sometimes mentioned, and I took it as the sheerest flattery. Nichols, though, was her true twin—maybe that was the problem—the man who was as smart as she was, who knew theater and film, the difference between Little Santa Monica Boulevard and Santa Monica Boulevard, the Beverly Hills hills from the Beverly Hills flats, the Upper West Side from the Upper East Side, the cafés of Paris, the works of Bernhard Schlink as well as the writings of Liz Smith. He shared so much with Nora, even for a time their shrink.

Both Nora and Mike had a surfeit of talent, almost too much to handle, big and small ideas sloshing around in their brains, searching always for the meaning—the hidden meaning—of anything, its essence. Nora and I would sit and discuss something for what seemed liked hours, searching for the point—the point of a column, the thing that was hidden, the thing she could reveal, the point, the point, the point—while Nichols, with a wry observation, could get to the essence of a play or a movie with a snap-of-the-fingers metaphor that materialized even as he spoke it, and his actors immediately knew what the point was.

I met with Nichols from time to time, nearly always at Nora's suggestion. I had a script I was pushing, an idea that was perking. He always read my stuff, sweetly passing—"It's very, very good, Richard, but not for me"—and once saying, astoundingly, that he wanted to make a movie with me and Nora. I was flattered, but not quite convinced. Whatever my talent, I was above all Nora's friend. And he loved her.

Somewhere along the line, Nora's relationship with Mike reached an inflection point. The mentor (Mike) and the mentee (Nora) became near equals, although Mike always remained the dominant one. Mike sought Nora's counsel, but he always remained the one who had made more successful movies, more successful plays, and, of course, had been an entertainer. What Nora lacked in résumé, she more than compensated for in decisiveness. It could be as good as wisdom.

But their relationship did not start on an even keel. After all, it was Nora who came to interview Mike, not the other way around. It was Nora who went to Mexico to write about the famous director, the man who was doing what she'd always wanted to do. So it was Nora who sought approval from Mike and who, in the way she judged these things, did not get it back. *Catch-22* was over. It was in the can. Nora and Mike had become close. Yet he was not inviting her to dinner.

So Nora asked Mike to lunch. They met at a place on Madison Avenue, across the street from the Carlyle Hotel, where Nichols was living. Nora said there was something she wanted to talk to him about. "And I said, of course. And I said, what do you want to talk about?"

She burst into tears.

"'I'm not on your A-list.'"

"What are you saying? I don't have dinner parties. I live in a hotel."

Nora's belief that she had not made Mike Nichols's final cut was a rare false reading on her part. It was also additional evidence, if any be needed, of the centrality of the dinner party in Nora's thinking. It seemed inconceivable to her that Nichols was not giving dinner parties; it was only conceivable that she was not being invited. It's actually inconceivable that Nichols would have ever had a dinner party without her.

In time the mentor and the mentee fused. On a given day, one became the other, and just as Nora would look to Mike for his experience—he was, after all, older and already established when she was starting out—he learned to rely on her, her judgment, and the ferocious certainty of those judgments. They usually talked several times a week, not always about work, but often about food—the hot dogs from Nate and Al's, for instance, and were they, as Nora insisted, the best. They reviewed various ice creams and restaurants as well, and, knowing Nora, the floundering marriages of people they either knew or heard about. They were both great gossips, not because they were vindictive or spiteful but because gossip was theater by another name. Such characters! Such behavior! Who could have guessed? Not in your wildest dreams. Actually, *only* in your wildest dreams.

In fact, one of Nora's dreams was about Mike. She mentioned it on the Dick Cavett show in 1971. In a very jolly manner, she told Cavett that she dreamed her husband had died and she was free to marry Mike Nichols. It was tossed off as a joke, a joke that's not a joke, a joke that seemed more of a wish than some wild dream, Nichols himself was watching. It brought him up out of his chair.

Why didn't it happen—if not marriage, then an affair? Maybe because when Nora met Mike he was already successful in an industry where a perk, along with a chair with your name on it, was an abundance of women. Maybe because Nora was married much of the time—and so, for that matter, was Mike. Maybe because their chemistry was entirely cerebral or maybe because one or the other feared sex would ruin a perfectly wonderful relationship (the theme of *When Harry Met Sally . . .*). Whatever the case, while many people wondered about it, I never got the slightest hint that Nora and Mike had ever had an affair. I have to add, however, that my record in these matters is dismal. Caesar and Cleopatra could have gotten by me.

As close as they were, though, Nichols, too, was kept in the dark about Nora's condition. He later accepted her decision with equanimity; she had not only done the right thing, but—should there be any doubt—in matters such as this, Nora always did the right thing. Somewhere toward the end, though, Nichols learned that something was wrong. They were planets in the same showbiz solar system—and Nora, inexplicably, went dark. She was working with the movie and stage producer Scott Rudin and he couldn't find her. He checked with Mike. Alarmed, Mike called Nora. She lied, and then quizzed J.J. about the source of the leak.

Near the very end, Nora's son Jacob got in touch with Mike. Nora was dying.

From the hospital, I conferred with Mike. There was this matter of a memorial service. Mike was to speak. I was to speak. He wanted to talk about that. He was distraught—adrift. I felt the same, but Nora's condition was not a surprise to me. It was, though, to Mike. His despair was palpable. He was disconsolate, and nothing he was in life seemed to matter—not director, not producer, not writer, not intellectual, not entertainer. Momentarily, his confidence was gone. His voice wavered. He was eighty-one and in bad health.

A bit later, the phone rang. I was in the hallway of New York Hospital, a pace or two down from Nora's room. She had just died. It was Mike. His voice broke.

"What are we going to do now?"

Baseball Wives Forever

I don't want to be misunderstood. Nora knew many famous people. Some of them were close friends, even intimates. But Nora also had friends who were not famous—some of them dating from her college days and one, in particular, going back to when she was the showbiz version of a baseball wife. That's how she met Judith Corman.

Judy died of cancer in 2004, a hideous nine-month ordeal from the first little bump on her tongue to the end. Nora suspended the shooting of *Bewitched* so she could attend the memorial service, where she spoke and declared Judy to have been her "best friend." She said substantially the same thing in her penultimate book, a collection called *I Feel Bad About My Neck*.

"My friend Judy died last year," Nora wrote. "She was the person I told everything to. She was my best friend, my extra sister, my true mother, sometimes even my daughter, she was all these things, and one day she called up to say, the weirdest thing has happened, there is a lump on my tongue. Less than a year later, she was dead."

In order to know Nora—to really know Nora—you had to know Judy. She was the wife of Avery Corman, the writer of the novels *Kramer vs. Kramer* and *Oh, God!* and many other works, but when they first met, Nora was not yet famous and Judy Lishinsky of Brooklyn was married to Avery Corman of the Bronx and he had not yet written his first novel. At the time, in fact, he was partnering with Nora's fiancé-cum-husband, Dan Greenburg. They had a comedy act.

The act was Greenburg's idea, and it was good enough for the two to have played both Merv Griffin's and Dick Cavett's TV shows, and like many comedians, as well as other entertainers, they honed their act at the Improv, a club in the old Hell's Kitchen neighborhood of Manhattan. The place was run by an impresario named Budd Friedman, who seems to have discovered much of the 1960s and 1970s comedy talent. But he did more than merely present the comics. He also managed them, and it was the suspicion of those who were not managed by Friedman that at the Improv they were the last to appear.

Corman and Greenburg virtually closed the place. It was Corman who used the term "baseball wives." Like those spouses, Nora and Judy waited for their men to be called to the plate. This, in the haze of cigarette smoke and the rebuke of stale beer, was how Nora and Judy got to know each other. Corman dropped out of stand-up and Greenburg did the same—it's very hard work, after all—but Nora and Judy remained fast friends, best friends, until the end.

By then, Judy had gone in and out of several careers. She was an extremely *hamish* woman, a Yiddish term of very high praise which often gets defined as "cozy and homey." Judy was all of that—exuberant, bubbly, a central casting Jewish mother (she had two boys)—but her chubby frame obscured an awesome competence and talent. She worked in both the music business and publishing, doing public relations; she ran a quilt and wicker furniture store in Bridgehampton. (For a while, she had a Manhattan store as well.) She had reliable, unerring taste in clothes, furniture, jewelry, fabric, and of course, quilts. She was Nora's Nora.

Judy was an aggregation of common sense, and in the maelstrom of conflicting advice Nora would receive—agents saying one thing and studios saying another, stars demanding the extravagant and others demanding only what was due them—Judy stood above it all, rendering a judgment that was informed by seeking only the best for her friend. Nothing in her life intersected with Nora's. In no sphere did they compete. As far as Nora was concerned, Judy's judgment was entirely based on what was best for Nora. Judy was neither jealous nor competitive. She was, however, astute. And she had been around.

In the late 1960s, Judy had worked as a publicist for RCA Records. She handled pop music, and her eye fell on a regional performer who was being treated with disdain by the established New York rock critics. This was Elvis Presley, who was then opening in Las Vegas. Judy flew the important New York rock critics out to see the show. They were dazzled by Presley, and suddenly, the Presley song "Suspicious Minds" got airplay on rock radio stations. The King had been anointed.

Nora's love for Judy was intense. It complimented both women—Judy because Nora was a good friend and remained so even after she became famous and wealthy, and Nora because Judy was neither of those things. In fact, while Avery's success was hardly a flash in the pan—he was a gifted writer—the novelist's life is a hard one and not a long one, either. The Cormans never made it to rich, never made it to famous, and yet as a couple they always remained in Nora's inner circle—Judy because she was Judy, Avery because he was Judy's husband.

Following Judy's funeral at the Steven Wise Free Synagogue, Nora immediately enlisted my girlfriend, Mona Ackerman, as Judy's nominal replacement. "You're now my best friend," she told her. For a while, it was just a title. Then they both got cancer and it was a title no more.

A Navaho Ceremony
in Foley Square

Bob Woodward had hired a limo. For some reason, he sat in the front and the rest of us piled into the back—my wife Barbara and I; Bob's wife, Francie Bernard; and Carl. It was April 15, 1976, and we were on our way down to the West Village, to Mildred Newman's place to pick up Nora at group therapy. In an hour or so, she would be married to Carl.

Mildred Newman and her husband, Bernard Berkowitz, were famous A-list shrinks. Both Mildred and Bernie were psychologists. Together they had written the best seller *How to Be Your Own Best Friend*, blurbed not only by Nora but also by Tony Perkins the actor, Rex Reed the critic, and Neil Simon the playwright. The two shrinks were as celebrated as their celebrity patients.

If you knew them—better yet, if they knew you—you either had it made or were on the way. Nora often dropped their names but rarely attributed to them any particular piece of wisdom. Still, I could tell. For instance, if I said I would *try* to do something, Nora would seize a nearby ashtray and say, "Try to pick that up." See, you either do it or you don't.

Thereafter, I avoided the word "try" as the weasel word it was asserted to be. I found it a useful insight, if not a life-changing wisdom, and it did not take me long to realize that the whole try-to-lift-that-ashtray bit had come from Mildred and Bernie. That was all right with me, although I distrusted celebrity shrinks, and in Mildred and Bernie's case my cynicism was deepened by the conspiratorial mist that seemed to envelop them—members of the group were forbidden to identify other members of the group or even talk to them about the group when they were outside the group. It reminded me of the Communist Party with its secrecy and smug incestuousness (as if being in need of a shrink was not enough for admission—you had to be famous, too).

Indeed, some pretty famous people belonged to the group, including, of course, Dan Greenburg and Mike Nichols. In fact, when Nora went down to Mexico to report on the filming of Nichols's *Catch-22* for the *New York Times Magazine*, she had effectively joined a Mildred and Bernie group on location. Many of the actors were the couple's patients, including Tony Perkins and Richard Benjamin and his wife, Paula Prentiss. Perkins brought in Joel Schumacher, later to become a director, and still later Bob Balaban and his wife, Lynn Grossman, enlisted. Schumacher was so broke he told Mildred he could not pay. Don't worry, she told him. Someday you will. Little wonder her patients were so loyal.

Mildred and Bernie, so easy to mock, who created something so much like a social clique, were nevertheless revered by their patients. Their methods were unorthodox; they insinuated themselves into the lives of the group's members. They would, for instance, come backstage to comfort Paula Prentiss before a performance. She could freeze with stage fright, and Mildred would get her to the point where she could perform. Witnessing that was what impressed the actor-director Balaban enough to join the group. Some former members laugh about Bernie and Mildred, but no one disparages them. They were extremely effective.

On this day in April 1976 Nora bounded out of the West Village building. I can't recall what she was wearing, but I do know she was ebullient, having just told the group that she was getting married. In her autobiographical novel,

Heartburn, if not in real life, there was applause and there were many congratulations, and then we were off to the courts in Lower Manhattan, where Surrogate Millard L. Midonick was going to officiate. Suddenly, Nora turned anxious. Maybe it was when Carl mentioned that, after talking to his mother, he suspected that Midonick and his mother, Sylvia Bernstein, had long ago had an affair. "He's going to want to perform some Indian ceremony," Nora said out of nowhere.

I was mystified. New York's surrogates were powerful judicial officials and occasionally the subject of vicious patronage battles. This was the era of weird weddings with exotic religious ceremonies, but the surrogates were usually Democratic Party stalwarts, chosen for fidelity to the organization and not for their anthropological creativity. As if to drive the point home, the surrogate's chambers were a baronial, high-domed affair with massive pieces of furniture, including a long, heavy table suitable for a medieval feast. It was covered by a suitably heavy tapestry.

Midonick himself, however, was a reformer. He greeted us warmly and said to Carl, "I knew your mother." Carl shot me a wink.

Midonick stood at one end of the room and readied himself for the ceremony. Normally, he said, he did the standard marriage ceremony, but this day—this very special day—he would like to try something different. Something from an Indian tribe. I think he mentioned the Navahos.

Oh my God, Nora's right, I thought. I was stunned. How did she know? How could she have known? Were we now going to be asked to do a rain dance?

Instantly, Nora objected. The conventional ceremony would be fine with her, she said sternly. Midonick hesitated and then acquiesced. He reluctantly handed his clerk the printed material he had been holding and, after a moment, began the familiar marriage vows. When he had finished, he nodded to the clerk, and the young man moved to the heavy table and threw back the tapestry. Underneath were about a dozen copies of *All the President's Men,* Carl and Bob's book about their Watergate reporting. Midonick wanted them autographed. The new bride cooled her heels as Carl and Bob dutifully did what was asked of them. We soon piled back into the limo and headed to a small reception in a suite at the St. Regis Hotel.

It was a Nora day from beginning to end—from the pickup at Group to the kibosh on the nontraditional Navaho ceremony and then, in the limo heading uptown, a display of her need to control . . . or panic. The limo driver had headed uptown on Third Avenue. Nora thought he should have chosen the FDR Drive. Third Avenue had lights. The FDR did not. Third Avenue had a twenty-five-mile-per-hour speed limit. The FDR's forty or maybe fifty.

She erupted. She berated the driver for choosing the wrong route. He mumbled some sort of explanation, maybe something about traffic on the FDR—I don't know. Whatever it was, Nora was not placated. She homed in on the driver, reprimanding him almost all the way up Third. (*See, the FDR would have been quicker.*) Woodward, who had served in the navy and just helped bring down the government, was awed.

Nora and Carl, Carl and Nora. They had gotten married in the face of second thoughts. Nora had been warned about Carl. He was a prowler, and Nora, who had already been betrayed by men (and with women she considered friends), was in over her head. They had broken up once, reconciled at Carl's pleading, and now—her cynicism be damned—she was going where her friends had told her she should not. Like the limo driver, she was taking the wrong route.

In the *New York Times* account of the wedding, Carl was the headline: BER-NSTEIN, CO-AUTHOR OF NIXON BOOKS, WEDS. The item mentioned that the couple had met in December 1973 and that "Mr. Bernstein would resume his book promotion tour with Mr. Woodward." It ended ominously with a quote from Nora: "Nobody's moving to the other person's town."

Dinner with Betty, Harold, and the Pope If He's in Town.

Nora did not so much move to Washington as accept what diplomats call a posting. She was only in D.C. temporarily, a Washingtonian by virtue of having been assigned there. She talked about the place as if it were a bit third world-ish. It lacked not only world-class restaurants but good physicians as well, the latter being only slightly more essential than the former. When she became pregnant with Jacob, born in 1978, she saw New York doctors, pronouncing them the best, and she gave no consideration at all to delivering her child in Washington, where countless babies had been born over the years—among them John F. Kennedy, Jr., my own son, and Carl himself—but insisted on New York. When Nora talked about the Washington medical establishment, one could conjure up a Civil War–era ward, mosquito netting over the beds and bearded orderlies cleansing wounds with whiskey. Nora's child would be born in New York, and that was that.

As with all of Nora's pronouncements, I accepted this one both as revealed truth and with a grain of salt. She did not wonder about the state of medicine in Washington, ask around about doctors, or in other ways consult. She simply said that the town was inadequate and implied that giving birth there would risk the life of her baby not to mention herself. I had to wonder if she was on to something. Her certainty was compelling. She brooked no contradiction. When the time came, she went off to New York.

Nora's life after marrying Carl could be summed up in a single screenplay. It would be called *The Eastern Shuttle*, and it would be about a couple who commuted between New York and Washington, going back and forth on the shuttle service maintained by the now-defunct Eastern Airlines. Nora and Carl wrote most of it and, when they got stymied, called me as sort of "play doctor." We fixed the screenplay but not the underlying problem. In retrospect, the marriage was in trouble.

It would be some time, however, before things would go haywire. In the meantime, Nora adjusted to the loss of New York by simply bringing New York down to Washington. Her dinner parties became half Oval Office and half Round Table.

Carl accommodated that. He poured some of his Watergate riches into a dowager of a four-bedroom apartment located in a grand old Washington institution called the Ontario. The cooperative was built in 1903, high on a hill and overlooking the National Zoo. (The nighttime roaring of the lions was an unadvertised feature.) Carl immediately gutted the place, tearing down walls, rearranging the layout, bringing in more sun and creating a dazzling all-white apartment.

He festooned the apartment with colorful quilts and American antiques, for which he had an unerring eye. It was a style not yet so fashionable, and it worked perfectly with the surgical austerity of the construction. Fresh flowers arrived daily, or nearly so, and a service periodically polished the new copper pans. Music from an intricate concoction of woofers, subwoofers, amplifiers, and preamplifiers suffused the place. I used to call the rig Ol' Sparky after the Sing Sing electric chair which dimmed the prison's lights when the switch was thrown. I feared Carl's elaborate stereo would do the same to the neighborhood.

What Carl knew about music, Nora knew about entertaining. She was already a foodie, but beyond that, she had an absolutely amazing Rolodex. I did not know back then of the hostessing confidence that had so awed Dan Greenburg. All I knew was that when Nora and Carl threw a dinner party, it was unlike any other in Washington. Sure, the odd politician or Georgetown fixture would show up, but so would someone from New York or Hollywood. One night, Harold Pinter and his wife, Antonia Fraser, stormed out. Pinter, the English playwright, and Fraser, the historian, had been offended when someone steered the conversation to the bizarre sexual antics of a mutual friend. They bolted the apartment just as I was arriving.

In 1978 Lauren Bacall published a memoir, *Lauren Bacall by Myself*. I loved the idea of Bacall, and I used the book as an excuse to vent my awe of her in my *Washington Post* column. To my surprise, a man claiming to be Bacall's father called the day the column appeared. He disputed much that Bacall had written about him, and I, properly skeptical, questioned his credentials. Come on out and see me, he said. He lived in an apartment house in the Washington suburbs. We would meet in the lobby.

"How will I recognize you?" I asked.

"You won't have any trouble," he responded—and indeed I didn't. In the lobby stood Lauren Bacall as a man. He had her long face and brooding eyes.

My next column gave his side of the family story. He had not left his wife, but she him. He was not a bad father, but a good one. And so on. The night of the second column I went to Carl and Nora's for dinner. Before I could get into the building, someone stopped me in the driveway with a warning: Bacall was there. She was going to gut me.

Washington dinner parties had certain rules. One of them was to avoid confrontations—say what you will about someone during the day, but at night hatchets are buried as canapés are eaten. Only once was I accosted on a buffet line and asked to account for something I had written. It was a shocking but refreshing breach of the rules. (Someone cared.)

I did not expect Bacall to play by Washington rules. She was a formidable woman and stories about her volcanic temper were legion. I hesitated about going inside, but I could not pass up the chance of seeing her in person. I circled inside the apartment, keeping away from Bacall. Finally, I took a seat and was munching something when she abruptly plopped down beside me. Her timing was stage perfect. She glared at me, then broke into a smile, took my hand, and said, "It's all right."

Nora was a Washington anomaly. She was a woman who was not, primarily, "the wife of" whomever she had long ago married, who had since worked his way to Washington—elected, appointed, or just showing up. She had crackling wit, a New Yorky cynicism, a knowledge of theater and movies and literature—almost anything, actually. She did not know the nickname of the undersecretary of whatever, but everyone else knew that. In a town of dormant women, a city where the seat to the man's left or right was sure to be occupied by some belligerently unhappy woman, someone who might just announce herself by saying, "I do nothing," Nora was a woman who not only did something but could talk about it. She was always on the hunt for the universal—the stuff that could make a column in *Esquire*, something the meaning of which would not evaporate in a news cycle.

Little wonder then that the few women like her in Washington gravitated to her. Foremost among them was Sally Quinn, who had been hired for the *Washington Post*'s new Style section and overnight, or so it seemed, became the journalistic enfant terrible of Washington society—or, to their regret, those deluded souls who somehow thought they should be included in Washington society. (Sally soon set them right.)

Quinn had gone off to New York to become the co-anchor for the troubled *CBS Morning News*. It was a spot that Nora had sought for herself, but, as a favor to literature and cinema, CBS had rejected her. Quinn, a requisite blonde but never a perky morning person, got the job and, soon, the approbation. She was vilified and, like almost everyone before—and after—her at CBS, failed. Sally returned to Washington and the *Post* and in 1978 married the paper's editor, Benjamin C. Bradlee.

Quinn and Bradlee personified "power couple." Betty Ford and then Rosalynn Carter got the title of first lady, but it was only titular. Washington's actual first lady was Sally Quinn. As the daughter of a three-star general, she not only reveled in the role but came to it naturally. She and Ben eventually moved into an appropriately grand eighteenth-century mansion in George-town, where she entertained in a manner befitting the house and its provenance (it had once belonged to Abraham Lincoln's son, Robert Todd Lincoln), but at the time Sally and Nora became close friends, the Bradlees had been living more modestly, in a nineteenth-century town house in the slightly raffish Du-pont Circle area.

Nora and Sally had much in common. They were both writers, of course—although Sally had not been one when the clearly smitten Bradlee had hired her at the *Post*. ("Well, no one's perfect," the *Post*'s editorial page editor, Philip L. Geyelin, wryly commented.) Nora and Sally were also both gutsy. Each came from her own kind of royalty—Hollywood or military—and they both could take a punch. Years before Nora would write *Heartburn*, Sally got up off the canvas to write "We're Going to Make You a Star," her account of her humiliation at the hands of CBS and Clay Felker's *New York* magazine.

But before Nora and Sally would become friends, they would become ri-vals. They had known each other, of course, crossing paths in New York and the Hamptons, noticing each other, saying the polite hello while doing a size-up, and then in 1973, a CBS-TV executive named Sandy Sokolow asked Nora if she would be interested in being the female host of the network's incessantly revamped morning show. The male anchor would be Hughes Rudd, an ap-pealingly crotchety non-morning type, and his female partner was yet to be chosen. Was Nora interested?

Yes. No. Yes and no. She was already an established writer and she had done some TV—not very well, she thought—and she knew that success on TV would mean failure: It would hurt her writing and kill her romantic life and she didn't much respect the medium, at least what she saw on it. Yet, could she say no? The money. The fame. The limo. Probably a clothing allowance.

Who else was in the running? she asked.

Sally Quinn, she was told.

"There is no way for me . . . to convey the exact pain I felt at that moment,"

Nora later wrote in *New York* magazine. She not only immediately knew that she had lost but that she had lost for the same reason she had lost so many other times in her life: She was not a blonde. She was not a looker. Here it was once again, the breast thing—or, to be more precise, a variation thereof. It wasn't that Sally was some buxom blonde, it was that she was definitely a blonde. She was pretty, sexy, and, worse yet, she knew it and used it to her advantage. She had even said so. At the very same journalism conference where Nora and I had had our brief encounter, Sally revealed how she got her interview subjects to open up. "Being blonde doesn't hurt."

This was at a panel on women in journalism. This was said during the high age of orthodox feminism. This was said at a time when saying such things—never mind their truth—was forbidden. The audience was shocked. Nora was furious and instantly she said so. In fact, she said so to one of Sally's colleagues at the *Washington Post* who, seeing her duty, printed it.

In due course, which was to happen very quickly, Nora and Sally became fast friends. What Nora did not know at the time was that she was about to move to Washington as Mrs. Carl Bernstein. Upon rumination, however, she did come to realize what had so irritated her. It was not, exactly, Sally's veering from feminist orthodoxy and it was not even losing the CBS job, it was the unavoidable truth.

"I realized that what had gotten me was that Sally Quinn was right. Her way worked. My way didn't."

Well, of course it did. Her way did not work when it came to getting the CBS job, but it did at so much else. And one of the things it worked at was becoming the poster girl, the anti-pinup, for the ordinary-looking woman. It was to some extent a pose—although Nora was sincere in her insecurity—but it did make her tribune of the ordinary, the woman who spoke for all women who resented the other women who got the guys. She spoke for them and she spoke with such humor and keen observation that it ultimately propelled her to the sort of success that certainly would have eluded her had CBS chosen her for the morning show anchor. Nora could be an essayist, a screenwriter, a playwright, a blogger, a columnist, and a film director, but she could not be—in the fullest sense of the word—a blonde.

Two other women of importance showed up at Nora and Carl's—Katharine Graham and Meg Greenfield. The former was the publisher-owner of the *Washington Post*. The latter was the paper's editorial page editor after Geyelin. Graham was routinely called the most powerful woman in Washington, which was part truth, part cliché since her power was severely limited by tradition; the publisher did not interfere with the news department. Meg, in contrast, wielded real, visible power. She wrote or approved the *Post*'s editorials and she chose the paper's op-ed columnists. Underneath her avuncular façade was a remorseless killer.

Graham and Greenfield were worldly women. Graham, an heir to a sizable fortune, had done her radical days in San Francisco, and Greenfield had come down from New York trailing an oft-mentioned but entirely vague love affair. I was thoroughly terrified of both women and perplexed by the rules, if there were any. What could I say? What should I say? Could I use the word "fuck"? If I did, it was probably after Katharine did.

Nora knew both women as "girls." I do not mean to either trivialize or patronize. These were tough, talented women. But whereas I knew Katharine and Meg as bosses and powerful Washington figures, Nora knew them as women as well. They knew the sexism of men. They knew the sexism of men who did not think of themselves as sexist. They felt the dank touch of the patronizing compliment, the feeling of being the rare or only woman in the room. They had that in common and they exchanged experiences with a knowing glance—as Jews once did and blacks still do.

Washington hardly humbled Nora. She brought her New York ways with her. She demanded acknowledgment at the restaurants where, through frequent patronage, she thought she had earned recognition. For instance, we were all regulars at the Palm, a New York steak house that had opened a D.C. branch. We had planned to celebrate one of my birthdays there. A cake had been ordered, but when I called on the appointed night, I was told that no table was available. The restaurant conceded that I had ordered a cake, but I had failed to book a table.

I was prepared to show up and wait, but Nora insisted that if anyone should wait it ought to be someone who was not a regular. Call them back, she softly ordered. I called.

"No can do," Tommy, the maître d', said.

"Tell them we're going to eat somewhere else, but you'll stop by to pick up the cake," Nora told me to say.

I said it.

A bit later, I showed up with my game face on and asked for the cake. The maître d' handed it to me. "You know where you can put it," he said.

It was years before I returned to the Palm.

Someone called a meeting—I don't know who. It was called to discuss whether Bob and Carl should permit their book *All the President's Men* to be made into a movie. The idea for a movie had come from Robert Redford, who was the very embodiment of the cliché "not just a pretty face." Redford did have the prettiest of faces, but it masked a restless intellect and a compulsion to make very good, as opposed to merely popular, motion pictures. By the time he approached Woodward, he had made nearly twenty feature films, starred in most of them, and had been directed by some of Hollywood's best—Arthur Penn, Sydney Pollack, George Roy Hill, and, significantly, Alan J. Pakula.

The meeting was convened in Carl's apartment to consider a matter of grave importance: Would Carl and Bob be selling out? The concern seems laughable now, but it was keenly felt at the time. Would Redford and Pakula cheapen the story? Would the *Washington Post* suffer? How about journalism in general? After all, Carl and Bob were constantly being scrutinized for the least ethical or moral lapse: Was Bob really in the CIA? Was Carl a commie, as his parents were rumored to be?

Seymour Hersh was at the meeting. I found that odd because Hersh, who had won the Pulitzer Prize for exposing a massacre of Vietnamese civilians by U.S. Army troops at My Lai, was then with the *New York Times* and ostensibly a competitor. But here again relationships were intertwined. Hersh had been represented by David Obst, whose Dispatch News Service had syndicated the story of the massacre. Obst was also Carl and Bob's agent—and would become mine as well. (He would later marry Lynda Rosen, who as Lynda Obst would become a Hollywood producer, *Sleepless in Seattle* being one of her movies.) Above all, Hersh often played tennis with Woodward. Bob knew he didn't cheat.

Hersh questioned Redford's offer. Nora, on the other hand, was all for it. It seemed only natural to her that a book would become a movie, and it was likewise natural that in the process some facts would be changed. A book was a book. A movie was a movie. The worst thing a director could do was film the book.

Nora's voice was the one of authority. But it was also oddly the voice of a Hollywood where fidelity to the truth was not as valued as a good story. This was the wrong approach as far as meticulous Washington journalists were concerned. When it came to moviemaking, who could argue with Nora? It turned out that Pauline Kael could. She was the film critic for the *New Yorker*, the goddess of the cineaste, and in the middle of the meeting Woodward casually dropped her name. I was dumbfounded. Pauline Kael! Woodward knew the great Pauline Kael! I said nothing, but after the meetings was adjourned, I went over to Bob and asked how he knew Pauline Kael and when he had met her. He didn't know her, he replied. He had called her earlier that day. I understood. Carl had his Nora. Woodward needed one, too.

The movie went ahead. Redford, who would play Woodward, and Dustin Hoffman, who would play Carl, descended on the newsroom of the *Washington Post*. Redford and Pakula were sticklers for accuracy—they even had the newsroom's trash scooped up and shipped to the Hollywood set. The two actors came to visit me, sometimes sitting in my office, whiling away the time. Hoffman was just going through the motions. He was not going to imitate Carl. He was not going to study how to be a reporter. He was going to do something else, he confided to me. "It's called acting."

All the President's Men premiered in Washington, at the Kennedy Center no less. Redford and Hoffman were in attendance, most of the *Post*'s top editors and, as I recall, Nora, although she was not mentioned in the next day's newspaper. Woodward pronounced himself pleased with the outcome since the film, he said, "is about reporting—the procedures and not the personalities." Whatever it was, it was a triumph. It was nominated for the Academy Award in eight categories and won in four (including Art Direction, for the meticulous re-creation of the newsroom). William Goldman got one for his screenplay and Jason Robards won Best Supporting Actor for his role as Ben Bradlee. The film made plenty of money, turned journalists into latter-day cinematic cowboys, and reaffirmed Bradlee as a folk hero. The *Washington Post* itself became fabled. All in all, it was a glorious time to be at the *Post* and in Washington.

Washington, however, is where I lived, not where I worked. By day, I got into the car and drove to Annapolis, Maryland, where I covered the State House—the governor's office and the legislature. Maryland was a small state, but it was capable of huge scandals—two governors back-to-back were convicted of corruption. The first was Spiro Agnew, who served as Richard Nixon's vice president until he was forced to resign and plead no contest to corruption charges. The second was Marvin Mandel, whose conviction was later overturned on appeal—but not before he had gone to prison. For a journalist, Maryland was a feast.

Along with my *Washington Post* colleague Jules Witcover I did a book on the Agnew affair. As unprecedented as it was for a vice president to be proven corrupt and have to resign, the scandal soon got overwhelmed by Watergate. It became a footnote, sinking to the bottom of the page, where it has remained ever since. A vice president is a pretty big fish, but a president is a whale.

I came back from book leave and was peremptorily assigned to the city desk. I was apparently deemed in need of humility, and so a trash fire in an apartment house was my first assignment. I soon became bored, incapable of doing just any story. A torpor set in. My production was meager; my attitude was lousy. Nora noticed. She took me to lunch.

The restaurant was called the Big Cheese, located on M Street, N.W., in Georgetown. We sat toward the back, and I wondered what the agenda was—why I had been summoned for lunch. It was not all that rare that I joined Nora for lunch, but dinner with Carl and my wife was our usual fare.

Nora came to the point. I had to become a columnist. She had had her eye on me, it seemed, and discovered that I was no good at taking orders and not much good, either, as a reporter. Once I saw the outline of whatever story I was working on, my enthusiasm flagged. Then I wanted to write, since writing was fun and a way of expressing myself.

Nora's suggestion was both intriguing and preposterous. I had always wanted to be a columnist—my boyhood heroes were Nora's old colleagues at the *New York Post*, particularly Murray Kempton—but, still, I had no idea how to make this happen. Nora, though, not only knew that it could happen, but that it should happen. She enveloped me in her confidence. She even picked up the check.

Sometime later, I asked Bradlee to lunch. I was going to quit the *Post* and accept a job with Cox Newspapers covering the White House. But before I could quit, Bradlee surprised me by offering to try me out as a columnist. Did Nora have anything to do with it? I don't think so, but whether she got to Bradlee is almost immaterial. What matters more is that she got to me. She made me think of myself as a columnist.

Bradlee's offer came with a condition: Submit five sample columns. He would look them over and then decide whether I had what it takes to be a columnist. But I needed the adrenaline of a deadline and, besides, Nora had already decided I was a columnist, so rather than submit five columns to Bradlee, I submitted one to the city editor. I'm the new local columnist, I told him. You can check with Bradlee.

The next day, my column appeared in the paper.

From there on in, I had the best editor in the world working with me. Nora would call with suggestions. She would call with hints, tips, and choice pieces of editing wisdom. She taught me how to end the column, often by circling back to the beginning, closing the circle. She taught me that a column was a bit like a play or a short story. It had to have a beginning, a middle, and an ending. A writer had to respect and honor the reader's expectations. Just as Chekhov said, "One must not put a loaded rifle on the stage if no one is thinking of firing it," so the columnist must not raise an issue without making a point.

Not long after I began writing my column, in 1976, it was revealed that Marvin Mandel, the governor of Maryland, had borrowed $54,000 so he could divorce his wife and marry his mistress. That was enough in itself to make a column, but in this case the devil was surely in the details. Mandel had borrowed the money not from a bank or even a political crony but from a Catholic religious order called the Pallottines, who were headquartered in Baltimore's Little Italy neighborhood.

Marvin Mandel was Jewish. His mistress was Catholic. When he remarried, his new wife converted to Judaism.

I hurried to Baltimore. I scurried around Little Italy, which I knew from my days covering Maryland politics. I talked to everyone I could, people on the street, women coming out of St. Leo's Roman Catholic Church, and even the parish pastor, Nicholas D. Rinaldi, a Pallottine priest. I returned to Washington with a notebook bursting with gorgeous quotes. And then I wrote and rewrote—polished and polished until the column glistened with detail and facts and the utter absurdity of it all. My editors loved it. They actually said so, which they almost never did.

When Nora called the next day, I was expecting even more praise. But, no, she was critical. What had wowed my *Post* editors was my reporting, the accretion of detail. They liked that. Nora did, too—up to a point. But then I had not turned the corner, brought the column home: said what it all meant. What was the point? What was the point? My column, Nora said, had no point. It was a little feature story. It was not a column. My editors were wrong. Nora was right. That, too, was the point.

Nora Wishes Naples a Ba Fungu

We flew into Rome on some sort of charter flight which landed at the secondary airport, Ciampino. How we got on that charter is something I cannot recall, except that it must have been Nora's doing. Everything about that trip to Italy was Nora's doing since Nora either knew the best way to go or the best place to be. Besides, she had mentioned our forthcoming trip to Katharine Graham, who gleefully said she had to tell her friend Johnny that we were coming to Italy. At that moment, I had no idea she was referring to Gianni Agnelli, the chairman of Fiat and without a doubt the most important and influential man in Italy. Johnny would take care of us, Katharine Graham said.

Johnny was on the spot. Almost wherever we went—Rome, Venice, the Amalfi Coast—a telegram was waiting at our hotel from Johnny. A duly impressed hotel manager would intone that Signor Agnelli—our Johnny—was unable to meet us for dinner or lunch that day but surely we could meet another day. With that, our reserved room was instantly upgraded at no charge and we were properly installed as friends of the most important man in Italy.

At one stop, our friend Johnny suggested by wire that he send his helicopter to fetch us for lunch. He was on his yacht somewhere in the Mediterranean, but he'd make sure we'd be back by dinner. Before I had a chance to say yes—yes, of course, the yacht, beautiful women, a smattering of dyspeptic royalty, a movie star or two, possibly even Cary Grant—Nora put her foot down. No. Who would want to do that? We were in Italy to see Italy, not to schmooze with decadent Euro trash.

In Rome, we hired a car for the drive down to the Amalfi Coast and the Hotel Palumbo in Ravello. I drove, my wife Barbara sat next to me, and Nora and Carl took the back. Nora chose to consult her many guidebooks rather than look at the steep drop into the Mediterranean. The serpentine road hugged the cliff, making for an exhausting and tense ride, but I was then the owner back in Washington of a BMW 2002 with a stick shift, and so I rather enjoyed the opportunity to downshift and take the turns in just the proper gear. Nora, however, had scant appreciation for my driving skills, and with the fate of the hapless New York limo driver in mind, I slowed the pace. Nora was a horrible backseat driver. It wasn't that she always knew the best route. It was that she was always fearful.

Traveling with Nora was a bit like joining an organized tour. The only thing she lacked was one of those brightly colored umbrellas that tour guides hold up. She had the requisite guidebooks, which she occasionally consulted but which she had mostly committed to memory. But she also had the many suggestions of her many friends who were experienced travelers and foodies. They knew the best hotels and the best restaurants, and so then did she. We went where we were told.

In Venice, Nora and Carl's contact person was a woman named Olive Behrendt. She was the widow of George W. Behrendt, a Los Angeles insurance tycoon who had done, as they say, quite well in the business. Olive was a tall woman, well dressed and possessed of a bouncy charm, who had been an opera singer in her youth and was then on the board of the Los Angeles Philharmonic Orchestra. She lived part of the year in Venice, where, as she told it, she had become the city's first and maybe only woman licensed to pilot a powerboat. As Nora pointed out, she was also the only person capable of saying "Zubin" twice in one sentence. Referring to her friend, the Philharmonic's musical director, Zubin Mehta, she would say, "So I told Zubin, Zubin . . ." Once Nora said that, we all started to count Zubins.

Behrendt was a real find. She was a delightfully knowledgeable guide, ferrying us around Venice in her sleek powerboat and slipping lira notes of undermined denomination into the hands of countless expectant Venetians. The money seemed to come out of her sleeve like fish flapping down a sluice.

I had been to Venice once before with my wife, coming in on a vaporetto, the boat that serves as a bus. The vaporetto had been crowded, and while open on the sides, it had a sloping roof that hindered getting a good view. This time, though, we had hired a private motor launch. It made all the difference.

Our boat took a route that the vaporetto did not. It slid into a narrow canal and then, clearing its throat, varoomed toward the heart of the city, where it made a wide, sweeping turn into the Grand Canal. I had a difficult choice to make: either look at Carl's face and watch it become engorged with delight or see Venice on a sparkling day. There is no forgetting seeing Venice for the first time. There is no forgetting Carl seeing it for the first time, either.

In Rome, we plunged into Italian cuisine—or rather cuisines. At a place off the Via Veneto, we discovered spaghetti alla checca, a gorgeous, summery dish which in *Heartburn*, Nora described as "hot pasta with a cold tomato and basil sauce."

In the book (and the movie) Barbara and I are Julie and Arthur Siegel. In the book, we spend quite a bit of time delving into pesto. It was 1977 and "everyone was eating pesto. As Arthur Siegel said one day: 'Pesto is the quiche of the seventies.'" I have no idea if I said that or not, but I like the line and I did develop an addiction to pesto. Up until that trip, though, food was just something I ate, usually—but not necessarily—when I was hungry. I came from a family where absolutely no one looked forward to a meal as a sensuous—as opposed to necessary—experience. We ate because it was time to eat.

Italy and Nora—Nora and Italy—changed all that. Food became not something you ate but something you did. The day was arranged around our meals, and the meals themselves were prolonged affairs in which we tasted just about everything interesting a particular restaurant had to offer. Sometimes, too,

Nora would cadge a recipe, as she did for the acclaimed spaghetti alla checca, modified in *Heartburn* as linguini. It's a happy dish, bursting with the Italian countryside (tomatoes, olive oil, and basil), and it became my go-to recipe, so simple to prepare that even I could manage.

Some days it seemed we did nothing but eat. We consumed Italy, gulping it down restaurant by restaurant. Some we went to twice—the little place with the outdoor tables in the old Ghetto—great food, but really no Jews—and the spaghetti alla checca joint a block off the Via Veneto, which, when we went back years later, had inexplicably dropped it off the menu—and refused to make it. We ate, of course, at Dal Bolognese, the celebrity spot, to see who we could see, which, as I remember, was absolutely no one. (I once saw Audrey Hepburn there.)

Italy was an introduction to the supreme importance of food in Nora's life. Many years later, as if I was still digesting what we had eaten in Rome, we drove from L.A. to the Napa Valley and went almost immediately to Thomas Keller's French Laundry, the restaurant that's occasionally called the best in the world and always called *among* the best in the world. Nora had secured the reservation, and while the French Laundry's lunch is renowned for its many courses, it soon became clear that the additional ones had been added on account of her.

The food kept coming. Delight turned to duty, a trudge through pastries and meats, fish and vegetables, all of it too enticing and delicious to reject. It was impossible to say no. Everything was extraordinary. Besides, Thomas Keller would be hurt. He was in the kitchen. We had met him. We had to keep eating. For the experience of it all. For Tom. For the sake of afterward—a good anecdote.

Normally, the restaurant served a nine-course tasting menu. That day I think I counted seventeen. (I also had a lot of bread.) It was Italy all over again—food consuming us instead of the usual way around. Satiation turned to discomfort and discomfort to mild agony. We were paradigms of the bourgeois barbarian, gourmands rather than gourmets—yes, we were aware of that.

Yet Nora was always the very model of moderation. She ate everything but sparingly and never drank to excess, either. No matter what came at us, an assembly line of the succulent, Nora was able to parse, taste every ingredient, and declaim on the cooking method. She loved the food not because reservations were nearly impossible to get or because the place had more stars than Patton's parade uniform, but because it was *sooo* good.

Italy was my first trip with Nora. Later came Spain and England and the Caribbean and of course the Mediterranean on David Geffen's divine dreadnought, a one-boat flotilla of luxury. Later, too, came Paris and back to Italy several times more and California and Vegas, more Nick's town than hers, and then Paris once or twice more. But Italy is where our splendid romance blossomed. Nora put it best in *Heartburn*.

"Arthur and Julie and Mark and Rachel. The Siegels and the Feldmans," Nora wrote. In real life, they were the Cohens and the Bernsteins, four former or current newspaper people, all of us writers—close, so very close. "It's not just that we were best friends—we dated each other. We went steady. That's one of the things that happens when you become a couple: You date other couples. We saw each other every Saturday night and every Sunday night, and we have a standing engagement for New Year's Eve."

Yes, and Christmas, too. That first one, when Barbara was away and I had stayed in Washington to work on the Agnew book, Nora had cooked a goose dinner. It seemed appropriate to her, Dickens and all that, and so for years afterward we had goose for Christmas and sometimes for New Year's and sometimes for both. Usually, the goose was bought locally, but one year we got one that Sally Quinn's father, the formidable General William "Buffalo Bill" Quinn, had downed at his place on Maryland's Eastern Shore. The poor bird was riddled with buckshot. We poor diners had to chew with caution.

At Ravello, we checked into the Hotel Palumbo, perched on a cliff overlooking the sea. The proprietor was waiting for us. On our terraces, he served us his homemade wine and then some ice cream made from local peaches, a taste so vivid it lingers still. Church bells summoned the fishing boats home for the day. Above us, brazen yellow lemons hung heavy from the trees. We were two couples, in love with one another, in love with our lives, and in love with life itself. The collision of sights, sounds, and emotions was too much for me. I cried.

We ate at the San Pietro in Positano, yet another hotel chiseled out of the cliffs, admired the table setting, flipped over a plate—and were soon off to Vietri, where they made the stuff. On the way, we got lost and hailed a middle-aged woman to ask directions. She was going to Vietri herself and so she climbed into the back of the car, sat on Carl's lap, and spouted the English she had undoubtedly learned from the erudite soldiers of George S. Patton's Eighth Army.

"Fuck you," she would chirp, and then laugh.

"Fuck you," we would cheerfully reply, and then laugh ourselves.

We found Vietri, bought all we could afford of the colorful plates, espresso cups and saucers, and such, and had it all shipped back to Washington, where it arrived cracked and smashed and pulverized. The crate sat, sad and collapsed, in the middle of a vast warehouse, the pottery bleeding from it. We salvaged what we could and laughed some more.

Ring My Bell

On March 28, 1979, Margaret Thatcher, the leader of Britain's Conservative Party, called for a vote of no confidence in the Labor government of James Callahan. She won by one vote, forcing Callahan to call an election which he subsequently lost, costing his son-in-law, the economics writer Peter Jay, his ambassadorship in Washington. He and his wife Margaret decided this called for a party.

Margaret, who would become Baroness Jay of Paddington and hold various positions in the House of Lords, was tall and charmingly ungainly, but smart and ironic and energetic and funny. In Washington, I used to see her from time to time—usually at dinner with the flood of British writers who augmented those already stationed in Washington during the glorious Watergate years. They were all lefties of some sort—Margaret's father, after all, was the socialist PM—although some moved right as they aged and the urge to mount the barricades presumably faded, along with the one for afternoon sex.

The British ambassador was the titular head of the diplomatic corps. He was not the so-called dean—the longest serving ambassador, who was invariably from some amiable dictatorship (Nicaragua, the Dominican Republic,

Spain, Iran, etc.), but he was the most important because Britain was America's most important ally and because its ambassador entertained a great deal. The embassy itself was a handsome Georgian-style structure on prestigious Massachusetts Avenue, N.W. (Embassy Row), a huge affair built for entertaining and to suggest an English country house.

Carl and Margaret had met at the home of Fred and Nancy Dutton, both lawyers of great zest and charm who wound up with a single client: the Kingdom of Saudi Arabia. I was a regular at the Duttons, but my only time at the embassy came after Callaghan's loss, when the embassy's capacious wine cellar was about to be turned over to the Tories. Defeat was drowned in drink.

I'm sure Nora was at the party, but I don't remember anything other than Margaret gleefully taking Carl by the hand and prancing him onto the dance floor. The song was the disco classic "Ring My Bell," with its suggestive lyric and its insistent beat. It played over and over again that night—

"You can ring my bell, ring my bell."

The song, although immensely popular, was new to me, and when I mentioned it later to Carl, he vehemently denounced it as trash. I was surprised because Carl was always leading the way when it came to music. I had dropped out of popular music while in high school, using my pay as an afternoon counterman in a luncheonette to buy one classical album a week. (Beethoven's Fifth was my first purchase.) I looked down on popular music, especially rock, for its juvenile lyrics—"I wanna hold your hand"—and its intimidating sexuality.

But Carl embraced it all. He heard sounds I did not, and sometimes we would sit in his pre-Watergate car, a fatigued red Datsun, and listen to the radio. He thought that the car provided a perfect sound chamber—and it really did—but the sound quality aside, what impressed me was the absolute joy he got out of music—all music. I wanted to believe in a music hierarchy, with classical at the top and contemporary rock 'n' roll at the bottom. Carl disabused me of that. It was possible to appreciate Beethoven and Little Richard, Schubert and Frankie Valli.

Carl approached music as he did life. He sampled it all and was innocent in his enthusiasms, and like a child, or a puppy, he would taste almost anything. On vacation with Nora and Barbara and me on the Caribbean island of Martinique, he unthinkingly reached into the floral centerpiece at our lunch table, withdrew a lethal hot pepper, popped it into his mouth, and instantly, rocketed out of his chair, howling. He seized the water pitcher and drained it into his mouth. His mouth was a three-alarmer.

The man Nora had married was, in a phrase once intended for Hemingway, "a consumer of life." He grabbed at it all—music, books, experiences, women. He was alive in a tingly sort of way, and surprises popped out him like jacks-in-a-box. At a party once in West Virginia, he sat down at a decrepit upright and played the piano. Who knew? Other times, he played the guitar, once challenging a Tennessee-raised *Washington Post* colleague, Richard Harwood, to join him in singing "Great Speckled Bird," a hymn of the Protestant South. Harwood was stunned by the challenge: Bernstein? The Jew? The red-diaper baby?

C'mon, Carl challenged him, waiting, and then began by himself.

"What a beautiful thought I am thinking / Concerning a great speckled bird / Remember her name is recorded / On the pages of God's Holy Word . . ."

Reluctantly and then with more enthusiasm and delight Harwood dropped his reserve and, providing the requisite twang, joined Carl, whose own accent was an admixture of his parents' New York and his native Washington.

This anecdote is really about Nora. It is about the man she married. The marriage came to ruin, a scandal of Krakatoa proportions, and Carl went off looking like a fool. But he was not a fool, and neither was Nora. She had not married wisely, but she had married well. She wrote the history of their marriage, but she did not tell it all. I loved Nora, but I loved Carl also. And I am not a fool, either.

I can only assume that the night at the British embassy had gotten away from Carl. I was there, Barbara was there, Peter was there, and, most important, Nora was there—and Carl's inamorata, the future Baroness Jay of Paddington, was playing this salacious, suggestive song. Did Nora notice? I don't know. But I do know that she was a fervid non-dancer, someone who eschewed the dance floor, preferring the sidelines, the anteroom, where the music was distant and she could do with repartee and wit what the dancers were doing with their bodies.

Nora did not dance and for all her humor about it, she was deeply insecure about her attractiveness, her sex appeal. And here was Margaret, for all her ungainliness, exuding a kind of Old Vic ribaldry and having, for all her lefty credentials, that upper class proprietorship of sex. It was theirs. They had long ago disconnected it from love or marriage because what mattered most of all was consolidating and safeguarding property. Marriage could be just a business plan.

Indeed, at that very moment, Peter Jay was himself carrying on with his children's nanny, by whom he would have a child. In due course, Peter was chauffeured out to the Washington suburbs, where he met with a psychiatrist associated with the famous St. Elizabeth's Hospital who had earlier met with both Carl and Margaret. I, too, had sought her counsel—her Patient Zero having been a *Washington Post* colleague of Carl's and mine. Nora enlisted her as a character in *Heartburn*, in which she became "a Guatemalan shrink over in Alexandria" named Dr. Valdez, who had a Chihuahua named Pepito.

In the fall of 1980, Nora called my house. She was leaving Carl, she said. Suspecting he was having an affair, she had rifled his files—breaking into the cabinet with a letter opener or something—and discovered incriminating receipts and an American Express bill. They were for flowers and jewelry— and in *Heartburn* a children's book—the usual stuff, and the recipient was Margaret Jay.

Nora confronted Carl and he confessed, but they stayed together, barely. Carrying on as if nothing was amiss, they accepted an invitation for an informal dinner at Sally and Ben Bradlee's home. They ate in the kitchen and at one point discussed, of all things, extramarital affairs. A woman the Bradlees knew was cheating on her husband—boldly, flagrantly. How was it possible that her husband did not know?

"I said that there was absolutely no way a spouse could be cheating and the other spouse not know about it. It's just not possible," Sally recalled. "You have to know about it. You may not want to know about it, but you have to know about it. You may be in denial, but you have to know about it."

They were eating fish and drinking white wine.

Nora asked for red wine. Ben was puzzled. "Red, you want red?"

She wanted red.

He fetched a bottle from the bar, opened it, and placed it on the table.

Nora stood.

"She took the bottle and walked behind Carl and she started pouring the red wine on top of his head," Sally remembered. Carl was wearing a brand-new tweed sports jacket that just moments before he had proudly shown off. His hair was long and blown dry.

"The wine ran down all over his clothes and he just sat there. He didn't move. And she just kept pouring, glug, glug, glug. It was like slow motion. Nobody said a word. Ben I were staring at each other. Finally she finished emptying the bottle and put it down, and Carl was sitting there with his hair all down. It was this long silence, and finally Ben said, 'Well, we all go through troubled times.' One of them said, 'I think we better go,' and they got up and left."

For the scriptwriter-director, this was a fabulous scene, more riotous than sad, although Nora was certainly hurting and Carl reeling from the pain of ridicule and sudden uncertainty. Here she was, taking charge of the situation, finding the humor, the drama, playing it out before the mighty executive editor of the *Washington Post* and his star-reporter wife. The incident was bound to go wide, to leave Washington and then New York agape. It was a foreshadowing of *Heartburn* itself, a chuckly book about betrayal interspersed with recipes for the most delicious food.

Yet Nora had not done the scene quite as she wanted. In the book and the movie, she changed the wine to a Key lime pie. She would have preferred a blueberry pie, "but Betty [the name Nora gave Sally Quinn] said bring a Key lime pie, so I did." (She then provided the recipe.)

But even the Key lime pie or the wine was a variation on something her friend Rusty Unger had done years before. Rusty had been stood up for a New Year's Eve date, and the next day, in a snowstorm, she hurried down to Greenwich Village to meet a friend for lunch. As she ate, she looked up to see the date breaker from the night before. He was at another table, engrossed in conversation with a woman. Rusty dashed out into the street, scooped up a large snowball, snuck back into the restaurant, and approached the guy from behind. "I tapped him on the shoulder and when he turned around I smashed it into his face."

Rusty had told Nora that story, and Nora, as was her wont, put it through rewrite. "She told me that when she poured the bottle of wine over Carl's head, she was thinking of that snowball," Rusty said.

Virtually before Carl could get the wine out of his hair, Nora was gone—back to New York. She fled with alacrity, moving from one friend's to the next and then to her father's temporarily available apartment and then to another and finally to the storied Apthorp where, by dint of both her writings and the movie *You've Got Mail*, she became queen of the Upper West Side. But before any of that could happen, she returned to Washington, and I drove her out to the faceless Virginia suburbs and a warehouse where she had stored her stuff. She arranged for the shipping, and then, after a stop at a coffee shop for something to eat, I drove her to the airport and the return to New York.

Her move had been swift, almost precipitous. She had not so much returned to New York as fled Washington. She had the strength to take action; she had the acquired fear of being hurt again. Carl was acting unpredictably. He was both famous and infamous. I loved Nora, and while I did not hate Carl, I hated what he had done. On paper, he was my best friend, but I came to realize that I knew so little of his life.

Carl was in a vertiginous plunge, drinking and clinging to whatever self-esteem he had left. He was a good person, he insisted to me. And he was—good in his instincts, great in his talents, and wanting to be better than he knew he had been. He babbled the argot of shrinks and he waxed expansively about his future. I had no idea what was real and what was not—he was, after all, capable of so much—but our friendship was in tatters. We had been two couples, Carl and Nora, Barbara and I—so much fun, so many good meals, so many laughs, so much . . .

Nora, pregnant and her infant son Jacob in tow, went off to New York. In November of 1979, Max was born. She was essentially a single mother.

From Coup de Foudre to Heartburn

Nora's bereavement was total.

She returned to New York with some baggage—the one-year-old Jacob and the about-to-be-born Max. At first, she moved into her father's apartment, and after Max was born, she accepted an invitation from the book editor Robert Gottlieb and his wife, the actress Maria Tucci, to stay with them. The Gottliebs had two young children of their own, and Nora arrived with one child, one infant, one nanny, and one nurse for her preemie. Things were a bit cramped but never tense. By then, the Gottliebs were enamored of Nora. Many years later, they were among the very few Nora told about the sickness that would take her life.

Bob Gottlieb and Nora had met back in 1969 when, on assignment for the *New York Times Book Review*, she wrote "Where Bookmen Meet to Eat." It was about the lunch habits of New York's important book editors and publishers. It began oddly enough with the book editor Evan Thomas, Sr., who had confessed in an earlier *Times* piece that he didn't do lunches at all. Since an expensive lunch was an industry perk as well as a customary way of wooing authors, Thomas's confession was taken as akin to admitting celibacy or, worse, abstinence.

It was for this frivolous piece that Nora made a date to interview Gottlieb, then the publisher of Knopf and a man who projected great seriousness. (He was a music, dance, and literary critic as well as a book editor.) They wound up sitting on the floor of his office, eating sandwiches.

Gottlieb's feelings for Nora were ardent, and he describes them much as Mike Nichols later would: love at first sight. It was not some zingy chemical attraction but a meeting of the minds where a nod meant *Yes, yes—we agree and, what's more, there are very few of us who do.* "We just loved each other on sight and we never looked back" is the way Bob put it.

And so, ten years after Nora interviewed Gottlieb about publishing industry lunches, she and her children moved into his East Side brownstone. It was a full house, maybe too full, but Nora was not merely on the move, she seemed to be on the lam, fleeing (if she could) a stinging combination of hurt and mortification. Her husband had confessed his love for another woman—and she, to Carl's incomprehension, had gone to the tabs with the news. The affair was overloading phone circuits in all the usual places—New York, Los Angeles, Washington, the Hamptons, and, given who Margaret was, London and the whole British Empire. The sun never set on this scandal.

Carl asked for reconciliation. Come back, please. And she did. But then Carl found himself unable to give up Margaret and so Nora fled the marriage. Her life must have seemed like it was in a washing machine's tumble cycle. She tried to make sense of it all, but she couldn't. After all, it made no sense.

Soon, Carl called me. "The baby's come," he said. Barbara and I flew to New York. We saw tiny Max—underweight, crinkly, appearing ahead of schedule—and Nora, dazed and smiling wanly. Carl, steadying himself under the weight of conflicting emotions, wasn't himself, not at all. He was a new father, clinging to the debris of a marriage he himself had torpedoed, afloat in indecision and confusion. We met later, at Elaine's. The place was just opening for the night and was completely empty. Still, I was denied a table until I mentioned that I was meeting Carl. He might have suddenly become a man scorned, but he remained a celebrity.

Nora's life, always so carefully organized and planned, had gone flying off the page. She had gone from rich to something else. She was not poor, but the financial umbrella her parents had provided was gone. Her mother had died in 1971, and her father was still reeling around, making no money, spending what he didn't have, showing up drunk and crazed on occasion. (At his death in 1992 he was apparently worth less than $50,000.) She had two kids and no husband. She had tried and then abandoned a book on the American liquor industry, and Viking Press was pushing her to either come up with the book or repay the advance. She could do neither.

Nora was a broken woman, abandoned, scorned—all the usual purple adjectives. She tried to find the humor in her plight, but initially she couldn't. She had been pregnant when she discovered the affair, and now she was the mother of a toddler and a newborn. She cried often and deeply. She cried when she stayed with Amanda Urban, a close friend and her agent, and her husband, Ken Auletta, and she cried at the Gottliebs. She steeled herself for a new life, making her decision irrevocable by offering news of her breakup to the widely read columnist Liz Smith, yet another Mildred Newman acolyte.

"Liz, I have a story for you," Nora said. "Carl and I are going to divorce. Please write it." On December 19, 1979, Liz reluctantly did as Nora asked. "Writing this scoop makes me feel sick," she wrote.

Carl did not want a divorce—he tried to talk Liz out of running the item— but Nora was clearly moving on. By 1980, her relations with Carl had reached their nadir—where, more or less, they stayed. My own friendship with Carl became episodic, encumbered by what had happened and my closeness to Nora, but Nora never inquired about it or protested when I mentioned his name. Occasionally, she would ask about something Carl had done—often something she had read about in the tabloids: Was it true? Often, I didn't know.

As the years went on, my friendship with Carl revived some, and yet Nora and I became closer and closer. We talked on the phone frequently—she in New York, me in Washington—and I rented summer places in the Hamptons to be near her—and Carl, originally, and then whomever she was with. She became my manager, my agent, my career counselor, my romantic adviser, my marital therapist. Our only breach came when my marriage broke up. Nora took it hard. I expected her to understand. Initially, she did not. That summer the Hamptons did without me.

At the Gottliebs' Nora sat down at the typewriter. "The first day I did not think it was funny," she wrote. She called the book *Heartburn*, punctuated it with recipes, and had it published by Bob Gottlieb's Knopf. In due course, it became a script and then a movie and somewhere along the line a how-to book for women trying to pick themselves off the floor after a betrayal.

"She took the worst thing that can happen to one personally, wounded to the quick, weeping for months, and turned it around," Mike Nichols said. "I've always thought that people don't survive being publicly cuckolded, but she caught the knife in midair and turned it around. She turned it around, and she wasn't the one that was harmed.

"She did it by writing every day and crying all the time, but writing the next day, too. She made it funny. There's no one else on earth who could have made it funny and have cried all the time. I think that everybody saw her do it. Some were scared by her because it was incredibly powerful. She had an iron will and she was able to do something that had seemed impossible."

Before writers write on paper, they write in their head. Nora wrote *Heartburn* in conversations with herself and others. She did not say she was thinking of writing a fictionalized account of her marital breakup, but she started to recount it, to shape it, to see what worked and what did not. She tried it out one day in San Antonio, Texas, on the writer Marie Brenner. Nora had gone down to Houston to promote her new book, a collection of media pieces titled *Scribble, Scribble*, and then hopped over to San Antonio to see Marie, who had come home for medical reasons.

The two had a lot in common. They both were writers. They both were committed New Yorkers who had come from elsewhere—Nora from Beverly Hills, Marie from San Antonio—and Marie had dated Carl. It was at a party Marie gave that Carl and Nora met. Marie saw it happen—a locking of the eyes, a meeting of the gaze.

"I saw the coup de foudre," she said, using the French phrase for passionate love at first sight. "It happened right in front of me. He took her number down."

Nora called Marie the next day with a question. "'Are you really sure you're through with him?' she said. 'Trust me, I am.'" And then Marie added a caveat: "Trust me, this is not going to work."

In San Antonio, Nora and Marie went for a drive. Nora wanted to see the Alamo and other sights. Marie played tour guide, but her mind was on her own condition. She had recently been diagnosed with melanoma and was recovering from massive skin grafts. As they drove, Nora recounted her breakup with Carl. Much of it was news to Marie. The story was gripping, sad and outrageous, and Nora cried some of the time—and then, it seems, never again. But this was one writer listening to another, and Marie could detect that tragedy was being nudged into comedy. Nora was shaping the material, blanching it of pain and seasoning it with humor. This was her story and she would not be the victim. She would not play the fool. Carl would.

Get the Bromo—
Heartburn All Around

*H*eartburn has attained the status of a classic, but when it was published in 1983, it was considered controversial and occasionally denounced as tasteless. Carl certainly felt that way, and he greeted the news of a movie sale by getting a lawyer and having the case moved from New York to Washington. In the end, he got pretty much what he wanted—which was, above all, joint custody of his boys and to be portrayed "at all times as a caring, loving and conscientious father." Those words are from a curious document titled "Attachment A to the Marital Separation Agreement Between Nora Ephron and Carl Bernstein." In other words, if Nora wanted a divorce, she was going to have make some changes to *Heartburn*. She did.

So did Mike Nichols and Paramount. The attachment was the culmination of a legal tussle. Carl not only demanded that he be portrayed as a dutiful and loving father, but he insisted that his kids not be portrayed in the movie or, if they were depicted, that they would be shown as females. His real children, meanwhile, were not to be allowed to attend any publicity event for the movie, and Nora was prohibited from ever writing about them. Nora agreed.

She agreed further on inserting a description of Carl's exemplary behavior in the immediate aftermath of Max's premature birth. "Carl, over the objections of the hospital staff, remained with me during the delivery of our child," she stated. "During the following five weeks, in which our son was hospitalized, Carl spent almost every day feeding, holding, and caring for our baby."

Carl got a first look at the script. He got to meet with Nichols and offer objections, if any. None of this was necessarily unique—scripts often become legal tugs-of-war—but it was possibly the first time such a document was inserted in a divorce agreement. Paramount Pictures and Mike Nichols signed off on it, Mike thinking Carl had a case. At Carl's insistence, "The Attachment" was filed with the court and remained public. It was 1985. After more than five years of often bitter and always expensive negotiations, Carl and Nora were finally divorced. *Heartburn*, a work of more or less fiction, was ready to shoot.

The attachment was liberally quoted in the *Washington Post* and almost entirely reprinted in *Harper's* magazine. It made for juicy reading, but to those who knew Nora and Carl at the time, it made for painful reading. Carl's wariness about Nora's intentions were manifest and raw. He didn't trust her one bit. And, in essence, was vigorously asserting his rights as a father.

As far as she was concerned, she was being compelled to guarantee that she wouldn't do what she would not have thought of doing in the first place—using her children to get back at Carl. Sadly for Nora, though, Carl was hardly alone in thinking that *Heartburn* had crossed a line.

In *Vanity Fair*, the critic Leon Wieseltier, writing under the nom de plume Tristan Vox, found the book disgusting in all respects—even the writing—and rendered the most hurtful judgment of all: "The infidelity of husband toward a wife is banal compared to the infidelity of a mother toward her children. Here is Carl Bernstein and adultery; there is Nora Ephron and child abuse. It is no contest."

Nora was devastated.

Wieseltier is an especially powerful and occasionally viperous writer, but his was a common refrain: What about the kids? What about Jacob and Max? When they grew up, what would they think of their father, not to mention their mother? What would they have to endure in school, on the playground?

They would be the talk of the crowd at the Upper West Side's sliding pond, the sandbox, the lox line at Zabar's. They would be ruined.

Nora insisted otherwise. She furiously refused to concede that she had risked her kids' well-being in an attempt to make a buck and get back at Carl. What's more, she resented the implication that there was something untoward or unsporting in not suffering her betrayal in stoical silence . . . as a good wife supposedly should. Some wondered why she had acted—overreacted actually—and made such a big deal over what was, to many people, a run-of-the-mill infidelity?

The book troubled me as well. I was, as usual, torn between Nora and Carl. Nora was in pain, but so was Carl, and the case he made about the book's effect on his kids hardly seemed nonsensical. On the other hand, Nora was certain it would do no harm—and Nora's certainty was vault-like. She never paused in her determination to see the book become a movie, not a moment's hesitation. She insisted she knew what she was doing.

Here again I was talking across a cultural gulf—and so was she. My preference, I admit, was for silence, for her to have treated Carl's affair with Margaret Jay as a secret—this stinky thing to be buried out in the backyard. The book, though, was one thing, the movie something else again. It raised the stakes considerably—premieres and spotlights arching the night sky. Movies mean interviews and television commercials and a final product that is shown on a screen that is appropriately immense, twenty feet high and forty feet wide. We all respect books; we adore movies.

Nora had been raised in the maelstrom of Hollywood banality. The extravaganza was just another day at the office for her parents. Pictures came and pictures went—and so did stars and, of course, screenwriters. It was all very big but as evanescent as the articles in last month's fan magazine. A movie opened bombastically with a premiere and a dinner and many interviews—and then, as all Hollywood knew, often nothing happened. It died. It evaporated. Gone. The hurt of the flops could last longer than the joy of the hits. Failure was always watching from the balcony.

Nora had had her own experience with the uninvited spotlight. Her letters home from college were expropriated by her parents for their play *Take Her, She's Mine*. She was twenty when the play opened on Broadway, twenty-two when it became a movie and she metamorphosed into Sandra Dee, a 1960s-era movie star of insufferable cuteness. Nora had been older than her boys when this all happened, but she had experienced the leers of her college classmates and the unavoidable sense of having had two existences—the real one and the reel one, which audiences of course, felt was even more real. Still, it came, it went—and that was that. Her boys would become men and they would understand, as indeed they did. But it took some time.

In the meantime, she put her head down, tucked in her chin, and just kept on going. She was modestly accustomed to being in the center of a storm—the blowback from Dolly Schiff and the concussive effect of "Breasts." Another piece comes to mind in that respect. It was a trifle she wrote in 1975 and it was called "Crabs." It was about how the sexually transmitted little crustaceans were passed around a group of friends.

The friends were "neither fact nor fiction," Nora wrote. But to people in the know, which was New York's Nora set, they were fact and not fiction. They were real people. I knew that. But I was a Washingtonian, and I needed to have the piece annotated so I could know who was who. I could not ask, because that would amount to a confession of being a rube, and I was, in my bones, a New Yorker.

So I guessed, listened at the dinner table for clues, and wondered if a comeuppance was in the offing. It never happened. She had virtually named real people as having this awful ailment, this condition—this thing out of a horror movie with scratchy stuff crawling around one's crotch (Is this what crabs is?). And they, moreover, had gotten it sleeping where they should not have with people they should not have. And Nora, who had presumably learned some of this in confidence, had written it all.

"Crabs" left me in awe, not to mention flabbergasted. It was written in disregard of any consequences. The people alluded to were not defenseless civilians but were armed to the teeth with typewriters of their own and with regular publishing outlets. They could retaliate, if not in print then in the corner of the room at a cocktail party. Nora could be whispered to death, shunned, banned, banished—from Elaine's and other places that mattered.

She didn't seem to care. The article, the piece—the facts and the non-facts—was like a tank, impregnable, and so was the person who wrote it. I still recall one of the characters in "Crabs," a writer Nora expanded upon at dinner, gallivanting around someone's bedroom trying to hoist up *his* pantyhose. My God, the thought of it almost made me dizzy, not to mention apprehensive:

What might she write about me?

Nora was my friend. I loved her. But she was a killer.

Heartburn, of course, was her most famous bunker-buster endeavor. Nora not only wrote it in flamboyant disregard of the consequences, but while driving straight at Carl, she casually ran over some other people as well. One of them was Dan Greenburg. Their divorce had been amicable, but *Heartburn* put it on the rocks. Nora invoked a thinly disguised Dan as a walk-on—an ex-husband who kept hamsters and dressed them up in adorable little outfits. The character was a complete invention, a version of Nora and Dan's attempt to dress their two cats, Bernie and Arnold, in tiny sombreros they had bought in Mexico. The cats preferred to go hatless and that was that.

The Ephron-Greenburg marriage lasted nine years, some of them—especially the early ones—quite wonderful. It was followed by the nicest, most pleasant divorce possible, handled by a single lawyer. Nora and Dan had simply grown apart, but they still liked each other and, amazingly, occasionally even dated. Their relationship was so amicable that when Nora told Dan that the people in her therapy group said she should have received a larger share of the house the two had owned in East Hampton, he wrote her a check on the spot. Still, all good divorces must end for some reason and this one did. *Heartburn*, it turned out, got two husbands with one shot.

Nora alerted Dan to what she had done and assured him it was harmless. At first, he agreed. But then Mildred Newman, on whom the character Vera was based, went to work on him: "How could you stand what she did to you? She mocked you. She made fun of you, she lampooned you. She made a fool of you."

Mildred had few rules—she socialized with members of her groups, for instance—but mocking the shrink herself could not be countenanced. Nora was effectively named a "non-party person," an old Communist Party term which applied in this case because as with the old CP, membership in the group was secret and thrillingly subversive. Nora became anathema. To Mildred she was a skunk. (Nonetheless, when Mildred died in 2001, Bernie asked Nora to do the eulogy. She was, everyone remembers, terrific.)

Mildred got to Dan. When Craig Horowitz of *New York* magazine called to ask what he thought of *Heartburn*, he allowed his resentment to get the better of him. "Nora is a much classier person and a much better writer than is evident in this book," he said.

Nora cut him dead.

"That was the end of our relationship," he said. "She and Mildred got back together again. I never resumed my relationship with Nora."

The publication of *Heartburn* left me flummoxed. I didn't know what to make of the book. For guidance, I looked to Nora's then boyfriend, Joe Fox. He approved of the book. Fox was an esteemed senior editor at Random House, a product of the Waspy Philadelphia Main Line, an elegant man of simple tastes (while traveling, he eschewed complicated dishes for simple ones that invariably tasted better), a Harvard graduate, and a proper member of proper clubs.

For all of that, Fox was an odd fellow who seemed to collect idiosyncrasies as a hobby—he wore a ratty, moth-eaten tennis sweater, carried his tennis gear in a straw basket, chain-smoked unfiltered Camel cigarettes, and drove a Volvo so fatigued it had the automobile equivalent of fallen arches. His city apartment was on Central Park South, a duplex with lofty studio windows overlooking the park, which he furnished in pedigreed hand-me-downs—a Sheraton-era desk, for example, which at auction would refill his depleted coffers. He had been married and had four sons.

Out on Long Island, Fox had a squat, utterly suburban house on a cul-de-sac in Sagaponack. The front was pure Levittown, but the back was pastoral Hamptons. It looked out on Sagaponack Pond and a lazy creek that oozed to the nearby ocean. He furnished the place in a shabby-chic style which Nora abhorred and would, if she could, have had condemned on health grounds alone. She installed a new kitchen with a beast of a Garland stove and deposited a handsome master bedroom over the garage, with floor-to-ceiling bookcases. Nora would have gotten to the rest of the house in good time, but the relationship didn't last long enough.

Fox had impeccable literary credentials. After Fox died, John Irving, the novelist, wrote about him in the *New Yorker*. The article was titled "Fox Here," which was the way Fox announced himself on the phone, and it mentioned not only his brilliance as a book editor but also his role as the center of a Hamptons literary set. Irving listed some of those he had met through Fox: James Salter, Peter Matthiessen, and George Plimpton just for starters. Fox had introduced me to some of the same people as well, and so his influence on me was great. Writers listen to great editors. I listened to Fox.

What did Fox think of Nora's book? He wore bespoke suits with an inside jacket pocket for cigarettes. He reached down for one, lit up, and as the smoke rushed from him, exhaled a gleeful giggle. Fun, he said. The book was fun, he pronounced—as if it were adultery itself. But he was a book editor, which meant both that he was accustomed to handling controversial books and that the book itself came first. If feelings were going to be taken into account—even matters of taste—then many good books would not be written. Fox was an editor, and Nora, while not his writer, was a writer. He nonchalantly dismissed the book as no big deal.

Nora was a woman of many talents, but she was inept at public displays of pain. She seemed too confident, too successful, too powerful, and too disdainful. But she could be hurt. With *Heartburn*, she was under attack, defending herself against an accusation that could only be disproved over time. If her kids turned out all right, she would be exonerated—not that the critics would track them and then, years later, write an apology.

No one wrote in those terms, raising the question and then saying only time would provide an answer. The conditional tense was eschewed. It was for the literary faint of heart. No one was permitted to wonder, to wait and see, to write that stale phrase, "Time will tell." The critics criticized and moved on, but I stayed, and once—just once—I oh so tentatively ventured that I could understand why Nora's critics were saying what they were saying—nothing stronger than that, I assure you. She whirled on me. "Do you think I would do anything to hurt my kids? Don't you think I'm a good mother? I know what I'm doing."

From everything I could see, she did.

All these years later, I retain a residue of doubt about *Heartburn*. In his documentary about his mother, Jacob acknowledged that those were tough years for him, but he is fine, his brother is fine. Jacob is a writer and filmmaker, accomplished at both. Max is a musician—guitarist and arranger, and much in demand as both—and splendidly married. Their success thrilled Nora— a mother's expected love, certainly, but something more, absolutely. Maybe vindication.

Heartburn endures. Lines from it get quoted to me all the time. It was written under incredibly difficult circumstances—"a tear on every page," Nichols said—and it was a tour de force in literary judo, using the weight of mortification to produce humor. It was most certainly not a scathing jeremiad—if it had been, it would be forgotten by now—but it has been embraced as one by women for whom betrayal is either in their past or feared for the future. In terms of staying power, *Heartburn* is a classic.

The Paper Eater
Makes a Picture

A story about Karen Silkwood in a 1975 issue of *Ms.* magazine caught the attention of Sam Cohn, an important film and theatrical agent who, besides absentmindedly eating paper when under stress, represented Nora. Cohn, who died in 2009, was one of those semi-mythical figures who seem created for colorful obituaries. In addition to eating the occasional napkin, he was a movie agent who loathed Los Angeles, who rarely returned a phone call, who eschewed the limo for the subway, who dressed one notch up from a derelict, and who, rather than having a tiresome contempt for his clients, was in absolute awe of their talents.

Cohn was renowned for structuring fortress-like deals that could withstand the sappers of any movie studio's legal department. He was phenomenally loyal to his clients, and he was, almost without a doubt, the single most important film agent in New York City. In fact, he was the indifferently dressed, if unheralded, center of the New York film world.

At the time that Cohn read that *Ms.* magazine article, he was representing Paul Newman, Meryl Streep, Robin Williams, Liza Minnelli, Lily Tomlin, Whoopi Goldberg, Roy Scheider, Hume Cronyn, Zero Mostel, Jackie

Gleason, and Macaulay Culkin; among directors his clients included Robert Altman, Robert Benton, Mike Nichols, Bob Fosse, Arthur Penn, and Louis Malle. He also represented Woody Allen and his writing partner (*Annie Hall*, *Manhattan*) Marshall Brickman, as well as the playwrights John Guare, Arthur Miller, and for just about everything—plays, books, movies—the acclaimed novelist E. L. Doctorow.

Nora had written an article for the same issue of *Ms.*, the feminist magazine co-founded by Gloria Steinem. Nora's piece was a review of the book *Naked Nomads* by the relentless antifeminist (his description) George Gilder, also an extremely conservative economics writer who, for a short while, was to the Reagan administration what Marx was to Lenin's. He was so many fish in Nora's barrel. She reloaded many times.

Nora's piece is both funny and smart, but it's the one about Silkwood that holds our attention here, and that—not that she could have known it at the time—changed her life.

At the age of twenty-eight, Karen Silkwood died in an automobile accident when her car ran off an Oklahoma highway and careened into a culvert. She was on her way to meet David Burnham, a *New York Times* reporter, to tell him about allegedly unsafe conditions at the Kerr-McGee plant in Oklahoma where she worked and where she had become a union activist.

The plant manufactured highly radioactive plutonium for nuclear reactors. It was amazingly dangerous stuff. It could kill. In fact, it was apparently killing Silkwood. She had been contaminated.

Almost no aspect of the Silkwood story was straightforward. How had she been contaminated? Had it happened at the plant or had she contaminated herself? Had she died in an accident or was it actually murder? Was she high on drugs that night, a touch drunk, or solemnly sober? Had she started out to see Burnham with a file of material she was going to show him, and if so, what had happened to it? (It was never recovered.) Was she a stable woman, and, if so, why had she surrendered custody of her kids to her ex-husband, merely remarking that he would provide a calmer environment? For a heroine, Karen Silkwood had much to answer for.

But for *Ms.* magazine, the story had much going for it. In Silkwood it had the stigmatized woman, sexually active and therefore considered immoral, the (very) bad multinational corporation, the good union guys, the hideous nuclear threat, and an indifferent or corrupt criminal justice system that could not see the supposed accident for the murder it might have been.

Cohn asked Nora to write a screenplay about *Silkwood*. She had already done a TV movie and was clearly aiming for a big-time career as a screenwriter. When, in fact, she and Carl got their hands on William Goldman's script of *All the President's Men*, they had the epic chutzpah to rewrite it. (Goldman, a volcanic figure, predictably erupted.) Still, *Silkwood* was a particularly challenging project if only because Silkwood herself was a particularly challenging character. As ultimately played by Meryl Streep, she was coquettishly charming but explosively foul-mouthed, a beer-swigging pill popper. She presented a challenge to any screenwriter, especially one who was fairly new at the game.

Nora knew nothing about Oklahoma. But sometime before Cohn had handed her the *Ms.* article, she had run into the budding screenwriter Alice Arlen on the Washington–New York shuttle. They struck up a conversation, the usual lunch followed, and following the usual lunch came a discussion in Nora's office at *Esquire*. Alice, it turned out, had been studying film at Columbia and writing screenplays. In addition, she came from the Midwest—not exactly trailer trash Oklahoma, but Chicago and one of its foremost families, the Medill Patterson clan, publishers of newspapers (the *New York Daily News*, the *Chicago Tribune*, *Newsday*, the *Washington Herald*) and patrons of the arts, crafts, and everything else worthwhile. Still, she would do.

Alice was atypical in so many ways, but not as a Nora friend. She was connected to almost everyone who was anyone. She had been married to James Hoge, editor of the *Chicago Sun-Times*, later to be editor of the *New York Daily News* and then editor of *Foreign Affairs*, the publication of the august

Council on Foreign Relations. (His brother, Warren, had been the longtime boyfriend of Sally Quinn and later would be a high-ranking editor at the *New York Times*.) Alice had since married Michael Arlen, the highly regarded television critic for the *New Yorker* and the author of *Living-Room War*, the classic account of television's coverage of Vietnam.

Alice flung herself into the project. She went down to Los Alamos, New Mexico, sort of ground zero for America's nuclear weapons program, and came back with a box full of notes. She and Nora completed a first draft and then Cohn completed the deal. He got Nichols. He got Streep. He got the movie made.

Nora and Meryl had met only once before they all convened in Grapevine, Texas, for the filming of *Silkwood*. The initial meeting must have taken place at Sam Cohn's office, but Streep has only the dimmest memory of it. What she remembers, though, is Cohn saying to her, "Nora is an investigative reporter. She has a journalistic background. Let's get her to write this."

Nora had done some hard reporting and she certainly knew how to use the phone, but she was by no means an investigative reporter. Nonetheless, within a year, the script was ready, Streep had signed on, and Nichols was ready to go. They all assembled on a set built in a warehouse. The place had a little kitchen which became the clubhouse for the women—Nora, Alice, Meryl, Cher (in her first major screen role), and Ann Roth, the costume designer. Streep called the group "this little coven of women."

Nichols was not a dictatorial director, not some authoritarian auteur. He would take suggestions from anyone, but once filming was completed, he went into the editing room and the film was his and his alone. Until then, he convened a jolly group of stalkers, the women watching their leader, Nora watching Mike the most—or most intently. She was going to direct someday, and she was going to learn (if she did not already know it) that the movie belonged to the director and that the character who was born in the writer's imagination—a person who, on the page, did precisely as the writer wanted—rebelled when filming began and answered to someone else entirely.

Any movie is in danger of sudden death—if the script doesn't work, if the star balks, or, as happened to Nichols on a 1975 movie called *Bogart Slept Here*, if the star just doesn't understand the part. On the fifth or sixth day of shooting that movie, Nichols concluded that Robert De Niro was not working out and the dailies looked like "shit." To De Niro's everlasting dismay—and considerable anger—Nichols abruptly abandoned the project. The script, by Neil Simon, was later reworked as *The Goodbye Girl*, and Richard Dreyfuss won the Best Actor Oscar for it.

At the time Sam Cohn was assembling *Silkwood*, Nichols was hardly in any position to walk out on anything. He had not made a feature film since 1975, and his two previous efforts, *The Day of the Dolphin* and *The Fortune* had bombed, both critically and at the box office. (*The Fortune* had starred both Warren Beatty and Jack Nicholson, a seemingly failure-proof pairing.) Nichols needed a hit.

In other words, he needed Meryl Streep. Streep was well on her way to becoming the dominant and most successful female actor of her era. She had already appeared in seven movies, all in starring roles, including the just-concluded *Sophie's Choice*, for which she won an Oscar for Best Actress. (*Sophie's Choice*, budgeted at $9 million, had taken in more than $30 million.) Before that, she had won Best Supporting Actress for *Kramer vs. Kramer* and been nominated for her performances in *The Deer Hunter* and *The French Lieutenant's Woman*. She had also appeared in *Julia*, *Manhattan*, and *The Seduction of Joe Tynan*, choice roles all.

For Streep, the project was the fortunate marriage of ideology and juicy role. Silkwood had feminist credentials. Meryl Streep was—and remains—a feminist. (She at one time asked Nora to write a script based on the life of Elizabeth Cady Stanton, a founding American feminist and suffragette. The project went no further than lunch.)

Silkwood was hardly formulaic. The usually fetching Streep was not going to fall in love. She was not going to get the guy. She was not even going to survive the end of the movie. Karen Silkwood was an activist who could well have been a man. A man, though, would not have had his sex life held against him—a certain promiscuity suggesting a certain instability.

The movie was a women's project all the way, beginning with the *Ms.* magazine piece, itself written by a woman (B. J. Phillips), which was then made into a screenplay by two others and a movie starring two more. None of these women were oblivious to the feminist statement being made.

This was especially true for Streep, who for the first time in her career had come in early on a project—not merely handed a script, but allowed to participate in its development. She had expressed such a strong interest in *Silkwood* that she was momentarily unsure in retrospect if, in fact, she had brought it to Cohn and not, as she finally came to realize, the other way around. Whatever the case, something magical happened to her on the *Silkwood* set. She went into wardrobe as Meryl Streep and came out as Karen Silkwood.

"She was wearing cowboy boots with no socks, an extremely short denim skirt, no stockings, no socks; a T-shirt, very tight, no bra, and her cigarettes rolled into the T-shirt sleeve, a pack of cigarettes, and a cowboy hat," Mike Nichols remembered. "I had to sit down. I got dizzy.

"It was so fucking carnal. It was so, 'Are you ready to fuck me?' It was one of those movie experiences. It is everybody falling in love with everybody. It was wildly sexual just being there. We were all having a good time. Everybody was discovering everybody else. It was the first time I worked with Meryl, and I couldn't fucking believe what it was like. I could not."

Ann Roth, the costume designer, had conjured a transformation. She had roughed up Streep, and then Streep on her own decided to go from blond to mousy brown, changing her hair and her social class with one or two rinses of dye. The Vassar-educated Presbyterian from horsey Bernardsville, New Jersey, became a shit-kicking Oklahoman in a flash. Nichols had opposed the dye job, but not after he saw it. Streep was a triumph of trash.

Nora, meanwhile, was holding down two jobs. Along with Alice, she was reworking the script, but she was also keeping an eye on Nichols, watching a director direct so that she could someday do it herself. "She was just a huge pair of eyes and ears," Nichols remembered. He imagined Nora following him with a camera. "I heard clicking all the time."

Roth noticed, too. "She's learning," Nichols told her.

"And then I started watching Nora learn. That was pretty interesting. There was no question. She knew what she wanted out of that."

Silkwood was budgeted at about $10 million and took in a bit more than $35 million—a success by anyone's reckoning. It was a stupendous achievement for Nora and Alice, and they were nominated for screenwriting Oscars. Nora went to the ceremony insisting that she would not win. She was right. The Academy Award went to the veteran Horton Foote for *Tender Mercies*.

Foote had won once before, for *To Kill a Mockingbird*, so it was hardly a disgrace to lose to him. It was virtually an Oscar in itself for Nora and Alice to be nominated right off the bat. As proof of that, she and Nick and Alice and Michael Arlen were invited to the exclusive après-awards party given by the famed agent Samuel "Swifty" Lazar. Nora was nominated two more times as a screenwriter, for *When Harry Met Sally . . .* and *Sleepless in Seattle*. She never did win.

Nora accepted her loss—actually, Foote's win—with equanimity. She knew that she had already won entrée into the select group of screenwriters who could deliver. In fact, two of the other "losers"—Streep had been nominated for Best Actress and Nichols for Best Director—were already heading to their next project. Nora would write it, Nichols would direct it, and Streep would star. She would play Nora.

Where's My Kitchen?

It turned out that my Washington house did not look like a Washington house. This was the judgment of Paramount, the studio that made *Heartburn*, and so my expectation that my weary kitchen would be updated and the outside of the house given some badly needed paint was dashed. As far as I was concerned, this was yet another sad Hollywood story.

In fact, the movie wasn't really filmed in Washington at all. The lone exception was an exterior shot of a house located in the city's Capitol Hill section and owned by a *Washington Post* colleague of mine—probably the richest person on the staff and undoubtedly someone not in need of a new kitchen. Another scene was shot in Alexandria, Virginia, a Georgetown clone across the Potomac from Washington. The rest of the movie was filmed in New York.

Heartburn opened in the summer of 1986, by which time Nora was living with Nick Pileggi—or he with her, actually. Nick had moved into the apartment in the Apthorp where he, in time, would establish an office high in one of the building's rooftop aeries. Nora would take yet another Apthorp apartment for her own office.

With three apartments, Nora and Nick quickly established themselves as major Upper West Side figures. The neighborhood was to her liking. Zabar's, the celebrated and nearly mythical food emporium, was a mere one block north and Nora was one of its more famous patrons. (She made a cameo appearance in a film about Zabar's attempted by Rachel Zabar but never completed.) Citarella's, not quite as renowned but better for rotisserie chicken, was only four blocks to the south, and when a union threw up a picket line blocking its entrance, Nora had a genuine, if somewhat comical, crisis. She was constitutionally unable to cross a picket line. On the other hand, the fish at Citarella's was nonpareil, especially the baby clams. Nora did what she could. The strike was precipitated by the firing of three employees who allegedly walked out over working conditions. Fire them, the shop's lawyer suggested. Nora had a better idea. Fire the lawyer, she told the shop's owner on the phone.

The Apthorp was built between 1906 and 1908 and covered a square city block. It was a massive structure, twelve stories high, with a rare interior courtyard that, for all its Old World charm, meant that some apartments were deprived of light. Not Nora's, however. It looked out over West End Avenue and, beyond it and Riverside Drive, the thrilling Hudson River. After that, came Jersey, which, on a clear day, was still Jersey.

Nora wrote about Zabar's. She wrote about Citarella's. She had Tom Hanks and Meg Ryan walk the streets of the Upper West Side in *You've Got Mail*. It's hard to say she made her neighborhood famous—it had been featured in numerous movies, including Woody Allen's *Hannah and Her Sisters*—but she helped to make it chic—so fashionable that the Apthorp's zooming rents eventually forced her out. She decamped to the Upper East Side, where, with the same enthusiasm, she discovered another Citarella's and numerous other stores catering to what has to be the world's most affluent and demanding customers.

In *Heartburn*, the character based on Nora repairs to her father's spacious Apthorp apartment, but for most of the movie she's in Washington. For this movie, I again had to play the role of the Carl Bernstein expert. This time it was not Dustin Hoffman who came to see me in my tiny, airless, glass-enclosed office at the *Washington Post*, but the extravagantly talented singer and actor Mandy Patinkin. He stuffed himself into my cramped office's only guest chair—and confessed himself puzzled: Why had Nora left Carl?

He was having an affair, I said.

So what? Patinkin said.

I understood what Patinkin was saying. Extramarital affairs are common and not always reason enough to sunder a marriage. I know Carl felt that way— not that he had not grievously wronged his wife but that she had overreacted. Patinkin, in any event, never made it onto the screen. Nichols fired him for lacking the requisite chemistry with Meryl Streep. Patinkin took his firing hard—"I thought my life was over," he told the *New York Times* in 2013—and discomforted everyone by showing up somewhat dazed on the set anyway. He apparently was surprised by his firing. Maybe for the wrong reason, I was not.

Patinkin's replacement turned out to be no less problematic, but in a different way. He was Jack Nicholson, who was not, as was Patinkin, a stage actor looking to make a name for himself in movies, but already a titanic Hollywood figure. By the time he signed for *Heartburn*, Nicholson had been nominated for eight Oscars and had won twice—for Best Actor in a Leading Role for *One Flew Over the Cuckoo's Nest* (1979) and for Best Actor in a Supporting Role for *Terms of Endearment* (1984). He was not only one hell of an actor, but unlike Patinkin, he had an outsized off-screen persona as a gadabout and roué. In a clichéd, tabloid sense, he was perfect to play Carl, but bringing him on changed the chemistry of the cast. Nicholson was no mere actor. He was a movie star.

Almost imperceptibly, the story started to drift his way. Nora probably noticed, but she was the writer and in no position to countermand Nichols. Streep was, and she stepped in. "I said, 'This is about a person who got hit by the truck. It's not about the truck.'

"They forgot about that for a minute, when he first came in," she said. "They really did."

Among the subjects I did not discuss with Nora were the challenges and difficulties of being a female director. We talked movies and moviemaking plenty of times—the inhumane stinginess of the studio, for instance, or the demands of stars for something another star had (John Travolta wanted a third trailer, just like Will Smith.)—but not the challenges of being a woman in a job usually held by men. It took Meryl Streep to provide some insight.

Meryl Streep has spent a lifetime being directed by men. Of her approximately seventy films, only a handful were directed by women—one of them being Nora's *Julie & Julia*. As a result, she is keenly aware of what happens when the character of a woman—the story of a woman, the emotions of a woman, the very soul of a woman—gets interpreted by a man.

"It's harder for men to imagine they are women than for women to imagine themselves on the male trajectory through a story. I'm not sure why that is, but I do know that with directors, having a female protagonist is a bigger leap than for a woman to imagine what it's like to be the guy."

Nonetheless, not even Streep could fully contain Nicholson. He was a riveting screen personality, and he endowed Carl with a winning humanity that was entirely lacking in the book—and that, at Carl's insistence, had gone into the movie script.

Still, for all the attention the movie got, *Heartburn* was no blockbuster. It was, at best, a modest hit and it garnered no awards. The critics were not kind. In the *Chicago Sun-Times*, Roger Ebert panned it. "This is a bitter, sour movie about two people who are only marginally interesting," he wrote.

Ebert was an important critic. Walter Goodman was less so, but his newspaper, the *New York Times*, was more important than either of them. "It isn't the actors' fault," he wrote with apparent regret. "*Heartburn* stands as testimony to the limitations of star power."

The pallid reviews notwithstanding, *Heartburn* was a huge success for Nora. As a screenwriter, she now had two movies to her credit—a lifetime's for all too many writers. Nicholson had expanded a small picture into a huge one, but he was not even remotely Carl. Streep, though, became Nora, and Nora emerged through Streep as a distinct personality in her own right. She had written the movie based on her own book, but what mattered most was that in the addled mind of the American public, she had been given substance on the very big screen.

"I highly recommend Meryl Streep play you," Nora said at Streep's AFI Lifetime Achievement Award tribute. "If your husband is cheating on you with a carhop, get Meryl to play you. You will feel much better. If you get rear-ended in a parking lot, have Meryl Streep play you. If the dingo eats your baby, call Meryl."

In 2007, secretly sick with cancer, Nora called Streep one last time. She asked her to read the script for *Julie & Julia*.

Cover for Me Kid, and You Can Use My Bathroom

I need to be upfront: In writing this book, I discovered nothing I did not already know about Nora. Sure, I found a detail here or a detail there—and there a lover and here a lover and everywhere a lover. But that was when she was young, and anyway, she had hinted at most of these affairs in her writings. Simply put, Nora was exactly who she claimed to be. It was the same with her marriage to Nick Pileggi. It was as splendid as she claimed.

Many marriages are lies in one way or another. Either the couple is not as happy as they pretend or not having sex as often as they hint—or they hate their kids or are having affairs or have no respect for each other or are harboring seething resentments from something that happened long before you ever met them.

Not Nora and Nick. Nora's son Jacob once said that he never saw Nick and Nora fight. No doubt. But I did. It happened just once, and it was over so quickly that I cannot remember what it was about. I do remember being shocked that it had happened at all. We were at some restaurant, Nora seated across from me, Nick on my right. He said something. She sharply rebuked him, and he instantly shut her down, more by manner than by words. She retreated, and it was over—as swift and as clean as the report of a rifle. It never happened again—not in my presence and not, I would guess, anywhere else, either.

Nora and Nick were in a swoon for each other. I saw them both frequently, incessantly, ate with them, boated with them, and flew with them. I went to Italy with them and France with them and England and Spain and the Caribbean, and Miami and California over and over again. I stayed at their apartment in Manhattan and their place in the Hamptons, and although I looked, I peered and sometimes wondered, I detected not a mite of disaffection between them. They loved each other. They respected each other. They found joy in each other. It was a grand affair.

The daily newspapers were printed for Nick and Nora. That's the way it seemed. They read them all and discussed what they found interesting, and if I called later in the day—say, mid-morning—Nick would tell me what Nora thought and Nora would tell me what Nick thought, and rarely, if at all, did one think differently from the other, and if they did think differently, each thought the other was cute.

My calls were often made out of necessity: I needed a column. Something had happened. It was in the papers. What did it mean? Between Nora and Nick—more often Nora—I usually found some meaning in what had happened. If she was not right, she was at least interesting. I'd settle.

Nora met Nick not long after she ended her relationship with Joe Fox. She had been hospitalized for the removal of her thyroid gland. It was a minor but emotionally fraught procedure because, as always, Nora knew everything that could go wrong. Above all, she feared cancer. She did not fear it in some abstract way, as we all do, but always as an imminent possibility. She'd talk about the high rate of breast cancer on Long Island and wonder if it had anything to do with overhead power lines or whether, as later became clear, it was the large number of Ashkenazic Jewish women, who have a genetic disposition toward breast cancer.

Later, when cell phones came along, Nora worried about whether they could cause brain cancer. There were reports about this in the press at the time, and it seemed somewhat plausible that holding a little radio transmitter to your ear could ultimately do some damage. I kidded her about it, saying there was no escaping fate. If the person next you on the street was using a cell phone, the impulses would go through you on the way to him. And, I would add, if that person was speaking a guttural language, such as German, the waves would necessarily be more powerful. It was best to stand next to a French-speaking person, I advised. It took her a minute or two to catch on. She laughed—always a great triumph for me.

Nora both recognized that her fear was unfounded and recognized at the same time that the fear was real. Her uncle Dickie had died very young from cancer, and his death had a profound and deleterious impact on Phoebe Ephron, who had virtually raised her much younger brother. Nora summered on Long Island. Nora was an Ashkenazic Jew. Nora worried.

Joe Fox did not. He had been good to Nora as well as being good for Nora, but he was a man of resolute, virtually metronomic habits. And so when the time came for him to get into his weary Volvo and drive to his weekend place, he did so—leaving Nora in the hospital.

That did it for her. She ended the relationship, and they both seemed to suffer little afterward. They were an odd couple to begin with. Nora could not get over Joe's WASP ways, including membership in an exclusive Manhattan social club that she insisted was anti-Semitic (Joe insisted it was not), and moreover, he had an impecunious approach to food. He hoarded leftovers in plastic containers that he ferried back and forth to New York City.

Joe moved on—another marriage, a son, and, too soon, a nap in his office from which he never awoke. He was sixty-nine. He had been a father, soldier, baccarat player, ladies' man, book editor, muse to many writers, and, for all time, the Tom Hanks character in Nora's *You've Got Mail*. She forgave him.

Nicholas Pileggi was nothing like Joe Fox. Nick was Brooklyn, not Main Line. His father, Nicholas, was an immigrant from Calabria, in the poor south of Italy; his mother, Susan, was also Calabrian but only by descent. She had been born in America. Both of course were Catholics, not WASPs like the Foxes. Nick's school was Brooklyn-based Long Island University, not Cambridge's Harvard. Joe belonged to the Raquet; Nick covered the rackets. All the rest is commentary.

But not ordinary. A bit like Nora, Nick also came from a writing family. Gay Talese, a splendid and justly celebrated nonfiction writer, is his cousin. Nick's mother and Gay's mother were sisters, and even their fathers were first cousins, from the same Calabrian town. The cousins went their own ways in America—Talese to Philadelphia and then the Jersey Shore and Pileggi to Brooklyn—and they split also on politics. Talese veered right and Pileggi went—or remained—left, both men reflecting the split in the Italian-American community, where the Fascist regime of Benito Mussolini was not universally despised. During World War II, first generation Italian-Americans had to face the anguish of fighting an army that, just some years earlier, had been their own.

Nick and I had met in 1967. I was working for United Press International and he was working for the Associated Press. We represented competing wire services, and we were both sent to cover the showdown between the TV networks and the American Federation of Television and Radio Artists, the union representing television performers. At stake was the telecast of the Academy Awards, scheduled for Monday, April 10. An anxious nation awaited the outcome of negotiations.

Few things in life are as boring or tedious as covering labor negotiations—even those involving television. You don't actually cover the negotiations. Instead, you hang around waiting for someone to tell you something. Leaks are not unknown, but news is made usually whenever a representative of management or labor—or a mediator—decides to talk to the press. The AFTRA negotiations were held at the Barclay Hotel in Manhattan, now the InterContinental. The most interesting thing about the assignment was watching the hookers stroll through the lobby. They looked like a million bucks, which judging by their appearance was not far from their yearly take.

Nick had taken a room in the hotel. He was working on a freelance piece about Rome for *Holiday* magazine, and way before the phrase was in common usage, he made me an offer I could not refuse: In exchange for covering for him, he'd let me use his bathroom. A deal was made, a bond was forged. From time to time, I would venture out into the hallway where the press was gathered, check around for any tidbits, and return to Nick's room, where I would sit and watch him type. I was content. My only competition was the AP, and its man was sitting in front of me writing an article about the glories of Rome.

The way I met Nick was far less dramatic than the way I met Nora, but it left a lasting impression. He was the senior man, a seasoned reporter. I was his junior, still learning. I don't know what I called him, I suppose Nick, but he called me "Kid." Way into my seventies, he was still calling me Kid.

Journalists are like cops. The average person is familiar with what they do and is therefore free to criticize. But just as it takes a cop to know a cop, it takes a reporter to know a reporter—not only to know what news is and isn't, but what constitutes a story, how it's built, its ingredients, the G-force of deadlines, the demonic demands of editors, and the severe limitation of space in print or time in television (when Nick and I met, the Internet was not yet a factor).

So journalists, like cops, hang together. They often avoid civilians because they weary of explaining what they do and why some story that has offended some reader had to be written the way it was. Or maybe not. Either way, it is gone and nothing can be done about it.

Nora had been a journalist, a member of the club, and knew that within that club Nick was considered something special. Working general assignment for the AP meant that Nick was well known to other reporters—not to mention cops—and while he had never toiled for the tabloids himself, he covered the same stories they did. This is how his reputation spread.

Nick was very good at what he did. He had very specific, quite specialized knowledge, which was about the mob. The romance of journalism has to do with the story behind the story. A newspaper prints the story. But it does not print everything because not everything can be proven or is in good taste. So the journalist knows things that the reader does not. The mob writer knows even more. He knows what the mob controls or influences, which for a time in New York City, was pretty much everything, including of course a good deal of politics. Nick knew these things.

Nick was affable. Nick was genial. But Nick was not easy to know. He held himself at a remove. He watched. He observed. He studied. He did not talk about himself. He did not say that he had been a poet of sorts, winning the odd literary prize while at college (LIU), that he had written a novel (*Blye, Private Eye*), that he read interesting books voraciously, that he traveled with older, accomplished women who valued his comportment. He had been married to *Sports Illustrated*'s celebrated golf writer Sara Ballard, who was doing what only men had done before. Nick was accustomed to strong women.

The same detachment that commended Nick to the cops commended him to Italian mobsters as well. Nick, of course, was Italian himself and spoke their language, particularly their body language. The wiseguys had their attributes—love of family, loyalty to friends and neighborhood, all the *Godfather* stuff—and Nick recognized who they were and what they did. That was all right with the mobsters; Nick had his job, they had theirs.

His breakthrough came with the book *Wiseguy*. It was the story of the mobster Henry Hill, who was squirreled away in the Federal Witness Protection Program when he opened up to Nick about his life in the mob. "Once he realized I was nonjudgmental about his life, he was unbelievably open and full of details," Nick told the *New York Times* back in 1986, when *Wiseguy* was published.

Some people only knew Nick as Nora's husband. He was the guy who preceded her, dispensing cash to head waiters and such, like some sort of Manhattan Johnny Appleseed, and then sometimes took care of even more people on the way out. He was a promiscuous and generous tipper, a characteristic Tom Hanks and Rita Wilson lovingly portrayed at Nora's memorial service. This was one of Nick's jobs. He took care of Nora.

But outside a small circle of people who saw him mostly as a spouse, Nick was known as a brilliant screenwriter and producer, a one-man idea shop, turning out proposals that wound up on the movie or TV screen. Nick was relentlessly self-effacing. His mob connections remained as confidential as any source more famous reporters had—Bob Woodward, for instance. The mob operated by the rules of omertà. So did Nick.

I vaguely knew about Henry Hill. I sort of knew when Nick was in Vegas, but not what he was doing there or, certainly, whom he was seeing. Nora, though, knew it all. Nick's material was not Round Table stuff, no Parkerish witticisms from stone-cold killers. Still, Nora thrilled to it. She had a taste for the demimonde, and the denizens of that world, hardly literary, had an eye for her. They knew of her and her movies, and like any American, they were infatuated with Hollywood.

By the late 1950s, the Mafia was going from an obscure collection of (mostly) Sicilian thugs to recognition-cum-celebration as the nation's premier crime syndicate. In 1972, the release of *The Godfather* clinched the mob's hold over the American imagination—and clinched the movie's hold over the mob's imagination. The wiseguys saw themselves up on the screen, huge and hugely romanticized. They started to use *Godfather* quotes like "I'm going to make him an offer he can't refuse" in their daily life and played the movie's theme music at their weddings, baptisms, and funerals.

"It made our life seem honorable," Salvatore "Sammy the Bull" Gravano, said. Gravano was in the business of killing people.

The Italian mob became a metaphor for American life—capitalism, family, masculinity, and, finally, a cowboys-and-Indians tale in which the good guys were the bad guys. When that happened, Nick was well placed. He knew the prosecutors, the lawyers, the lawmen, and the lawbreakers. *Wiseguy* became a best seller in 1986. The producer Irwin Winkler read it, thought it could make a great movie, and brought it to Martin Scorsese to direct. It was called *Goodfellas*, and it became a classic.

The script for *Goodfellas* was written both by Nick and Scorsese. Some of it, though, was ad-libbed on the set. Joe Pesci, who played the psychopathic Tommy DeVito, injected the word "fuck" into all of his scenes. (The word occurred 393 times in the movie itself, placing *Goodfellas* in the top ten of all movies in that regard—along with *Casino*, the film Nick did next for Scorsese.

Again, the culprit was Pesci.) At the premiere, Nick paced nervously as if waiting to be admonished for his dialogue. Instead, screenwriters now pay him
homage—not just for *Goodfellas* but also for *Casino*. They are masterpieces of
structure and storytelling.

It was 1983 when Nora and Nick began a love affair that never ended. They
had noticed each other out of the corner of their eyes, often at Elaine's. They
traveled in somewhat the same circles, although Nora, with *Heartburn* just
published and *Silkwood* in theaters, was the more glamorous of the two.
Washington was behind her—Washington and its huffy outrage over *Heartburn*—and instead she had New York, where writers were not supposed to be
influential, but merely brilliant. Nora was the latter, and New York, a cold city
of warm people, cosseted her.

A book has been done on Elaine's, and Frederick Seidel wrote a poem
to the place. "Remembering Elaine's" is studded with names and lurid with
cigarette smoke, and there's even a reference to Elaine Kaufman herself, "the
woman who weighed hundreds of pounds."

"The fat lady's" is what some people called the place, and it was to the fat
lady's one night that Nick and a pal repaired in a sudden spur-of-the-bache-
lor's moment—and there, finally, was Nora. They talked and they made a date
for the next night, drinks only because Nora was dining with Ken and Amanda
Auletta and Howard and Jennifer Stringer. Individually, they each knew Nick,
and so when Nora, still tingling a bit from the night before, told Amanda about
Nick, she was told to bring him along.

That dinner was a typical Nora event, even though it was not, strictly
speaking, Nora's event. While it might seem that she collected famous and
successful people—and she most certainly did—she was actually an amazing
talent scout who had met some of the famous well before they were famous.
Howard Stringer was one. He and Nora had met years before when, obviously
morose over the breakup of a relationship, she approached him at a party and
got him talking. They talked for a very long time, Nora focused on Howard
throughout, drawing him out of his gloom and leaving an indelible memory. "I

was completely bowled over by her and she just cheered me up immensely," Howard said.

A bit later, Howard would meet Nick. The two of them worked on a CBS documentary on Italian Americans which became one on the Mafia. Howard was the producer, Nick the consultant. Many years later, Howard became the president of CBS and then CEO of the Sony Corp. In that capacity, he supplemented Nora's fee for *Sleepless in Seattle* and overcame some studio opposition to get *Julie & Julia* made.

Ken Auletta became the *New Yorker*'s media writer and the author of eleven books, but when he and Nora met he was writing for the *Village Voice*. (He would later write political columns for both the New York *Daily News* and the *New York Post*. Amanda had met Ken when they both worked for the New York City Off-Track Betting Authority. Ken was so admired by Nora that some felt he paved the way for the even more Italian, Nick. Amanda, who encouraged the affair, went on to become a phenomenally successful and important literary agent.

Jennifer Kinmond Patterson (Mrs. Howard Stringer) was the only non-media person at dinner that night. She was a dermatologist, soon to have her own Manhattan practice.

The dinner was held at an Upper East Side Italian restaurant that Ken had booked. The food was forgettable but not what was happening to Nick and Nora. They were falling in love.

"You could feel it," Auletta remembers.

Nick had a place downtown, where, as Nora put it, he lived out of a Chinese takeout container. Within a month, he had moved into Nora's place in the Apthorp. In the summer, they took a rental in the Hamptons. The next summer they would have moved into Nora's newly purchased East Hampton house, except that it burned down—not quite to the ground, but the damage was extensive. They rented yet again, this time a massive Tudor-style house set up on a berm, not too far from Nora's charred dream house, which was located on the most Hampton of all corners, the intersection of Lily Pond Lane and Apaquogue Road.

In Nora's hands, catastrophe became opportunity. She had the dream house restored to her specifications. With the exception of the kitchen floor, which was done in black-and-white tiles, the other floors were painted white, which is what she did in all of her apartments. I used to joke that someday when people came across a New York apartment with white floors, they would exclaim "An Ephron!" and its value would instantly increase. Her response, as to all such witticisms directed to her peculiarities, was a weak patronizing smile. As with her fervent allegiance to the round table, she stuck with what worked.

She scoured much of the known world for quilts and colorful throw pillows with jaunty Early American motifs. The guest bedroom I sometimes occupied felt as if it has just been vacated by Betsy Ross, and the bed itself was buried under an avalanche of little pillows that I would study at bedtime with great intensity, trying to remember what went where so I could make the bed in the morning. (This was before smartphone cameras.)

A helpful insurance company contributed to the restoration, Nick chipped in some of his movie riches, and Nora provided the rest. The result was a happy place, pre–Martha Stewart but very much in her style, to which was later added a mudroom and an auxiliary kitchen, into which was placed . . . the mangle.

The mangle was the perfect Nora device. It not only was useful, but it was exotic, in a thoroughly boring way. After all, it was nothing but a hotel-style rotary presser used for ironing sheets. But Nora was very excited about her mangle—both because of its oxymoronic name and because it was useful. Nora showed it off the way some people do pictures of their kids at camp—although, at first, the mangle was more interesting. Unlike Nora's first food processor, however, it must have proved its worth. It remained in the mudroom.

Nora and Nick planted a sapling at the side of the house. It is now confidently established. She put her round dinner table in a corner of the kitchen and surrounded it with swell guests—sometimes the Spielbergs from across the street, sometimes the Bradlees from across the other street, sometimes the Hankses, Meg Ryan and her then husband Dennis Quaid, the Aulettas, on occasion her sister Delia and her husband, the movie and television writer Jerome Kass—and less frequently, her youngest sister, Amy, who lived on the faraway West Coast.

It is antithetical to who Nora was to drop the names of her weekend or dinner guests. She would never have done something like that herself. On the contrary, I never knew in advance who was going to be at dinner—but I always knew it was going to be someone interesting. One time a Harvard law professor. One time another screenwriter. One time an important agent or an actor or a novelist or a director or a chef or an artist. So, for many summers, I would start out from Washington with a great sense of anticipation. Somewhere around five hours into the ride—say, Southampton—I would enter Nora's ambit. I would either be staying with her and Nick, or I would have rented nearby, and I would be free of Washington, and its incessant talk of politics and government, and into this other place which was not exactly New York and was not Los Angeles, either, but was a mélange of the two, with just the occasional dash of Washington thrown in.

Sometime in March of 1987, Nora called: Come to a dinner party she was having in New York. It would be on the 28th, which was a Saturday. I turned her down. My wife was then the executive producer of *Meet the Press*, which broadcast on Sunday morning. There were no early morning or late night trains or planes from New York to Washington.

There was a pause on the other end of the line.

"Nick and I are getting married," she said. "It's a surprise. You two are the only ones who know."

Actually, by the time we got in the door, everyone knew. Nora's sons, brimming with excitement, greeted the guests with the announcement "They're getting married!"

Nora wore a polka-dotty thing she later came to regret and Nick, as I recall, wore an air of supreme calm. In due course, Richard A. Brown appeared. He was later to become the district attorney of Queens County, but that night he was still a judge who had earlier married Ken and Amanda. Without any attempted Navaho nonsense, he married Nora and Nick. Afterward, Barbara and I piled into a limo (authorized by NBC's storied bureau chief, Tim Russert) and were driven to Washington. We arrived a bit before dawn. It had been a delicious night. Including of course the food. For her own wedding, Nora had cooked.

I Am Not and Never Have Been Harry

I am not Harry. I need to say that because for a time—and continuing past Nora's death—it was sometimes rumored that the Harry character in *When Harry Met Sally . . .* was based on me. It was never clear to me when Nora and I had supposedly had an affair—before she married Carl, after she married Carl, after she left Carl, or some other time entirely—but it never happened. (*Richard, I love you, but not in that way*, I hear her say. Then we both laugh.)

It was true, however, that Nora and I had discussed the premise of *When Harry Met Sally . . .* , which is whether a man and a woman can be friends—"just friends," as the expression goes. It is also true that Sally Quinn and I had whipped up a four-page movie treatment about a relationship that went from friendly to sexual and had presented it to Nora at a lunch in Washington—and that Nora had based "Sally" on Sally Quinn. But it is also true that the idea for the movie originated with Rob Reiner, who would wind up directing *When Harry Met Sally . . . .*

Reiner, who had divorced the actress-director Penny Marshall in 1981, was going through the vicissitudes of dating. Along with his producing partner, Andy Scheinman, he had many stories to tell about the single life. Nora was all ears, and eventually they decided on a pitch that asked a question: Can sex be avoided in a friendly but intimate male-female relationship? The answer in the movie is no. The man (Billy Crystal) and the woman (Meg Ryan) even get married. My answer would have been just the opposite. Sex can be avoided—especially, as I hear Nora whispering—after marriage.

If one hand washed the other, then Nora was my other hand. There was nary a toast I made that she did not either approve or improve. She often contributed to my columns—especially the weekend one, which I tried to make humorous. After a while, I could not figure out where I left off and she began—or the other way around. Even in the book *Heartburn*, when she described her husband as capable of having sex with a venetian blind, I think I said it first. Even so, I'm not sure I know what it means.

In the same book, she referred to Mark's brief first marriage to a woman named Kimberly—"the first Jewish Kimberly," she wrote. My first marriage had been brief. My wife was named Kimberly. She was Jewish and she had, just as in *Heartburn*, locked herself in the bathroom (not a bedroom) just before our wedding reception (not the wedding itself).

In *Heartburn*, Nora says that Kimberly was stingy—so stingy "she once blew up the apartment and most of what was in it while making brandy out of old cherry pits." Neither is true. It was a turkey that caught fire in the oven as guests were coming for dinner. Cherry pits, I concede, is more colorful.

Just as she debriefed Rob Reiner on the folkways of being a male on the hunt, she did the same with me. She seemed genuinely shocked or surprised at some of my tales, and particularly enjoyed one where, after a night of having too much to drink, I awoke next to a woman with no idea of her name or, for that matter, what had happened to her eyebrows. In a panic, I slipped into the living room, found her purse, and rummaged through it for her wallet. I greeted her when she awoke with the name on her (obviously purloined) driver's license.

She flew into a rage: "Maria? Maria? Why do you call me Maria?"

In minutes, she was gone—one moment an object of considerable lust, the next a durable anecdote.

For Nora, *Sleepless in Seattle* was a stunning achievement. She had directed only one previous movie, *This Is My Life*, in 1992, which had starred Julie Kavner as a budding comedian who survives by pitching cosmetics at Macy's. The film may have been early Nora, but nothing about it suggests an amateur or a dilettante. For it, Nora assembled what could be called the Nora Ephron Repertory Company. It included her frequent cowriter, her sister Delia, and a bit part for her friend Diane Sokolow And for those in the know, the film contained an inside joke—the paper-chewing agent played by Bill Murray. That was Sam Cohn.

This Is My Life got respectable reviews, without the almost standard criticism of a novice director. On the contrary, Nora was praised for her direction and character development. Roger Ebert, writing in the *Chicago Sun-Times*, not only liked the picture but was on the money when he guessed that Nora was "possibly drawing from issues in her own life." What Ebert knew, of course, was that Nora, as did the Kavner character, had two kids. What he might not have known was that she had spent nights waiting for Dan Greenburg and Avery Corman to go on at the the Improv. She knew about club dates.

This Is My Life was both a success and a failure. It got made, which was achievement enough for a first-timer, and it was about a woman, which in itself was something, and the woman was not some buttery-voiced looker who defined happiness as the love of a man, but a non-looker with a voice suggesting horseradish. At the box office, the movie did meager business and Nora thought she knew why. She told Sally Quinn that the Kavner character was too Jewish. (Kavner was best known then for playing Brenda Morgenstern in the TV series *Rhoda*.)

Nora pulled back. From there on in, her leading ladies were going to be the likes of Meg Ryan and Meryl Streep—wonderful actors both, but not likely to be found ordering smoked fish at Barney Greengrass ("The Sturgeon

King"). Even when she again returned to film in New York, her characters were named Joe Fox and Kathleen Kelly and they were played by Tom Hanks and Meg Ryan.

Similar sounding names, as ethnically blanched as any in an Andy Hardy flick, occur in *When Harry Met Sally* . . . . Meg Ryan is Sally Albright (Alice Arlen's maiden name) and Billy Crystal, a genuine product of Long Island (yet!), is Harry Burns. He tries to play a gentile, but underneath that wry smile is the aftertaste of stuffed cabbage.

Not many people saw *This Is My Life*, but two who did not only liked it a lot but proved instrumental in Nora's career. They were Rita Wilson and Tom Hanks. Rita was already a fan of Nora's writing, and when *This Is My Life* opened, she suggested she and Tom take it in. They not only liked the movie, but Tom—watching with the practiced eye of an actor—saw a director in command of her medium. In one scene, Kavner and her two daughters move from Queens to Manhattan and Nora tracks their car.

"It was a geographically accurate movie montage," Hanks said. "They got on the 59th Street Bridge and they drove up First Avenue. They went across the Park at 79th Street or whatever it was. That always knocked me out." (In *Sleepless in Seattle*, Hanks's character is driven across the same bridge to his rendezvous with Meg Ryan at the top of the Empire State Building.)

So, when *Sleepless In Seattle* was offered to him, Tom was primed. He (and Rita) liked what they had seen from Nora and liked what they had read from Nora. Nora and Tom met at the Beverly Hills Hotel. It was 1993.

By then, Hanks had hit it big with *Big* and, before that, *Splash*. He had been nominated for an Academy Award for his performance in *Big* and was on his way to the Oscar itself the next year for his portrayal of an AIDS victim in *Philadelphia*. Hanks was both a journeyman actor and a movie star. He had been in the business since doing plays in high school. In college, he studied theater. He was the consummate professional, at the top of his game and lacking just one thing: edge. Tom Hanks was a nice guy. You could not imagine him slapping a woman or, as Jimmy Cagney famously did in *The Public Enemy*, pushing half a grapefruit into Mae Clark's face. It was this quality that troubled Nora. It did not trouble Mike Medavoy.

Medavoy was the head of TriStar, the studio behind the picture. He had seen Hanks and Meg Ryan work together in the not very successful *Joe Versus the Volcano*. The movie did not work, but he thought the pairing of Meg Ryan and Tom Hanks did. He had also seen a French movie called *Toute une vie* or, as it was retitled in English, *And Now My Love*. It was a Claude Lelouch vehicle, and it involved a man and a woman who, although in love, meet only at the end of the picture. Medavoy was charmed by the concept, and Nora made it happen in her rewrite of *Sleepless in Seattle*. Sam Baldwin and Annie Reed do not meet until the very end of the movie, when they come together on the Observation Deck of the Empire State Building.

If Nora had some qualms about Hanks, he also had some about her. For one thing, she scared him—virtually a universal experience before falling in love with her (yet another universal experience). Hanks saw Nora as the very personification of the sophisticated New Yorker—"a lifelong Manhattanite, privy to all things Gotham, John Cheever and the *New Yorker* and things like that." His California sense of inferiority, of not knowing one subway line from the other or a bagel from a bialy, came on like a rush, and it only abated when Nora mentioned that she had grown up in Beverly Hills. Hanks greeted a 90210 childhood as if it were Dorothy's Kansas farm. What mattered was that it was not New York.

"I didn't realize that she had grown up just down the street from the Beverly Hills Hotel. That was astounding."

And while Nora might have been a New York sophisticate, she was nevertheless a filmmaking neophyte. Hanks was not. He had done his time. He knew his craft. He knew more than a bit about directing, too. He had ideas about filming and casting.

"I thought I was a hotshot and I was supposed to have opinions and supposed to carry weight," he said. He described himself when he first met with Nora as "persnickety in the course of the meeting" because he was very nervous, and in addition, he had a very basic concern that now brings a chuckle. He would play the widowed father of a young boy. "I didn't want the kid to have better lines than me. I didn't want to play the pussy."

Nora and Tom had subsequent meetings, and they were occasionally contentious. Hanks weighed in on casting decisions, which wasn't in his purview at all. Nora listened. She was "incredibly gracious," clearly biding her time until Hanks came to realize that she knew precisely what she was doing. Certainly that became clear at the end of the first week of filming when Nora fired the cute kid that Hanks had worried might get the better lines. The boy froze in front of the camera. Over the weekend, he was disappeared.

The firing of the kid certainly got everyone's attention, but it was hardly something Nora did casually. She was bothered about it and mentioned it to several people. In fact, the treatment of children in films was something that bothered her in general. We discussed the awkwardness of casting a child who, say, was supposed to be homely, or the fat kid who the other kids bully. I expected her to say something like, well, that's part of the business, which is how journalists distance themselves from the sometimes innocent victims of their stories, but she was having none of it. It was still troubling.

In a way, Hanks was the odd man out on the set of *Sleepless in Seattle*. He had worked with Meg Ryan before, but never with Nora. Meg Ryan had worked with them both—with Hanks on a previous film and with Nora, who had been the writer of *When Harry Met Sally* . . . Rob Reiner had directed that one, and so he was responsible for the scene that is forever associated with that movie and with Ryan herself: the faked orgasm.

The setup is simple: Ryan and Billy Crystal are eating in Katz's, the storied Lower Manhattan delicatessen, when Sally asserts that women often fake orgasms, and their lovers not only don't know it but take credit for the orgasms. Harry is disbelieving, whereupon Sally goes into orgasm mode, eventually slapping the table over and over again and exclaiming, "Yes! Yes! Yes!"

Harry is both befuddled and embarrassed. For a while, he has no idea what's happening, but he starts to catch on just as the store's other customers become riveted by the orgiastic sounds coming from Sally.

As written, the scene was limited to Sally merely saying that women fake orgasms and Harry expressing disbelief. Ryan had a better idea. She felt that her character had to be funnier, but the humor had to be physical. "She doesn't necessarily have punch lines in that script, but she's behaviorally funny. It came out of understanding that," Ryan said.

The scene has numerous quick cuts to other bewildered customers, one of whom is Estelle Reiner, Rob's mother, a former actress and cabaret singer. A waiter is ready to take her order. With a glance at the orgasmic Ryan, she says, "I'll have what she's having." It's become one of the great iconic lines of American cinema, up there with *Casablanca*'s "Round up the usual suspects." It was explosively funny. But it was not written by Nora. It was suggested by Billy Crystal.

In the inevitable ranking of almost everything, the line is number 33 on the American Film Institute's list of the 100 Greatest Movie Quotes of All Time, along with "We'll always have Paris" and other gems. It is the only one on the list, however, that is not spoken by a main character. For Estelle Reiner, that—aside from Rob Reiner himself—was her sole contribution to the film. The scene is now lauded as a comedic gem and considered not in the least controversial or smutty. Yet that was not always the case. Airlines edited it out of their in-flight showings and some audiences simply did not get it. Nora reported on the phone to me that when the scene was shown to a Las Vegas convention of movie distributors, the men in the room did not react at all. They didn't get it.

The women, however, did. They laughed, and their laughter became infectious until, one by one, the men joined in. It was not clear to Nora whether the women had, in effect, given the men permission to laugh, or whether the men were being told that something up on the screen was funny and they had better laugh or look stupid. By the time Nora told me about the distributors, the movie was already in release and widely known.

"You know, men fake it, too," I told Nora.

That stopped her.

I was in Washington and she was either in New York or Los Angeles, but I could feel her perplexity coming through the phone.

"Men fake it?"

"Yes."

"Men fake orgasms?"

"No, not orgasms," I said. "Listening. They pretend to listen."

The response was instantaneous—a hoot of laughter and then, "Write it."

And so I did. I killed a column I had already submitted for the weekend magazine and replaced it with one based on *When Harry Met Sally . . .* My column was not about how women fooled men but about how men faked listening to women. It was a total put-down of the self-involved man, which took about as long to write as it did to type. I read it to Nora over the phone. She approved, and I submitted it to my editor (a woman), who also approved, and she submitted it to her editor (a woman), who gleefully tore up my previous column and substituted the new one. I braced for the applause.

Instead, I was vigorously denounced as a male chauvinist pig. A fellow *Washington Post* columnist, a woman of unimpeachable feminist credentials, pilloried me for purportedly saying women were not worth listening to. I was mystified. Nora was not. She said that's why she left Washington.

The orgasm scene became bigger than the movie it came from. It gets mentioned all the time, and countless parodies have been done of it—testament to its ubiquity and testament also to how big and iconic a figure Nora had become. When she died, the scene was shown over and over again on television, and I doubt if more than a few people knew that she had not directed the movie or that the line was not hers or that acting it out was Meg Ryan's idea.

In the mind of the public, *When Harry Met Sally . . .* became a Nora

Ephron film. This happened through the sheer force of her personality—how she was able to put her stamp on a film that was not hers. She did not do this deliberately, and Rob's only public complaint was to insist that he—and presumably not me—was Harry, but when the publicity interviews were over, Nora had taken the picture away from its stars and its director.

Eighty-six the Kid

Back in 1968, Nora had a "naïve" question for Mike Nichols: How do you direct a movie?

"I just held my nose and jumped in," he told her.

Nora did not exactly jump in—she had studied at Nichols's feet—but she had not attended a film school or worked as an assistant director. In addition to having almost nothing in the way of credentials, she was this rarity in the film business—a female director. There have never been very many of them—and there were even fewer when Nora was starting out than there are today. The causes are several—including, of course, plain old sexism and the belief that the job is just too physical, too demanding, too much like being a military commander, for a woman to pull off. Whatever the case, women have a harder time of it in Hollywood than do men.

Nora was hardly among the first female directors. Ida Lupino, who broke into the business as an actress and, really, remained one throughout her directorial career, made some pretty good movies, particularly *The Hitch-Hiker*, a film noir semi-classic. Still, she is remembered more for being an early female director than for any particular movie she directed.

Lee Grant was another female film director who had started as an actress. If she is remembered as a director, it is as a cautionary tale. In 1997, a project her husband had been nursing, a story about a washed-up hockey player, got green-lighted. She would direct and the very hot Bruce Willis would star. The movie set up shop in Wilmington, Delaware, and almost immediately things started to go wrong. The film's editor left for another job. Willis was not getting into his part. He didn't like his hair (the hairstylist had also left). He didn't like the way he looked on screen. He didn't, in short, like the way Grant was directing.

He called his wife, the actress Demi Moore, and asked her to come to Delaware to watch some scenes. In Grant's memoir, *I Said Yes to Everything*, she told what happened next.

"Do you think it's sexy?" Willis asked Moore. "Do you think I'm sexy?"

"No," Demi said, "I don't."

"And that, folks, was that," Grant wrote. She was fired.

Willis abandoned the movie. A $28 million picture—$18 million already gone—went down the drain. Grant was devastated, and although she thought Willis had overreacted, she understood. Willis said she had lost control. He needed a stronger hand.

"The problem when you are a star, when the money rests on you as an actor, is that your freedom to fail is gone," she wrote.

Would something like that have happened to a male director? Maybe. But the question is unavoidable because what Willis was demanding had "masculine" written all over it. Whatever the case, Grant's description of what a star risks in committing to a picture explains why they are so understandably cautious in approaching a project. The studio was in for well over $30 million, but Willis was risking his reputation. The studio could make back its money, but Willis could never get back his time or the damage to his career from a failure. He cut his losses—and went on to great success.

Nora was an oddity in one other way. She recognized that the script for *Sleepless in Seattle* was initially made workable not by her, but by a writer named David S. Ward (who won an Oscar for *The Sting*). He was one of several writers who took a whack at the project, and it was he who put his finger on what had gone wrong. In the earlier drafts, the Tom Hanks character had called a radio shrink on his own and confessed a loneliness and an aching longing for his dead wife. Ward changed that. He made the kid, Hanks's son, call the station and then Hanks, mortified, takes over. Ward recognized that the audience might feel that a man who calls a radio shrink is not a worthy hero. Nora recognized that the change saved the script. She fought for Ward to get a writing credit. He did.

Naturally enough, when Nora showed up in Seattle, all eyes were on her. Was she tough enough? Was she disciplined? Did she know what she was doing? Jim Wiatt, along with Sam Cohn, had set up the project, and what had clinched it—indeed what had gotten Nora in the door—was not her work as a director, but her brilliance as a screenwriter and her considerable charm. She was hard to say no to.

Sleepless, like *Silkwood*, was a woman's production. Nora was writing and directing. Delia was cowriting and Lynda Obst was a producer. All over Hollywood, women seemed to be coming into their own as studio heads—Sherry Lansing at Paramount Pictures, Stacey Snider at Universal, Dawn Steel and later Amy Pascal at Columbia/Sony. Lower down were many female producers of all kinds. Yet there were very few female directors. Maybe the studio heads were women, but the corporate heads were men.

On a couple of occasions, I went to the set to see Nora direct. She was clearly in command and completely at ease. Directing was her natural element; she did it on a daily basis, telling everyone in her life what to do and often how to do it. But with movies her role was official and her wisdom certified by the size of her name in the titles. She casually exercised her authority, sometimes with an almost childish delight. As she assumed control over *Sleepless in Seattle*, she ran into her friend, the art director Walter Bernard. Along with Milton Glaser, he had designed and redesigned many American magazines and newspapers (*Time*, the *Washington Post*, etc.). She asked him if he had ever done movie titles. He said no, but that hardly dissuaded Nora. She knew Bernard's work from *New York* magazine and hired him on the spot.

"Can you really do that?" he asked, somewhat startled.

"I can do anything I want," she replied gleefully. It was fun being a director.

Filming of *Sleepless in Seattle* began on a Wednesday. By the weekend, Nora had viewed three sets of dailies—and she did not like what she saw. It was then that she both impressed and terrified the members of the cast by firing the kid. She was protecting the movie.

If Hanks was impressed, Rita Wilson, a member of the cast as well as Hanks's wife, was apprehensive. She later appeared in yet another of Nora's films, *Mixed Nuts*, and worried if she was going to be the next "kid." "I kept thinking I was going to get fired," she said. "I was shocked that I made it through the whole thing."

By then, Rita and Nora had become close friends. They had met initially at a party in Los Angeles when Rita approached Nora, introduced herself, and said she was a fan. Later, Rita and Tom leased an apartment in the Apthorp for the New York filming of *The Bonfire of the Vanities*," which starred Tom and featured Rita. The two families got closer still. Years later, Tom and Rita temporarily moved into a second apartment Nick and Nora maintained in their Upper East Side building, when the Hankses had to move out of their own. Many a night, Nora would call and offer dinner. In Nora, Rita was finding just the person she had been looking for.

"I really think that Nora was the closest thing I've ever had to having a mentor," Rita said. "I always wanted that, someone who would see something in you that other people didn't see. She really did that, because she cast me in *Mixed Nuts*, which was a big studio picture."

Yes, but while Nora handed out bit parts to old friends (I appear ever so briefly in *You've Got Mail*) friendship was no guarantee of getting an important part. She made Rita, for one, jump through the standard hoops. "I had to do a lot of auditions. I had to do screen tests. I had to wait for two or three months."

In the end, Rita got the part, and in the end, *Mixed Nuts* bombed. It had been a $15 million or so movie, with a money-in-the-bank cast (Steve Martin, among others), and it just flopped, taking in less than $7 million. Martin irrationally blamed himself, but Nora was the director. Her name was above the title. *Mixed Nuts* hurt.

Nora rehearsed her movies as if they were plays. For interior scenes, she would put down tape to simulate walls and set down fake couches where the real ones would go. Her scenes could be up to eight pages long and sometimes be deceptively complicated. One in *You've Got Mail* took days to rehearse. It's the one where Meg Ryan has a cold and is repeatedly sneezing.

"It took at least a full day to shoot," Hanks said. "It was all very specifically plotted out. No other directors did that. It wasn't like rehearsing with anyone else. Rehearsing in other movies may be nothing more than sitting around talking about the script."

Steven Spielberg observed that Nora wrote the way Tom Hanks and Meg Ryan naturally talked. So in *Sleepless in Seattle* and *You've Got Mail*, their natural bantering was incorporated into the script. Sometimes that sort of thing can harm a movie because a rhythm established off-camera takes too firm a hold when the camera is rolling. "But Nora's scenes just played like natural conversations punctuated by humorous bits that Meg certainly could deliver, and that's sort of my bread and butter," Hanks said.

So Hanks was given license to improvise. He had a problem with a scene in the script where his character complies with the pleas of his kid and stays home rather than go away for the weekend with a woman. Hanks knew better.

"I said, Nora, there's not a man in the world who is not going to go off and get laid for the first time in years simply because his son doesn't want him to. And she said, 'Well, you should say that then.'"

And he did.

Meryl Streep, who starred in three of Nora's movies, saw Nora as a female director who directed as a woman. "Nora never lost sight of the power of being a girl," Streep said. "On the set, and how you command attention, there's a bunch of different ways to do it as a director. Sometimes, like with Mike [Nichols], it's through humor and his wit that he establishes himself. He doesn't even have to work to do it, he's just a little bit ahead of everybody, and smarter, funnier, everything, so we defer to him.

"Clint Eastwood [who directed Streep in *The Bridges of Madison County*] would do it by virtue of who he was and the persona he brought to the largely male crew, so he never ever had to raise his voice. In fact, the quieter he would get, the more on their toes everyone became.

"Women have to do a different thing to establish authority. Clint could say, 'Just bring me the light, just do it.' A simple sentence like that. 'Just bring me the light. Just do it. Do what I ask.' If a woman said that in just that same tone, just that same way, it would be soul-curdling for a crew.

"The very first female director I saw on a set was Penny Marshall. The way that she did it, to not take anything away from the crew, to not give a direct command which is difficult for people to hear, she'd say, 'Oh, I know this is a pain but can we just . . . Oh, I'm so sorry to ask this, but, oh my God, I forgot to ask you on the last take, can you just put the light in there?' It was clearly a request. It was not a directive.

"Nora did it in a different way. She would be funny and she would be soft. She'd say, 'I think if we just had a little light on it, it could be perfect.' Nora had a way of doing it that was completely charming, was feminine, and took nothing away from anybody's manhood to do what she asked. She was good at it and was naturally diplomatic and graceful and understanding—and because her intelligence sussed out the situation—she devised a strategy to get what she wanted."

In his telling, Mike Nichols created a little family when he did a movie. In his recollection, Bob Balaban remembered no such thing. Balaban had been flown down to Mexico for a small part in *Catch-22*. He was young, cash poor, and unknown. He would sit by himself in the commissary, sort of like high school where the popular kids take certain tables as a matter of (nearly) divine right. As Balaban sunk into a funk, Bob Newhart used him for an extended shtick. "Newhart would get up and say loud enough for everybody to hear, 'Did you hear about Bob Balaban? He died.'"

"They would go through this twenty-five-minute improv about 'Poor Bob Balaban," Lynn Grossman, Balaban's wife, recalled. Bob would just be sitting there. It was very funny unless you were Bob."

Nora, who was the sole journalist allowed on the shoot, befriended Balaban. Along with his wife, they became lifelong friends.

But—I hear Nora nagging—that is not the point of the story. The point of the story is that that sort of anomie—a Balaban on the verge—is exactly what Nora set out to avoid when she did her own movies. She not only mothered the cast, but when it came to the leading players—Hanks, Ryan, Wilson—she set up a mini-salon. Seattle is where, really, Tom and Rita and everyone else learned that wherever Nora might be, a round table was nearby.

An Intervention

I was going to make this chapter about how Nora's dinner parties took on great importance to people who were already important, but I am being reprimanded: Richard, it's time to say something about the kids.

Yes, of course—the children. Aside from her own, the children she had in mind, the ones who meant so much to her, were the kids of her friends. She always had time for them—not as an exasperating courtesy due their often important parents, but out of an almost incomprehensible urge to mentor, to mother, to listen and listen, and then to talk. She did not need to be asked—*Nora, would you mind . . . ?*—but she would offer her time, volunteer a lunch, and then say nothing about it. I, for one, knew nothing about her relationship with Calvin Trillin's daughters or Spielberg's kid until I began researching this book.

I also did not know about Juanita. She was one of several underprivileged kids Nora corresponded with. Their names were provided by the Writers Guild Pen Pal project, run by Tom Fontana. The letters were written in 2010 and 2011. Here's one of them:

December 7, 2010.

Dear Juanita:

I'm happy to hear that you're my Bookpal for the school year. When I was your age, all I did was read too, like you. I loved reading much more than watching television. My mother used to drive to a used bookstore in Los Angeles, where I grew up, and get us books that she'd grown up reading. So I read all sorts of classics, like The Little Princess *and* Anne of Green Gables. *I still like to read them, and I have a shelf of children's books in my house, some of which are the very books I grew up reading. A couple of them are so old, they're practically falling apart. I also loved going to the public library. I used to ride there on my bike and come back with a basket full of books.*

One of my favorite books growing up was called Homer Price *by Robert McCloskey, and whenever children come to visit, I like to read from it, especially from the chapter about the donut machine that wouldn't stop making donuts. I always loved reading about food, especially sweets, so it's no wonder I love food and cooking as much as I do.*

When my sons were growing up, I used to read to them, and they loved the poems of Shel Silverstein, which are really clever and funny.

If you are a good writer, which you seem to be, you should think about being a writer someday. It's a good job, and you can be just as successful at it as being a doctor.

I hope you have happy holidays and write me back soon. Do you celebrate Christmas or Hanukkah? Tell me about it.

Best

Here's part of another:

Dear Juanita:

To answer your question, I am now working on a screenplay. Sometimes a screenplay becomes a movie, and sometimes it's just a script that kicks around for a while and doesn't get made. I have had both experiences. I've been lucky that a lot of my scripts have become movies, and because I am also a director, that helps. I don't know if you've seen any of my movies. The most recent was called Julie & Julia *and it starred Meryl Streep and Amy Adams. It was all about food, which you know is one of my favorite subjects. I wrote and directed two movies you might like—one is called* Sleepless in Seattle, *and the other is called* You've Got Mail. *They are both romantic comedies and I think you'd enjoy them.*

I also write books and plays, so I don't have to count on the movie business, thankfully. I have three sisters and they're all writers. My parents were writers, and they wanted us to be writers, and they got their wish.

As for your question about what I celebrate, I celebrate Christmas— which is to say, I have a Christmas tree and Christmas dinner. I am not religious but I love Christmas. I'm sad I have to take the tree down this week, because it's so pretty. We have a very weird tree that is hard to describe. It's made of metal and it's an antique and was used as a department store display, probably back in the 1940s. I bought it at an antique show. Anyway, because it's not a live tree, you don't have to take it down, so last year I decided to redecorate it. In January I decorated it with icicles and snowflakes. In February I decorated it with red ornaments for Valentine's Day. I was all set for March—I was going to do birds, for the coming of spring—and then I realized I was getting a little nutsy, tree-wise, so I took it down.

Anyway, write me soon and tell me what's up with you.

Your Pencilpal and friend

———————

Sasha Spielberg was hardly an underprivileged kid, but Nora made time for her anyway. Starting about when she was five or six, Sasha Spielberg was permitted to cross Apaquogue Road in East Hampton to visit Nora. These visits continued for the next fifteen years or so and involved conversations lasting two or more hours. When Sasha was younger, an enticement was Nora's lemon cookies, which she kept out on the kitchen counter, or the chocolate chip ones, which were kept in a cabinet. For Sasha, these were powerful lures because her parents maintained a draconian no-dessert policy, except on weekends. Then came Sweet Saturdays.

Nora made tea for Sasha and whoever of her little friends were visiting the Spielbergs. These teas, too, were regular affairs over which Nora presided. When they were alone, Sasha told Nora her problems. At a very young age, she came to rely on Nora's judgment, and that did not change one whit as the problems became more complicated—more adult. Nora became Sasha's mentor and her confidante. "She was a sister, she was a mother, she was a friend," Sasha said. "She embodied every person in my life in one."

On occasion, Nick would pop into the kitchen. His appearance shocked little Sasha. She had come to think of Nora as being just Nora—not part of a couple, but her big and wonderful friend. This sense of possession, or having sole and unabridged title, was not simply the product of childish, somewhat magical thinking. Adults felt similarly. Nora's ability to concentrate on the person in front of her, to make even a casual friend feel singularly important, was a pronounced trait.

I focus on Sasha for another reason: time. Nora spent a lot of time with her, and at no age—not six or seven and not seventeen or eighteen—did Sasha feel that Nora was stealing glances at the clock. And yet always—always, always, always—Nora was on deadline for something. Always, she was writing or producing or going into production as a director. Always, too, she was a wife and a mother. She had her own kids.

———————

I sometimes still talk to Nora. I conjure her and wonder about questions that occur to me now but did not occur to me when she was alive. Sasha Spielberg was not the only girl who came to rely on Nora. There were other kids—some who will not talk about their relationship—but none of them were boys. There were, as I have mentioned, some young men, writers all, but they did not come over for tea or coffee or talk about their love life.

In fact, Nora rarely wrote about men. Her movies were about couples or, as in the case of *This Is My Life* and *Silkwood*, about a woman. Similarly, her first two plays—*Imaginary Friends* and *Love, Loss, and What I Wore*—were exclusively about women, with the latter being really about girls. Only *Lucky Guy* was about a man, and while the unproduced *Higgins and Beech* was ostensibly about both a woman and a man, it is the woman who is the more vivid character—both excitable and palpably sexual—while the man is customarily brave, sardonic, and stoical. *Lucky Guy* was her only project to explore what it's like to be a guy.

And yet at the center of her life were guys—her two boys and Nick. She split custody of her children with Carl, so they were sometimes in Washington and sometimes in New York, and then more and more often in New York, where, after a while, Carl had moved. She and Nick took the boys to ball games—Nora became a boring Mets fan—and Nick very early on took Max fishing in Alaska, a journey of pure joy for the kid.

But while Nora and I had friends whose homes were dominated by the presence of children—a riot of toys scattered around, the children themselves ricocheting off walls and furniture, eyes focused always on the next tumble or spill—this was not in the least Nora's house. She had kids. Understood. But they were not the whole of her life. Understood. Other women were mothers first and then whatever else they once had been or wanted to be again. Not Nora. As it had been with her mother before her, she was both mother and writer. Each had its place.

Meg Ryan, when she first came to see Nora's East Hampton home, was shocked to see it was so "girlie." It was the home of a woman, a very feminine woman, a woman whose tastes were white and frilly, conventional in that way, but garnished with idiosyncratic touches—Nick's Diane Arbus photos; kitschy snow globes; an antique weather vane; a collection of small, brittle teacups. Nora was a girlie girl. She loved being one, but she had none of her own.

When she wasn't in East Hampton with her parents, Sasha would send Nora her writings for criticism and suggestions. She wrote short stories and, later, screenplays, and Nora would send back detailed criticism, not something like "good job" but notes about character and plotting. They stayed in touch by email. This is Nora's final one to Sasha:

1. congratulations on your b.a. who spoke at your graduation? did you find anything meaningful out?

2. where are you?

3. where are you going to live?

4. will you have an apartment of your own so I can send you something or are you moving back in to one of the thousands of options available to you?

5. or are you moving in with max? breaking up with max?

6. i would love to read your screenplay.

It was June 6, 2012. Nora said nothing about being in the hospital. She died twenty days later.

Lavender's Blue

To understand Nora Ephron, to appreciate why so many people loved her and sensed a compelling sweetness and even shyness in her, you have to know something about the movie *So Dear to My Heart*. It was a children's movie, released by Disney in 1948, when Nora and I were seven years old. It was about a black lamb that gets rejected by its mother. I'm not sure I ever saw the movie, although I assume Nora did. But we both knew a song from it—a radio staple sung by Burl Ives that was a sanitized version of a seventeenth-century English folk tune originally about sex and drinking.

"Lavender's green, diddle, diddle" got Disneyfied into "Lavender's blue, dilly, dilly, lavender's green." As a child, I never knew what that meant. As an adult, I still don't. Still, it is one of my favorite songs. One night at dinner, Nora told me it was one of hers, too. I was struck by that and we sang it, sotto voce, together.

In the Burl Ives rendition, "Lavender's Blue" is a sweetly innocent tune, childish, almost infantile. To admit to a fondness for it suggests a Technicolor-hued romanticism and, more than that, a childhood that has not quit. For me, the song has lingered almost seventy years, and it invokes, when I think about it, short pants and polo shirts and chocolate milk and my Dick Tracy watch. Nora would recall different artifacts, of course—maybe a dress, maybe jacks, maybe a doll whose eyes rolled back when it was tilted.

"I love to dance, dilly, dilly, I love to sing / When I am queen, dilly, dilly, / You'll be my king / Who told me so, dilly, dilly, who told me so? / I told myself dilly, dilly, I told me so."

That's the last stanza. You might argue that nothing about it evokes Nora—certainly not that bit about loving to dance. She was a renowned cynic, adept at throwing a cloth napkin at the fool across the table who had not only said something wrong but insisted it wasn't. She was urbane in a film noir sort of way, not a doll or a babe or anyone's arm candy, but smart and wise to the ways of the world. She had a corresponding low opinion of men and thought that even the nicest of them were sexual marauders. She always had her eye out for the exception and she found it, I am certain, in Nick. She was not, in the argot of forties movies, a tough dame, but she was a swell broad.

And yet, if you asked me to sum up Nora in a song—an odd request, I grant you—I would sing "Lavender's Blue." This soft, nonsensical number comes to mind because it is so like her and yet, one might think, so unlikely of her. As almost always, both are true, but there was a softness to Nora, a sweetness, an endearing vulnerability that some friends occasionally saw and others just guessed at and that I knew to be there. The song said it all.

The "Nora Ephron movies" that she was famed for making, movies "with messages of toxic female sentimentality," as one critic put it in a review of the play *Imaginary Friends*—the layers of romance and schmaltz; the sound track with Jimmy Durante singing "You Made Me Love You" in *You've Got Mail* or Durante twice in *Sleepless in Seattle*; the ending on the Observation Deck of the Empire State Building, an homage to *An Affair to Remember*; the appeal to nostalgia; the goopy but effective romanticism of it all—got criticized over and over again, and not only in reviews of Nora's own movies but in reviews of movies made by others, when they were deemed excessively sentimental: a Nora Ephron ending, they would call it. And she would be stung.

Yet, just as Nora discovered that Erich Segal was not a pandering fraud, so too were her movies an authentic representation of who she was. They were concocted, sure. They were tidily written, certainly. But the reason they worked—the reason she knew they would—was that they worked for her.

"Lavender's Blue" is not the only song I associate with Nora. The other is "White Christmas," the Irving Berlin perennial. Oddly enough, the song both separates us and bring us closer. Nora loved Christmas.

I come from a family that not only did not celebrate Christmas but actively resisted it. This was not the case with the Ephron family. They embraced the holiday. They saw it as it had become, a onetime religious holiday that, if anything, had been transformed over the years by their Beverly Hills neighbors—Jewish songwriters and movie producers—into the loveliest of all holidays, as secular as a hug. It was seemingly created to Nora's specifications, and I don't think even she could have improved on it.

Christmas was about a meal—actually several of them. But the one that counted was the one Nora and Nick gave. I was not a usual attendee, living in Washington a good deal of the time and affecting a bah-humbug attitude toward things Yule. The meal was not just an opportunity for Nora to cook, but an explication of what amounted to her philosophy of entertaining: Always make the meal yourself. Strictly speaking, it was not necessary in a city like New York to cook everything—a pig on a spit could probably be delivered in a half hour. But Nora cooked it all. For her, the meal was an expression of love. The Christmas food was a Christmas gift.

Nora also loved Thanksgiving. It, too, was about family and friends, but it was not a season and was, when you came right down to it, about a single meal. Nora's meal was as unvarying as any concocted by some Midwestern grandmother. She served turkey, of course, and cranberries and all the usual stuff, but also the universally dreaded oyster stuffing. This white, oleaginous blob—oysters seemingly stuck in some cheesy muck like sabertooths in the La Brea Tar Pits—was nobody's favorite, but Nora never abandoned it. I would tell you what it tasted like, only I managed never to taste it. It would sit, rebuked, at the near end of a round table in the kitchen, the last (or the first) stop of a buffet that began and ended, as far as I was concerned, with dark meat turkey.

I would circle the table, sneaking past the oyster stuffing year after year, until Nora caught me. She insisted I at least try it. I plopped a dollop on my plate and made for the dining room. I never touched the stuff.

Nora did not have much in the way of family—no aunts or uncles ever showed up at Thanksgiving, but her oldest sister and frequent writing partner, Delia, was usually there, along with her husband, Jerome Kass, yet another screenwriter and novelist. (He died in 2015.) Her youngest sister, Amy, a novelist and food blogger, lived in Los Angeles and had children of her own and, presumably, Thanksgiving chores as well. A middle sister, Hallie, lived in Massachusetts. She was oddly known as the sister who did not write and whose husband didn't write, either, and who even took her husband's name, Tauger. Yet she emerged in later life as Hallie Ephron, a mystery writer of some note and some notable success, and when I was seeking an assistant, Nora called to tell me I had already found one—Hallie's daughter, Molly. She was, of course, hired.

Whatever Christmas was about for others, for Nora it was about just about everything she loved. Christmas was the opportunity to make people happy, to find just the right gift and show how much they were loved. Nora's gift-giving was merely an extension of her dining room table—yet another way to entertain, to be a host, to spread pleasure. Alas, I was not on her gift list. I think she took my Scrooge-like antipathy toward Christmas seriously—more seriously than I did—and anyway much of the time I was in Washington and not able to attend her Christmas dinners.

There were other Christmas parties, though. One was routinely held by Howard Stringer and his wife Jennifer Patterson in their Upper East Side town house. Later, these parties were moved to the Stringers' upper Fifth Avenue place with its drop-dead view of the Central Park South skyline. These were Gershwin nights, or if you will Rodgers and Hart nights—magical Manhattan celebrations, something out of a movie, something that combined the New York Nora loved with the friends she loved with the success she'd had and, of course, Nick, Nick. Always and forever, Nick.

Marvin Hamlisch, the composer and a friend of Stringer's, worked the piano, sometimes singing his standards, sometimes nonsense tunes of his own invention, sometimes leading us in songs of the Christmas season. He was a funny, erudite man, a Broadway composer of classical training, an impish man who was always suppressing a gag.

The Stringers would distribute song sheets—the usual Christmas stuff— and we would belt them out. Then would come what for me was the highlight of the evening. Nora would take a handheld mic and step to the piano. She had a sweet, innocent, voice, a bit girlish, and she would sing the little known introduction to Irving Berlin's "White Christmas," including

"There's never been such a day / in Beverly Hills, L.A. . . .

But it's December the twenty-fourth / And I am longing to be up north . . ."

The girl from Beverly Hills, L.A., gave the lyric authenticity. With a pause and an expression of immense satisfaction, Nora would lower the mic and we would all swing into the song.

BeeBee Fenstermaker could sing.

Bedeviled by Bewitched

Movies fail. Movies fail all the time, most of them swiftly forgotten except by cineastes and studio executives who seek any reason to drive down the salary demands of an actor or director. Nora's movies failed, of course—maybe more than they succeeded. The triumph of *Sleepless in Seattle* was followed by *Mixed Nuts*, a Steve Martin vehicle which was an adaptation of a French comedy—a very dark comedy. It didn't work.

Next came *Michael* with John Travolta. Nora and Delia did the screenplay, and while the movie made money, it is not remembered as an Ephron film because there is indeed little of her in it. After that came another of her signature hits, *You've Got Mail*—and then things went off the rails. She coproduced and cowrote *Hanging Up*, a box office and critical failure. One review, in particular, is worth noting because it blamed Nora for the film's deficiencies, even though she did not direct it. The critic, Emanuel Levy of the widely read industry weekly *Variety*, had liked some of Nora's earlier work—he was kind to *This Is My Life*—but he came crashing down on *Hanging Up* as if he was settling a score. "*Hanging Up*," he wrote, was "a shamelessly sappy" film "that bears the schmaltzy sensibility of Nora Ephron."

Nora was both mystified and hurt by such reviews. They went beyond merely commenting on the film and instead swung a roundhouse at her—in this case, as the cowriter of the screenplay. How Levy knew the "schmaltzy" stuff came from Nora and not from Delia—or, for that matter, the director Diane Keaton—is beyond me. In a way, though, it was a backhanded compliment and acknowledgment of her fame and power. Just as she came to be associated with *When Harry Met Sally . . .*—a movie she had not directed and a scene she had not fully written and a line that was contributed by another—she was taking the blame for a film that, once again, had been directed by someone else. (In fact, she had her own problems with the film.)

Nora felt reviews such as this were personal. She wasn't liked, she'd say, and there was nothing she could do about it. She'd throw up her hands in exasperation. She was mystified. She was hurt. It was painful to see.

Worse was to come. Nora's next film was another John Travolta vehicle, this one called *Lucky Numbers*. It was another attempt to veer from the allegedly "schmaltzy" to the dark side. But it went too dark and got miserable reviews. The shoot had gone remarkably well. The cast had a great time, hugely enjoying themselves. The movie was funny. Everyone was laughing. And so its critical reception felt like an ambush. *Lucky Numbers* cost an estimated $65 million to make. It took in $6 million.

By the year 2000 Nora had made two outright bombs. *Michael* was an interlude, but it starred John Travolta only a year after he had done the immensely successful *Get Shorty* and two years after the even more successful *Pulp Fiction*. The latter revived his career, and some of that aura carried over to *Michael*. But *Michael* was where Nora's movie career might well have ended. As a director, her career seemed dead in the water.

In 2003, Nora switched agents, going from Jim Wiatt of William Morris to Bryan Lourd of Creative Artists Agency. The move was a wrenching one for both of them, although harder on Wiatt for sure. He had been Sam Cohn's man where Cohn dreaded to go, Hollywood. Wiatt was Nora's guy—her agent, her friend—and even when he left Cohn and his agency (ICM) to go to William Morris (which became William Morris Endeavor), she stayed with him—managing to be represented by both Wiatt at one agency and Cohn at another.

Both Wiatt and Lourd were immensely important agents, but Nora was in trouble and Lourd and his agency were perceived as more powerful than Wiatt and his agency. Nora wrote Wiatt and then met him at the Peninsula Hotel in Beverly Hills. She told him she was leaving him for Lourd. This was both an emotional and clichéd moment. Agents get fired all the time, occasionally even for cause. Still, they were both overcome. She told him the decision was very tough to make. They held hands. They hugged each other. They vowed to remain friends. (Nora was godmother to one of Wiatt's kids.) Nora had a new agent. She lost an old friend.

As far as Hollywood was concerned, Nora was a great screenwriter but not necessarily a great director. And when *Bewitched* came along, offered by her longtime friend and Sony Pictures chief Amy Pascal, Nora seized the opportunity. *Bewitched* was not only a big payday but an opportunity for Nora to prove that *Sleepless in Seattle* and *You've Got Mail* were her rule, not her exception. She was made the proverbial offer that could not be refused: a huge fee. She signed.

Bewitched had much going for it. It starred Nicole Kidman and Will Ferrell, both proven box office draws. Beyond that was its provenance. It had what Nora's friend the producer Lynda Obst calls "preawareness." The movie was based on the hugely successful television series that ran from 1964 to 1972 and at one time or another must have cumulatively employed half the actors and writers in Hollywood. Almost everyone knew of the series or had seen it. Not Nora, though. She had to watch segment after segment—an IQ leveler if there ever was one—while Mary Pat Walsh, an assistant, took notes so that their script would be true to the idiosyncrasies of the TV show, lest its fans scream in protest.

The TV series was about a witch who married an ordinary man and occasionally—once an episode, as it happened—used her supernatural powers to help him out. She does it by wiggling her nose, which, as luck and casting would have it, Nicole Kidman could do. The premise was silly—even mind-less—and an artifact of a different era, the late 1950s, but it intrigued Nora, possibly because of its feminist—or antifeminist—themes and also, in her version, because it offered the chance to parody Hollywood. Three different screenwriters had taken a cut at the material and all had struck out.

Nora and Delia went for number four. They knew something of the sub-ject, or, if you will, the phenomenon, because they had grown up in an age when every wife was considered to be something of an adorable witch. Poof! She made dinner appear. Poof! She did breakfast. Poof! The bed got made and the kids got dressed and the TV repairman showed up and opened a physi-cian's bag of tubes.

Nora used to mock that 1950s ideal of domestic bliss which was based entirely on the mythically cheerful servitude of housewives. Her favorite phrase—her virtual call to action, which she incorporated into *Heartburn*—was the seemingly innocent question "Where's the butter?" It wasn't just a simple question. It was a lifestyle with a question mark.

Nora would take it and run with it: "Where does a man think the butter would be? The closet? The bedroom? Maybe the garage?" But in that era, all across the nation, wives would rise from the table, apologize for their in-eptness, and say, "I'll get it for you, dear." Then they'd go to the refrigerator, which in the kitchen of my childhood was located right behind my father's chair. But if my mother had not gotten the butter for him, if she had not made the food and set the table (after coming home from her job running the busi-ness office of a local hospital), my father would have sat in that chair until he was nothing but a skeleton, a bony hand holding an upturned fork.

So *Bewitched* was an opportunity to return to the 1950s–1960s and do the era justice. It was also a chance to revisit one of Nora's favorite movies, *I Mar-ried a Witch*. That 1942 charmer starred Veronica Lake and Fredric March, and the possibility of a remake had kicked around Hollywood for years. I heard Nora once mention it to Tom Hanks. He said that he, too, liked the movie. There it sat.

Over the years, I had learned to defer to Nora. I understood that there were things I did not understand. I did not understand, for instance, what she saw in the property that became her play *Lucky Guy*, which, to my great relief, I was wrong about. I felt the same way about *Bewitched*. I had never seen the TV series, but I assumed Nora had. I assumed, moreover, that she had a firm and unerring grip on popular culture and saw deep meaning in what I thought was meaningless schlock. She used to discuss the characters from the *Archie* comics—Archie, Reggie, Betty, and Veronica (nobody cared about goofy Jughead Jones)—as if they were evocative of the real America, which someone like her, I figured, knew something about. (I, as a New Yorker, not only knew nothing, but I felt not the slightest nostalgia about my high school days.)

It turned out, though, that I was not the only one who had doubts about *Bewitched*. As she was in the practice of doing, she sent the script to Steven Spielberg to ask him what he thought. Not much, he essentially said. "I didn't tell her not to do it. [She may already have been committed.] I asked her how she was going to put herself into the movie. She said she would do it in the character of Samantha [the witch].

"You can find Nora in everything she ever directed. I could not find her in this script. And as it turned out, there was less of Nora in *Bewitched* than in any of her other pictures."

The critics murdered her. As usual, some of the criticism seemed personal. "The artificiality of *Bewitched* is so exaggerated that it almost works in the movie's favor for the first twenty minutes or so, before that heavy synthetic Ephron odor really sets in," wrote Stephanie Zacharek in *Salon*. Others were less personal but no less scathing. The movie was universally disliked by the critics. Audiences agreed in surveys. Mostly, though, they just stayed away.

So did actors. Nora wanted to move on to the property she originally called *Stories About McAlary*. No one wanted to do it. Leading man after leading man read the script and passed. McAlary was a chancy role to begin with—and Nora, it seemed, was not the director with whom to take a chance.

———————

Coming on the heels of Judy Corman's passing, the failure of *Bewitched* was cruelly crushing to Nora. She was sixty-four years old. She was a woman. She was, in short, an old woman (by Hollywood standards) whose two recent movies had been flops. She blamed herself. She had let down her cast. For almost any other director, it would have been time to collect awards, be recognized by the industry, do a lecture of two, and—before it was done for you—call it quits. Nora, however, was a writer. She would write.

The Blessing of Bewitched

Something was happening. *Bewitched* had bombed, but nevertheless, Nora Ephron was becoming a cultural icon—a phenomenon, actually. Her core admirers were women, primarily but not exclusively middle-aged woman—or older. The explanations for that were many and obvious. After all, she had done the book on betrayal, *Heartburn*. She had written the manual, then done the movie. She had been betrayed, publicly and flamboyantly, and instead of hiding in shame or simply lying low, she had come roaring back with an eviscerating form of fiction which, of course, was the truth, the whole truth, and a bit more.

But *Heartburn* was not the whole of it. There were the movies, of course, and the plays and the blogs and the columns in the *New York Times*—and, above all, the books. One in particular stuck a chord: *I Feel Bad About My Neck*. Nora published it in 2006, when she was sixty-five. The title essay is about aging. For a woman, that, not philandering mates, is the inevitable betrayal.

"That's when she became an icon for women," said her longtime editor, Robert Gottlieb. "Until then everyone thought she's funny, she's brilliant, she's this, she's that. But that's when women started to identify with her. *Heartburn* was admired. *Neck* was revered.

Why? First of all, the title essay is pure Nora. It is funny. I have read it many times, and it still brings a smile to my face. When Nora says that you have to cut open a redwood tree to see how old it is, but you wouldn't have to if it had a neck, I smile—and so do you.

Second, the essay is wise in a between-us-girls kind of way. It is about truth, a sad, lamentable truth, which is that a woman's neck is a dead giveaway to her age, and that age, if it is over precisely forty-three, will announce itself with a neck that is sagging and mottled and . . . well, not youthful.

There is another thing about this essay: It is not one bit different than having a conversation with Nora. It has the same timing and the same observant wit. It is really no different than the conversations she had with Christopher Lospalutto, her hairdresser, when, invariably buried in a script, she'd direct him to shape her hair so as to better to hide her neck.

Nora never let me in on that little attempt at hairline prestidigitation, but we did talk a great deal about aging. It was, after all, what we both were doing—full-time, as it were—each day's inspection in the mirror bringing further alarming discoveries.

Aging is funny—until it isn't. (It does not improve over time.) Aging has a kind of pratfall aspect to it—not just the morning aches and the evening insomnia—but the sheer surprise of it: How did we get here? Nora would recall her childhood and hearing her parents talk about not being able to sleep, and we children, would wonder how in the world that was possible. All you had to do was put your head down on the pillow. Close your eyes. There!

She wore socks to bed. She'd mention that. She'd take half a sleeping pill. She'd mention that also. We would wonder how anyone our age could have an extramarital affair—we'd hear about such things—when you wore socks to bed or snored or kicked in your sleep because you took a statin just so you wouldn't die of heart disease before you awoke. Where was eroticism? Where had it gone?

She went on *The Oprah Winfrey Show* to promote the book and erupted in honesty about the travails of aging. The show was entitled "Great Women and Their Anti-Aging Secrets," and the other guests were Diahann Carroll, Geena

Davis, Susan Sarandon, Diane Sawyer (via tape), and Alfre Woodard. Oprah praised the book and then said, "I see you're covering your neck, Nora."

That was Nora's cue.

"I am. I wore this. [A scarf.] I wore this just to show you what it's like to go shopping when you're older. I was not prepared for many things because nobody tells you. And here's what I really wasn't prepared for: sixty-two. You know what you get as a present for your sixty-second birthday? No one tells you this. A mustache."

And then came a cavalcade of candor.

Her memory? Shot.

Her neck? A mess.

Her energy? Diminished.

Her sex life? Not what it used to be.

Her honesty? Coruscating.

She repeated much of what she had written in the title essay of her book. She confronted the tendency to deny the dreadful effects of aging. She did this in a culture obsessed with youth and the antics of youth. The actress-singer Marlene Dietrich, to cite an extreme example, became a recluse in her early seventies and would not even allow herself to be filmed for the documentary Maximilian Schell did about her. (He used only her voice.)

Nora, in a sense, was the other extreme. Yes, she had never been a famous sex symbol, and, yes, she was not an actress, but still she had a public persona, and, yes, she worked in Hollywood, where old was not venerated, and she appeared on television all the time. In the entertainment world, to be old and not dead was simply to be stubborn.

Nora not only (literally) faced up to aging, she rued it. She was not one of those who found chirpy compensation in decay—wisdom in lieu of youth, patience in lieu of energy, and the comfort that, yes, while passion was either gone or going, so, too, was the regrettable behavior it brought on.

"Is there anything right with getting older?" she said on *Charlie Rose*. "Wisdom when you can't remember anything? . . . Having more time to read when you can't see? . . . I don't think it's better to be older."

The honesty of Nora's approach to almost everything—she did some-times fib about others' work when she met them—is present in this essay. It says that this aging business, this stuff about the neck, was a woman's thing—and it was unfair. It comes on faster for women. It is more obvious and more consequential. Nora wrote that she avoided mirrors. But she did not avoid saying so. The essay bookends her piece on breasts. It is its (fraternal) twin, a deeply personal shriek written in a jaunty style, saying both "I care" and "I don't care," but finally, "The only thing I can do about it is turn tragedy into comedy." Which she did.

"I can't tell you how many women I know who never met Nora, who, when she died said, 'I can't believe it. I based my life on Nora,'" Gottlieb said. "'Everything she said was relevant to me.' That did not happen after *Heartburn*."

Heartburn, in fact, sold 102,568 copies in the original hardcover; *I Feel Bad About My Neck* sold almost 800,000. In total sales—hardcover, paperback, ebook and audio—both books broke the one million mark.

The whole aging process, this reverse puberty, everything going backward, so much so that sooner or later we would be returned to the diapers where we all started and the mental state of an infant, terrified us all. Nora wrote about her neck, because the neck can be seen (unless it is hidden by a scarf from Loro Piana), but the visible stands for so much that is invisible. The neck was only breasts elevated just a bit—yet another physical catastrophe that Nora was dead honest about and with which any woman could identify—women, that is, of a certain age and, of course, any who thought they would make it to that certain age.

"Are any of you feeling the pressure that time is running out?" Oprah asked.

"Oh, yes," Nora said. "This is one of the reasons I'm so in love with one of the most important things in life at the moment—carbs. You know, because I've been really good my whole life. What if you are hit by a bus and the last thing going through your head is, I should have had that doughnut? You know?"

Oprah repeated, "Carbs."

"By which I just mean, savor everything. I mean, we live, let's just stick to carbs. We live in the greatest era of bread since the dawn of civilization. You can get good bread everywhere. But everything, you should just savor everything in some way or other so that every day is, did I do the thing I really wanted to do today?"

The *Oprah* show aired October 5, 2006. I have quoted from the transcript—Nora being witty, relaxed, charming, and soaking up Oprah Winfrey's praise of her book. The eye, however, sees something the reader of the transcript does not. Nora's face is bloated. She had recently been told of her fatal condition. She had begun treatment—steroids.

The Cut of Her Clothes

In 1973, Lillian Hellman published the second of what would turn out to be three memoirs. This one was stylishly titled *Pentimento*, which was an exotic term regarding an underlying image in a painting. The book was true to its title. Buried in it was a story of the heroic Lillian Hellman bringing $50,000 in cash to an anti-Nazi in Hitler's Berlin. The story was made into the movie *Julia*, starring Jane Fonda. Lillian Hellman, who had been more or less famous most of her life, was now a celebrity, known to people who knew nothing of her plays or her books or her lovers, one of whom was the former Pinkerton cop turned writer of detective fiction, Dashiell Hammett. For Hellman, this was another of her high-wire acts. This time, though, she fell.

Julia was a lie. The woman who had brought the cash to Berlin was named Muriel Gardiner. She lived in New Jersey. News of *Pentimento* came to Gardiner slowly. Friends called. Acquaintances inquired. Gardiner wrote to Hellman. She never heard back. Finally, she sued, and while it might be said that Lillian Hellman was exposed as a liar, that was not quite the case. Many people already knew that.

But not Nora. The same year Hellman's book was published, Nora went off to Martha's Vineyard to interview the grand lady for the *New York Times Book Review*. As was often the case with Nora, the interviewee became her friend. The much older and much more famous Hellman was clearly charmed by Nora and, I imagine, impressed by her intelligence and her bona fides. She was a child of Hollywood screenwriters and Hellman had been one herself. The Ephrons worked in the movie business during the McCarthy period, when ten screenwriters went to prison for refusing to cooperate with the House Un-American Activities Committee. In that dark period for Hollywood, a spotlight shone on Lillian Hellman. She took a star turn.

Imaginary Friends is Nora's most interesting and revealing work. The play is about Lillian Hellman and Mary McCarthy and their famous, and famously vindictive, feud. It is to my mind more about Hellman than McCarthy but not, at bottom, about either one of them. It is about Nora—the writer, the woman, and particularly the woman who felt she was not as pretty as she was smart.

To a remarkable degree, Hellman kept reappearing in Nora's life. The Ephrons had not been Communists, but they were liberals and, despite their avowed atheism, they were Jews. The combination was sufficient to warrant suspicion. The so-called Red Scare—tinged with anti-Semitism—surely dominated their dinner table conversation. They knew at least two of the ten screenwriters who went to prison for not cooperating with congressional inquiries—and probably many others who feared a subpoena and subsequent ruination. Hellman was the ultimate target. She was both a Communist and a Jew, the former by enthusiastic choice, the latter at the insistence of others. She was sure to have figured in dinner table conversation.

Mary McCarthy was a less important figure. Younger than Hellman—and very pretty—she was also a leftist but, unlike Hellman, no fan of Stalin's. By the late 1930, McCarthy was a book critic for the *Nation* magazine and well known in New York literary circles. She was a talented and often biting writer and something of a sexual omnivore. She not only recounted sleeping with three different men in twenty-four hours, but when she finally paused, she chose two leading intellectuals as her lovers. She lived with Philip Rahv, an editor of the influential *Partisan Review*, and later married the critic Edmund Wilson, a rotund man with an astonishing talent for seduction. Theirs was a tempestuous, sometimes violent, union.

In 1952, Hellman appeared before the House Un-American Activities Committee to say she would not testify about anyone but herself. Her words—a tribute to her gifts as a dramatist—became even more famous than any of her plays: "I am not willing, now or in the future, to bring bad trouble to people who, in my past association with them, were completely innocent of any talk or any action that was disloyal or subversive.

"I do not like subversion or disloyalty in any form and if I had ever seen any I would have considered it my duty to have reported it to the proper authorities. But to hurt innocent people whom I knew many years ago in order to save myself is, to me, inhuman and indecent and dishonorable.

"I cannot and will not cut my conscience to fit this year's fashions."

The line—written by Hellman but spoken by her lawyer, Joseph Rauh, Jr.—resonated on the political left with the force of the *"La Marseillaise"* among French revolutionaries marching toward Paris. Hellman, short and homely, instantly was transformed into another Marianne, although she was hardly bare breasted, swaddled instead in what she called a Balmain "testifying dress" and white gloves.

Nora maintained her friendship with Hellman for several years. They were both great conversationalists, bright as hell, voracious readers, talented writers—and they loved to cook. On the political left, Hellman was an adored and admired figure who got a standing ovation in 1977 at the Academy Awards when she presented the Oscar for Best Documentary. She already possessed a passel of honorary degrees.

It's not clear when Nora caught on to Lillian or if she suspected anything at all until Mary McCarthy, promoting a book, appeared on Dick Cavett's TV show in 1979. McCarthy had wanted to be asked to name an underrated young writer. Instead, Cavett asked her to name an overrated older writer. She named three—John Steinbeck, Pearl Buck, and Lillian Hellman. She said Hellman was "tremendously overrated, a bad writer, and a dishonest writer, but she really belongs to the past."

"What's dishonest about her?" Cavett asked.

"Everything," McCarthy replied. "I said once in some interview that every word she writes is a lie, including 'and' and 'the.'"

The next morning, Hellman announced she was suing Cavett, his network, and McCarthy. She was asking $2.5 million in damages.

Hellman was a woman of great presence. She may not have been a great playwright, but she was a great dramatist. Her most original production was herself—a plain woman of metastasizing ugliness who nevertheless exuded a flamboyant sexuality. I had met her originally in 1968, when the *Post* sent me to the Institute of Advanced Study at Princeton to cover a meeting of the Congress for Cultural Freedom. Ironically, the Congress had been created by the CIA to encourage Europe's anti-Communist left. Hellman, a former and unrepentant Stalinist, was one of the attendees.

At the conference, we became friendly. Later I learned that she was always on the lookout for young men—and it may have been my youth and not my dazzling intellect that attracted her. For a brief time, we corresponded. She wrote me about her life—nothing that I can recall, but it was surely more exciting, more literary, than mine. I was mired in the Washington suburbs, covering the school board's interminable nighttime meetings, the zoning commission, the sewer commission, and erotically tinged anti–sex education rallies in high school gyms.

All this was either fodder for parody or the daily newspaper, but not—I thought—for letters to the great intellectual-playwright-screenwriter-activist-memoirist who was so famous she was a celebrity model for Blackglama, the maker of a line of tony fur coats. She posed in one, a cigarette dangling from her right hand. "What becomes a Legend most?" the ad asked. Not a pen pal from suburbia, I thought. I dropped the correspondence.

I next met Hellman at Katharine Graham's in Washington. Graham was giving a small dinner party—just me; my wife; Carl; Nora; Joseph Alsop; the Washington columnist who was almost as important as he thought he was; and Hellman. This was late 1976, the very night there was a struggle in progress for control of *New York* magazine. Katharine Graham was involved, trying to save it for her friend Clay Felker and thwart Rupert Murdoch. She not only failed to get the magazine, she missed a swell dinner party. (Her son, Donald, substituted.)

I may now write matter-of-factly about that night, but I was knocked out by it. I was hardly a regular at Graham's house—a Georgetown mansion, actually—and I was so unaccustomed to her regal style that when, a couple of years earlier, I had been invited for dinner, I mistook what the invitation meant by "informal" for, well, informal, and not Georgetown lingo for "not black tie." All the men wore dark suits, white shirts, proper ties. I wore a sports jacket. A turtleneck sweater. And a mortified expression.

This night was different. But what I remember most about it was not what I wore, but Nora. She was totally at home. Joe Alsop was an imperious, intimidating man, once possibly the most important of Washington columnists. (Certainly, he thought so.) He affected a concocted Etonian accent—not speaking but proclaiming. He was easy to dismiss as a Vietnam War hawk and a droll fool, but his was the home John F. Kennedy went to after his inaugural. His erudition was awesome. He took a keen and sophisticated interest in the local public schools as well as fine art, archaeology, and statuary. There was little he didn't seem to know. He awed me, but Nora awed him.

I did not know that night that Nora and Lillian were already pals, but by then I was accustomed to Nora knowing everybody and everybody in return knowing her. It sometimes seemed that she had lived in a different era or that she had started her career at the age of fourteen or so—that she had stepped out of the rotogravure section of a defunct newspaper—the *Trib*, the *Sun*—or a magazine only found in dusty attics. This was the only way to account for how she knew the people she knew and who knew her—these historic figures, of which Hellman was most definitely one. Hellman to me was a figure out of a newsreel, a woman of the 1940s and 1950s who had stood up to Joe McCarthy and his ilk—and McCarthy was long dead.

In that respect, Carl complemented Nora. He, too, seemed to know everyone, but then he was magazine-cover famous, downright likable, and hardly shy. It was only a bit more than two years after Nixon had resigned, and so when Carl entered a room, history seemed to accompany him. Still, the room belonged to Alsop and Hellman, virtually statuary figures, and while they had different politics, in the not too distant past they had united in the fight against Joe McCarthy.

Alsop and Hellman traded stories. Joe told about being interned by the Japanese in Hong Kong after America entered World War II and having had gems sewn into the collar of his jacket. She told how she visited the Eastern Front in Russia and stuck her head up from a trench to view the fighting. When her military escort did the same, he had his head blown off.

That and other stories were extremely dramatic and told with the flourish of a playwright making a pitch, but they were probably not true. Soon after, Hellman came out with the memoir *Pentimento* and I recognized some of these tales in it—and so did others, including, of course, Muriel Gardiner. She cried "thief!" and Hellman was undone.

It was never entirely clear why McCarthy went after Hellman. And it was not clear, either, why Hellman thought she could win a $2.5 million libel suit. But it was abundantly clear why the feud and the lawsuit intrigued Nora. As a story, it was uniquely rich. It was about her childhood. It was about female writers. It was about lefty politics and the political pogroms of the 1940s and 1950s. It was, in short, about everything—including the inexplicable hate that occasionally courses through the sisterhood.

Hellman was a human question mark. She personified so many questions: What would you have done? What would you do now? Could you sacrifice your Hollywood lifestyle—the house, the pool, the car(s), the Japanese gardener, the mistress, the club membership, your very identity as a screenwriter, producer, or director for . . . For what? Exile in misty, gray England and minor writing jobs under a politically compelled nom de plume?

Hellman, in fact, had done so. She had been blacklisted. Her earnings plummeted. She lost her farm in Westchester County; Hammett was sick, blacklisted in Hollywood and creatively blocked everywhere else. Lillian Hellman was a vainglorious figure, a liar, but also admirable. She was better than a dramatist. She was a theatrical creation.

It was not only politics and questions of conscience, though, that drew Nora into the story, I believe. And it was not, either, sexual politics—the fact that Hellman and McCarthy were often the only women at the table and sometimes playing musical chairs with the same men. I think part of the allure was that Hellman was highly and boldly sexual and yet handicapped by dismal looks. She had to attract men with her fame, her achievement, her literary standing, her wealth. She was the flipped coin—the female version of the ugly man with the pretty girl.

As for McCarthy, she dowdied as she aged, but she was once a smashing looker and always a marvelous writer. Along with her best friend, Hannah Arendt, McCarthy was a rarity—a female public intellectual. She traveled in interesting circles and slept with interesting men, but her life was not nearly as flamboyant as Hellman's, and while she was truthful, she had never done anything as brave as choosing to stand up to HUAC.

McCarthy's best seller was a novel called *The Group*, a fictionalized account of her Vassar days. Her classmates felt betrayed, much as Nora's did after she wrote about their tenth reunion. That, though, was not enough to balance a play. Hellman is the weightier, more compelling figure—a fabulous fabulist—who intrigued or repelled many of the people who knew her. One of these—indeed, maybe foremost of these—was the unavoidable Mike Nichols.

Nichols had acquired a raconteur's fortune in Hellman stories, some of them appalling, some of them humorous, but all of them gripping. He found her loathsome. Also riveting. It's not possible he withheld them from Nora. In fact, he could barely repress them. He felt conflicted. He admired Lillian Hellman. He also found her despicable and somewhat frightening.

"Lillian was ugly. She had to make you forget it, and she could. That's how good she was.

"I did, in a twisted way, love her, but she was a terrible person, which was a shame because she was so brilliant. Nobody can improve that sentence. 'I cannot and I will not cut my conscience to fit the fashion of the time,' and I will not, which is ungrammatical, is a genius . . . The whole thing is a genius thing to say that made everybody look like shit, and that's what she wanted, and that's what she got. . . . She finally fucked it all up. She couldn't stop. She couldn't stop, and she died alone and defeated. She made it work for a long, long time."

Nichols clearly had first crack at directing *Imaginary Friends*, but for some reason—possibly to protect his friendship with Nora—he passed. So he called Jack O'Brien, the artistic director of the Old Globe Theater in faraway San Diego. He asked him to come to a meeting at Nora's apartment at the Apthorp. It was an ambush.

"I was suddenly playing on an Olympic team," O'Brien said. "I mean before I even read anything, there's Nora Ephron, Mike Nichols, and Marvin Hamlisch [who wrote the music]. What am I going to say? No? So obviously I thought, sure, put me in, Coach."

It took O'Brien a beat or two to realize that he had stepped into Nichols's shoes. "I came in late to this project and obviously it had its genesis with Mike, I think."

O'Brien, predictably, was dazzled by Nora and later moved by her generosity. When he and a friend bought a weekend place they playfully called Imaginary Farms, Nora gave him cocktail napkins with "Imaginary Farms" embossed on them and then took him to the antique fair and made him buy a quilt. "And she said mysteriously something that I really never understood. She said 'All the colors you need in the house are right there in the quilt.' It was so Nora."

After O'Brien's country house was finished—after *Imaginary Friends* had closed—Nora and Nick drove up for the weekend. She had made a blueberry pie, and then, along with O'Brien, she cooked dinner. This was her gift to the director who felt he had failed her. It was her way of telling him he hadn't.

An unwritten rule of the theater was to move on from a flop. Nora, however, reached back.

"We had wonderful time and it was a great reconciliation," O'Brien said.

Jack O'Brien had won three Tony Awards and been nominated for seven more. His is not a household name, but in the theater world he is very well-known and immensely respected. Still, when he met Nora and entered her world, he reacted like he had just gotten off the bus from Saginaw, Michigan, his hometown.

"It was an interesting rite of passage for me, because it was the first time I had been invited into that room [Nora's place]," he said. "I have had success and I have had various kinds of success, but I never landed there before. Not that room. Suddenly I would go to a dinner party and there is Meryl Streep, Barbara Walters, and all of those people. It's pretty heady stuff."

Imaginary Friends was a minor failure. Marvin Hamlisch teamed with the lyricist Craig Carnelia to provide songs, but the critics didn't much like them and found them beside the point. The play had worked best in San Diego, where it opened at the Old Globe Theater. But the move to the larger stage of Broadway's Ethel Barrymore Theater hurt it. Ben Brantley, the critic for the *New York Times* (and virtually the only game in town), had a particular problem with the play: He didn't get the point.

Neither, I think, did Nora. "The point" was always her goal, and getting there was her self-imposed obligation. In *Imaginary Friends*, however, she drowned in too many points—the unreliability of memory, the jealousy of high-powered women, the bitterness of an ugly woman (no matter what her gifts), the arcane antagonism between Trotskyites and Stalinists, and, finally, the tension between the obligation to the truth and the simultaneous obligation to tell a good story.

"I believed in the truth," McCarthy says.

"I believed in the story," Hellman says.

Imaginary Friends ran for seventy-two performances, and I suppose that's a failure. I didn't see it that way then and I don't see it that way now. The material was rich, beguiling, and Nora could not pass it by. She was caricatured as a writer of Hollywoody comedies with syrupy endings, but here she had tackled some big ideas and the complicated personas of two celebrated intellectuals. She enthusiastically waded into a theatrical effort with a briar patch of historical exposition to master. And she did it.

Hellman and McCarthy were dead by the time the play opened in 2002, but they remained a living presence in theatrical and literary New York, fresh in the memories of people who still mattered. Nora's failure, if indeed she failed, was in her reluctance to say that the liar was the more interesting character and the lies made for a more interesting life.

But possibly her first encounter with Hellman, that *New York Times* interview from 1973, was the vaunted Rosebud of this play. In it, Hellman referred to the difficulties of writing about living people. "It's hard to tell the truth about the living," she said. "It's hard even to know it." And then as if to say, *Here, Nora, here is your play*, she confessed that she was, in one telling respect, a jealous person.

"Dashiell Hammett used to say I had the meanest jealousy of all. I had no jealousy of work. No jealousy of money. I was just jealous of women who took advantage of men, because I didn't know how to do it."

Hello Sweetheart, Get Me Rewrite!

```
FADE IN ON:

A ROOMFUL OF MEN

Men at desks. Men as far as the eye can see. We're
in:

INT: CITY ROOM OF THE NEW YORK HERALD-TRIBUNE—DAY

It's 1950. We hear the rattling of Underwoods, like a
forest full of mechanical crickets. We track through
the city . . . and finally we come to rest on:

THE ONLY WOMAN IN THE ROOM.
```

Thus begins *Higgins and Beech*, a script Nora wrote with Alice Arlen that was dear to her heart but which she could never get made. Marguerite Higgins was the once-famous war correspondent for the *New York Herald-Tribune*. Keyes Beech was a war correspondent for the *Chicago Daily News*. Higgins had won a Pulitzer Prize for her coverage of the Korean War. Beech had won a Pulitzer for his coverage of the same war. They were competitors. They were lovers. It was a movie.

Nora offered the part of Higgins to Meg Ryan, but she turned it down. (A decision she later came to regret.) George Clooney took a look at the part of Beech, but, as did other possible leading men, he realized that the star was really Higgins.

Besides casting, the script had other difficulties. It was about the Korean War, the war that seemed nothing but a World War II afterthought and a prelude to Vietnam. It required an exotic locale for shooting, if not Korea than somewhere that could pass for it. (Australia was mentioned.) In all, this would be an expensive movie about a dying industry (newspapers) and two already-dead newspapers, a forgotten war, and characters that no one still cared about. Sony Pictures, where Nora had a contract, was not charmed, and Kate Capshaw, who read the script in England on location with her husband, told Nora it was great but that she was then watching rushes of the greatest war movie ever made. It was her husband Steven Spielberg's *Saving Private Ryan*. Spielberg had done his war.

It's hard to say what the essential, the quintessential, Nora Ephron movie would be. Surely, most people would pick *You've Got Mail* or *Sleepless in Seattle* or even *When Harry Met Sally . . .* Others would choose her final film, *Julie & Julia*, which combined themes from her own life—a preoccupation with food, the delights of mature love, and, of course, the thrill of working yet again with Meryl Streep. None of those would be wrong.

And yet for me it is the one that never got made. It is the one about the lone woman in the city room and what newspapering was once like and how it was possible to be a reporter and have your name and face plastered on newspaper delivery trucks as they rumbled out at night and coursed through the city. Nora was a newspaper girl, and she admitted that time and time again. She might have quit the *New York Post*, but she never quite walked out the door.

So it should have been no surprise—and yet it was—that Nora returned to newspapers and a newspaperman for her final project. It was the play *Lucky Guy*, which had been written as a movie and which started for her on the morning after Christmas 1998. As usual, she went directly to the newspapers. She read fast, moving quickly through the *Times* until she reached the obituary page. There, she stopped, ripped out an item, affixed a note to it, and dropped it into her office outbox for her assistant, J.J. Sacha, to pick up when he returned from his Christmas vacation. Mike McAlary, the celebrated and notorious newspaper columnist, had died of colon cancer the day before. He was only forty-one.

McAlary had been a titanic journalism presence in New York. He wrote a reporting column—lots of legwork, lots of attitude—and he wrote in the style of his tabloid elders, particularly Jimmy Breslin, who, along with the quite different Murray Kempton, was one of his journalistic heroes.

At one time or another McAlary had worked for all the New York tabloids—the *Post*, the *Daily News*, and *Newsday* out on Long Island—jumping from one to another, and sometimes back again, each time for bigger bucks. In the end, he was a gargantuanly well-paid newspaperman, making upward of $350,000 a year in an industry where almost no one except top editors made more than $100,000.

McAlary was not only paid by newspapers, he was covered by them. He was a brawler and a drinker and a womanizer. He barely survived a predawn car accident in which he was probably impaired, and in 1995 he had to retract a series of columns in which he claimed that a purported rape victim had fabricated the incident to publicize a feminist rally. (He had been misled.) Later in his career, he left a chemotherapy session to report the story of Abner Louima, the Haitian immigrant whom cops severely beat and then sodomized with a broomstick in a Brooklyn police station. For that, he won the Pulitzer Prize. A year later he died.

McAlary was a much beloved and much reviled figure. He was enormously brave, sometimes foolishly fearless, but it was his courage and working-class affect that commended him to the cops and explains why they trusted him. One time he called his lawyer, Eddie Hayes, from a riot in Brooklyn. Hayes, who was essentially the house counsel to the New York tabloid types and was also close to the cops, pleaded with McAlary to get out. "I'm going to get wood," McAlary screamed into the phone, using the newspaper term for the biggest headline of all. "I'm going to get page one."

"Michael, you're going to get killed," Hayes replied. "Forget about the wood, you're not going to get out of there alive. The policemen aren't going in there. They're afraid to go in."

"Eddie," McAlary said, "I'm going to get wood."

McAlary was the sort of journalist who made the story happen. He attacked it. He created it. He didn't just cover it. These characteristics made him into that rare enough figure—a man among men. Other men liked him, admired him. He was one of the guys or, in the words of Tom Hanks, he was "a great hang." He was the very personification of the hard-drinking newspaperman, usually Irish in the New York manifestation, a figure out of the Ben Hecht–Charles MacArthur play *The Front Page*, which since its opening in 1928 had been made into several movies, including the 1940 classic *His Girl Friday* with Cary Grant and Rosalind Russell. There is nary a newspaperman (or -woman) who has seen that film and not winced from recognition and shuddered with envy. Hecht and MacArthur got some things wrong—but not the frenetic excitement of newspapering.

Mike McAlary was not, in any way, an updated version of Maggie Higgins, but his story did put Nora back into her beloved city room. She set to work doing what any reporter would do—she read the clips and then did the legwork. What she found, if she hadn't already known it, was that McAlary's colleagues and pals were protective of him. The McAlary they knew had glaring faults, but he was both a gifted journalist and a gifted friend. In his circle—mostly Irish with working-class roots—loyalty and generosity were greatly cherished. McAlary was the personification of both. No one was going to talk trash about Mike.

As a columnist myself, I both resented and envied my big city brethren. In New York, local columnists were widely read and an institutionalized part of the urban culture. Washington, which was a Sunbelt city that just happened to be located in the East, had no such tradition. In New York, local columnists were stars. I thought some of them were mere showboats. McAlary was one.

My consternation over Nora's interest in McAlary, however, was nothing compared to Tom Hanks's. He not only didn't appreciate McAlary, he plain out didn't like him. Nora initially developed the script with Hanks in mind. She had an ongoing collaborative relationship with him—a constant exchange of ideas and concepts. Her script did not get a good reception. Hanks told her he didn't much like tabloid columnists to begin with—he found them "scummy"—and McAlary was an exception only in that he was scummier than most—"a big jerk."

Nora persevered. Bryan Lourd, her agent, shopped the script to his clients. Sean Penn, George Clooney, Philip Seymour Hoffman, Ed Norton, Daniel Craig, and others said that while they were eager to work with Nora, not on this one, thanks. Nora wanted so much to do it that she even was willing for someone else to direct. Still, no takers. *Lucky Guy* needed a lucky break.

Just as McAlary had come back from career purgatory to win the Pulitzer with his columns on Abner Louima, so Nora's story about him got another shot. The catalyst for that turnaround was an Englishman-turned-American named Colin Callender. He had once been head of films for HBO, where Nora's script had come and gone, but by the winter of 2008 he was an independent producer of plays as well as movies. As a New York resident, he knew something about McAlary. As a resident also of the Long Island community of Bellport, he knew somewhat more. Mike McAlary had been his neighbor. Mike McAlary had been his friend. Callender called Nora.

Nora started to revise, to write and rewrite, to think "play" rather than "movie." She had written *Imaginary Friends* and, along with her sister Delia, the delightful *Love, Loss, and What I Wore*. She knew what needed to be done. In relatively little time, *Lucky Guy* emerged, adapted for the stage. Callender liked what he saw. So did Mike Nichols. A reading was scheduled for May 26, 2010. Hugh Jackman would play McAlary.

On 42nd Street that day in May, the actors—all volunteers—sat at a very long table. The audience consisted of maybe twenty people, including Mike Nichols, who had directed the morning's rehearsal. We all sat about three or four feet from the actors.

Jackman took his seat. By then, he had made more than twenty movies and appeared—mostly starred—in eight Broadway plays. His performance in the Broadway version of *The Boy from Oz* (2003–2004) earned him a Tony Award for best leading actor in a musical. He could dance, he could sing, and he could certainly act. That day he would also cry—huge, Aussie-sized sobs—as he muscled through McAlary's last lines:

"I have lived the life I dreamed about, but there's so much more I wanted to do. I want to dance at my daughter's wedding. I want to see my son Ryan graduate from college. I want to walk old and gray on the beach with my wife. . . ."

By then, Jackman could hardly get the words out. His body convulsed, he gulped for air.

"I know I am unworthy" he continued. "But please forgive me if I don't protest this Pulitzer Prize. This is a mistake I can live with."

A moment later, the reading was over. Jackman, spent, composed himself. The actors rose, happy, even buoyant. It had been a good reading, a sweet theatrical moment. I was ecstatic, so happy for Nora. They play was nearly perfect. She asked for "notes"—the term used for criticism or observations. Later that night, I emailed her one, mostly because I thought I had to. I believed *Lucky Guy* was ready for Broadway.

Nichols, though, thought otherwise. It turned out he had many notes and he felt that the play had not quite come together. There would be other table readings—one in London with John Hamm as McAlary—and a final one with an always apprehensive and cautious Hanks. Over time, the play was rewritten, revised, nipped, and tucked, a process paused for a reading and then resumed almost the moment it was over.

But as Nora worked, discarding other projects in a fierce determination to see this play mounted on Broadway, the cancer was biding its time. She rewrote a script called *Lost in Austen* but passed up the chance to direct it in England, preferring both to stay close to her doctors and to concentrate on *Lucky Guy*. She knocked off a script for a Reese Witherspoon project about the 1950s-era singer Peggy Lee, but had neither the heart nor the time to direct it. She worked on her *Huffington Post* blog and, except for clandestine visits to the Memorial Sloan Kettering Cancer Center for monthly infusions, kept up appearances and a daunting schedule.

The cancer was right on time. The clock had been irrevocably set about six years earlier. Adamantly, I repeatedly white-lied my insistence that fate could be cheated, and Nora, with a "mother knows best" look, would respond with an indulgent smile. On occasion, she would dangle the phrase "If I live long enough," letting it trail off into silence, as if she had broken her own code of omertà. She was in a race she would lose. The cancer was determined to bring down her curtain before she could raise the one on *Lucky Guy*.

Emails in the Night

Nora hovered. I would talk to her by day, but at night, often while I was asleep, she could confer by email with Mona. They had much in common—a love of food, a knowledge of cooking, an eye for the nice things to wear, and some of the same friends from the movie business where Mona for a time had worked. But their bond was the terrible and, for Nora, the unspeakable.

Nora and Mona became fast friends, maybe best friends. Both women had sisters (Mona had a brother as well), but those were complicated relationships. Nora and Mona's was easier, more direct. They were similar in some ways—a compelling energy, an eagerness to laugh, a sharp social eye, and a deep layer of self-confidence masking an even deeper level of insecurity.

And they both had cancer. But just as Nora did not choose the McAlary story because she, too, was a dying writer, so, too, she did not choose Mona as an intimate because they both were sick. In a short while, though, that turned out to be the case—"our true bond," Nora said to Mona. They had this horrible thing in common, but they were, as all the dying are, alone with their pain, their fear, and, some of the time, their rage.

Nick and I comforted, arranged for cars, escorted to doctors' appointments and lab tests and in and out of hospitals, but there were times when I—I am speaking now just for me—failed. And when that happened, Mona would email Nora and relate how I had screwed up her schedule or doses of medicine—eleven different ones per day and, after a while, injections as well—and how sometimes I could not read the notes I kept, a log of the dosage and the time taken, illegible entries made in a half-asleep state, struggling for alertness after I had been awakened by moaning or the tectonic shivering caused by a spiking fever that would send us hurtling to the emergency room.

The time. The dosage. I had to note it all. But I was afflicted with a wandering handwriting, the result of a pesky learning disability that I had short-circuited by moving to the typewriter as early as the eighth grade. Now this trivial thing, this nothing handicap, so low on the spectrum as to be a shrug, was threatening the life of this remarkable woman—and she was tattling on me to Nora.

"Ri-i-i-i-i-chard," Nora would say on the phone, my name elongated and her voice elevated to the register of rebuke. Her go-to phrase would come next: "Just let me say . . ." Then came a rush of directives, orders, recommendations, names of people to see, clinics, doctors, places discovered on the Internet, cures related by friends about friends. Her foot would come down: Hire a nurse. (Mona didn't want one.) Then came the scolding. I had to pay attention. Really pay attention. Take careful notes. Make Mona feel secure.

Yes, yes, I would say. Nora always had scant sympathy for my learning disability. She once sharply rebuked me because I could not remember her phone number—this after twenty years or so of calling it once or twice a week.

I knew that Mona and Nora were talking behind my back—talking only occasionally, actually, usually emailing. In the middle of the night, their messages would go zipping across the East Side of Manhattan. They would both be up, armed with iPads, or sometimes Mona would get out of bed and clamber down the hallway to the den and use the computer there. I could hear the clicking of the keys, and I would sometimes learn about these insomnia-fueled exchanges from Nora, who then, in her coquettish drill sergeant manner, would rattle off instructions. She was part scold and part buddy and totally my lovable friend.

From the moment Mona got sick, Nora took over. Mona had a daughter who was a physician in Colorado, and a son who lived downtown, and access to the best doctors. None of that mattered to Nora. She appointed herself chief resident, the second opinion to any opinion, the doctor who oversaw the doctors.

Mona had been misdiagnosed with diverticulitis, which had diabolically masked the cancer. She had been in and out of hospitals—NYU, Lenox Hill, and ultimately, New York Hospital—until, finally, surgery was scheduled. A massive tumor was found.

I instantly called Nora. She rushed to the hospital. Nick took longer. He stopped to bring sandwiches. The both stayed for hours.

Nora went home and attacked the Internet. She researched Mona's cancer. She recommended oncologists. She forwarded the names of other women who had ovarian cancer whom we might contact. She urged me to call Jerome Groopman, a physician on the faculty of Harvard and the extraordinary medical writer for the *New Yorker*. (So did his *New Yorker* editor, David Remnick.) I balked. I did not know Groopman. I did not even know that he was part of Nora's medical team—in some ways, its CEO. I would not call him. I placed him in this firmament of stars that Nora had called in or, through Nora, someone else had recommended. She was open to all possibilities. When the talent manager Sandy Gallin got the renowned new age guru Deepak Chopra to call me, Nora said, "Who knows? He's done some remarkable things."

Mona and I had an understanding: No quack cures. No going to Mexico or some such place for some Hail Mary treatment. No extract of figs or total blood transfusion, no miracle cure—the miracle being that desperate cancer sufferers kept using it even though death swiftly followed. No doctor in Pittsburgh who saved the life of someone's aunt. None of these.

And then Groopman called me, and as he was apparently doing for Nora, he read the charts from distant Cambridge. He conferred with the oncologist and steadied me when I needed steadying, when I didn't know what to say to Mona and felt I had to say something. Everywhere I turned, Nora or her surrogates were there—on the phone or the Internet. I was grateful. I was in awe. Nora was dying. Mona was dying. The dying took care of the dying.

Mona's grand Fifth Avenue apartment looked out on the Metropolitan Museum of Art. From one window you could see down Fifth Avenue and the Central Park South skyline. After Mona got sick and it was difficult for her to leave the apartment, Nick and Nora would sometimes come over for dinner, often bearing discs of the latest movies—an industry perk.

On New Year's Eve during that time, after first having dinner at Steve Martin's on Central Park West, Nick and Nora would cross the Park and join us. Mona would serve caviar and champagne—caviar from E.A.T. on Madison Avenue, immense dollops of it, with toast points and potato skins, sour cream, chives, chopped egg whites, and grated onions. Maybe too much. What the hell, it tasted great.

At midnight, fireworks would explode over the park, huge, happy, bursts of light. Once again, it was the four of us—and twinkling Manhattan out the window. We loved one another and we loved New York, but the two women were sick, one obviously, the other not. New Year's Eve was special for Nora; she included it in two of her movies, notably *When Harry Met Sally . . .* , but also *Mixed Nuts* because it met most of her standards for romanticism. But those nights, like the tears of fireworks extinguishing as they dropped, were coming to an end.

Most of the time that Nora was sick, Mona was sick, too. Nora was not sick like Mona. She was not repeatedly hospitalized and she did not undergo two serious surgeries, but when Mona lamented her plight—the loss of energy, the constant pain, the discomfort, the mugging of her dignity—Nora said she understood. This was 2010, when they both had about two years to live and Nora, secretly and without any drama, was undergoing chemotherapy every four weeks.

Nora never specifically mentioned the chemo to me, although maybe she did to Mona. If I was reluctant to probe, she was just as reluctant to get into detail. She communicated with shrugs and sentence fragments—"You know" and such—and so I mostly steered clear. Still, Nora would pop up to New York Hospital following her session at Memorial Sloan Kettering across the street. Mona often had room 242—large and bright, with sunlight bouncing off the river. It had a couch which backed up against the huge south-facing window, a table with some chairs, two recliners—and, near the doorway, an alcove which I used as an office. About 4 p.m. daily, tea was served in a common sitting area.

The fourteenth floor of New York Hospital's Greenberg Wing was fairly new and, for a hospital, downright opulent. From time to time, rooms were cleared out to accommodate some Middle Eastern potentate, and once the entire floor was taken by the king of Saudi Arabia. (All the nurses, most of them women, were replaced by Filipino men.) When Nora finally moved into room 242, her neighbors were David Rockefeller and Jean Kennedy Smith, John F. Kennedy's last surviving sibling.

In my presence, Nora never talked about her chemo and what it entailed. Even at Memorial Sloan Kettering, she refused to use the term "chemo." She called it Vidaza, which was its official designation: "I'm here for my Vidaza," she'd announce.

In her visits to Mona, Nora feigned nonchalance about her own treatment. Her goal was to make Mona feel better. She was visiting in her roles as chief medical officer, chief morale officer, and town crier. She related what was going on, who was sleeping with whom—less and less, with everyone growing older, as it turned out—and the usual mélange of politics and showbiz news.

Nora suffered. She suffered and she wrote. She suffered and took her girlfriends to lunch. She suffered and she worried about her kids and what would happen to them. She went on a book tour for *I Remember Nothing*, which she dedicated to Mona and me. (The book arrived one night by messenger. I looked, mystified. It was not even signed. I handed it to Mona. Minutes later there was a scream. Mona had found the dedication. Within a day, she must have ordered a hundred copies.)

Nora worried about bedbugs in the hotels where she stayed. She examined the bedding and she tried not to put her luggage on the floor, where, she had been told, the bugs lurked. Once, she found a dark spot on the blanket which turned out, upon very intense examination, to be a dark spot on the blanket.

Bedbugs were then her obsession de jour. Before that it had been radiation from cell phones or overhead transmission wires—or, for that matter and always, cancer. Her condition remained a secret. She said nothing to no one, attempting to contain her cancer so it became as small a part of her life as possible. She would not give it its due.

For a time, prednisone inflated her face. Once, she had to leave the Geffen boat under mysterious circumstances. Another time her arm inexplicably ballooned and she spent time in Cedars of Lebanon Hospital in L.A.—the only time, Spielberg recalled, that she asked him for a favor. (She had had difficulty getting a room.)

All the time she emailed Mona, affirming her friendship, making plans. It was odd then and remains odd in retrospect: She was going to die before Mona—June instead of December—and Mona, with Groopman holding one arm, her son Ari holding the other, and fatigue demanding her attention, bravely attended Nora's memorial service. Until just a month before, Nora had seemed the healthy one, the eternal one, the caregiver and not the caretaker, so that when her birthday approached, May 19, Mona made plans for dinner. She emailed Nora: Sunday the 20th or Monday the 21st?

"Monday," Nora replied.

On Monday, early, Nora canceled. She had a cold, she said. But Mona was wise to her. A cold would not stop Nora. She emailed Nora. This had to be bad.

Nora was in the hospital.

The Leukemia Ward

As far as most people were concerned, Nora just dropped out of sight, as if she had been kidnapped or placed in a witness protection program. With very few exceptions, no one knew where she was. For a while, she maintained an email presence, even a phone call or two, but soon that ceased, too. She was on the seventh floor of New York Hospital. It was for leukemia patients.

Nora was in bed much of the time, but she was not bedridden. She could get around, and when she did, she noticed that rooms that were occupied one day were vacant the next, the patient silently removed in a protocol of closed doors, hushed instructions—a soundless departure to the elevator and down to the morgue, with its huge, forbidding, refrigerator.

Nora of course went right to work. She and Delia set up shop on a small round table. They were writing a TV pilot for the producer Scott Rudin. It was called *George & Martha*. Delia sat at the table and worked on a laptop. Nora sat up in bed. The two turned out a snappy, jolly script that was very much to Rudin's liking. As far as he knew—as far as he could tell—Nora was fine. The script was sound. A deal with HBO was being negotiated. Rudin knew that Nora had gone into the hospital, but he did not know the true reason. She had offered him a lie, something about a blood cleansing that she did annually. It was nothing. She'd be out in a week. Then she went silent.

At first, Rudin suspected nothing. But then the week passed and he heard nothing from Nora. She and Rudin had not been in the habit of telephoning each other—emails sufficed—and for a time the emails kept coming. When they stopped, Rudin began to worry. He is famously impatient, a man who wore out his assistants, who awoke to his emails, went to sleep to his emails, and must have slept fitfully, knowing emails were either on the way or were then arriving. Rudin wondered what was going on or, to put it another way, what was going wrong.

Rudin called J.J., who said there was nothing to worry about ("I thought, 'Oh, you just gave me a reason to worry.'"), and then he called Mike Nichols, who, like almost everyone, was in the dark. David Geffen, too, was in the hunt. He kept calling Nora, but his calls were not returned. "I thought she was upset with me," he said. Nora emailed him, saying she would call soon. She never did.

At the hospital, a debate was in progress: Should the world be told? I said yes. I argued that leukemia was not some sort of social disease—nothing to be ashamed of. Besides, I insisted, it could be beaten. Nora seemed unpersuaded, but I could not stay to press my case. My mother had just turned one hundred. It was a milestone she never wanted to reach. She was dying. I left the discussion and flew off to be with her in Newton, Massachusetts.

Almost to the very end, Pearl Cohen was alert. She took an interest in Nora, whom she loved and who loved her in return. Once when Nora was wrapping up a speech to a full house at the Coolidge Corner Theater in Brookline, Massachusetts, she squinted into the lights, recognized my mother in the audience, and dashed down an aisle to give her a hug. My mother was a small woman, then in her nineties, and Nora lifted her in the air. In some ways, my mother never came down.

My mother died June 13, 2012, and I rushed back to New York—to Mona, who was sick at home, and to Nora, who was dying in the hospital. As soon as I could, I went to the hospital. I was an accomplished, nonstop liar, a totally counterfeit cheerleader, always assuring and reassuring, almost convincing myself that I could, with just the right pitch of my voice, some additional torque and the switched-on intensity that I brought to Mona, keep Nora's death at bay. I steeled myself to enter the room, prepared to go into my sunshiny act, but the moment I got inside the door, Nora leaped from the bed and engulfed me. I was stunned, unsure of what to do. Nora was not a hugger, but tentatively at first I hugged back, and then I drew her into me.

A moment later, the moment was gone, and Nora wanted to know what I had written about my mother. Nothing, I said. I had written about her several times over the years, and I had nothing new, nothing fresh to say. Nora was adamant. I must write something. I said my mother was special, buoyant, extremely competent, and could have—and here I am foreshadowing what I did write—been president of the United States had she been a man. "Write that," Nora ordered. I did.

Soon, Nora was moved from the leukemia floor, the seventh, to the fourteenth and the very room Mona had usually occupied. It was where Nora had visited her.

Mona was only able to make a single visit. She sat where Nora once had and faced the bed that she had so recently occupied herself. She gave Nora a cashmere throw. They talked of this and that—neither this nor that being what was happening to them both. Mona was weak and could not stay long. I put her in a wheelchair and took her home.

By then, the decision had been made to remain mum about Nora's condition. We had all become accustomed to maintaining silence, to becoming suddenly hard of hearing when asked about Nora, to brushing aside the mild and always tentative query. Some people gleaned the approaching tragedy. They knew enough not to insist on knowing.

A new, more powerful, chemo was tried. Nora had been reluctant to do that, having little faith that it would work. She went ahead anyway—as much, I think, to prove that she was right as to stave off death. She swiftly went bald, wore a Lana Turner–style turban, and seemed to get thinner. The numbers became important—the reds, the whites, the platelets. They were on the move.

Looking back now, her friends could see so many clues. Her appearance. Her unknowable schedule, her disappearances, and, of course, the rear-view-mirror hints dropped in what she wrote. In her final book, a collection called *I Remember Nothing*, the last essay was titled "What I Will Miss." It followed a chapter titled "What I Won't Miss" and only makes sense, really, if you know it was written by someone who knew life was coming to an end. The book was published in 2010; in less than two years, Nora would be dead.

Nora's list is mostly about family—Nick and her adored boys—and family events like Christmas and Thanksgiving and the dogwood tree that she and Nick planted on the East Hampton property. She mentioned New York several times. She'd miss "a walk in the park" and "the park" and "Shakespeare in the Park" and "the view out the window," which, in her New York apartment, was of that art deco wonder the Chrysler Building.

She said she'd miss Paris and "next year in Istanbul," where she had just been, and then New York again—"coming over the bridge to Manhattan." She had driven over that bridge countless times returning from Long Island and had filmed it at least twice, but to see the brazen city pop out of the brittle darkness of a winter's night was always to see it refreshed, as if scrubbed clean over the weekend.

As she grew older, Nora came to hate the geese that would fly low over East Hampton. She wrote about this. She wrote about how she'd take the kids out to Long Island when school got out and not return till after Labor Day. In July, the geese would show up, flocks of them whooshing overhead, honking incessantly. She wrote how the sight and sound used to thrill her—when she had endless summers to go.

As she got older—she wrote this when she was sixty-nine—the geese became a clock ticking out her life. The geese came to mock us, Nora and I decided one day. They honked of summers past and of people gone, of the Hamptons before the traffic on Route 27 got intolerable and private jets screeched insolently overhead. The geese. The geese had the traffic beat.

Late in Nora's life, she and Nick avoided the Hamptons in August and repaired to Los Angeles. They had a house in Beverly Hills, not too far from where Nora had grown up. It, too, was home.

In that same essay, she mentioned the beach parties and the Fourth of July fireworks. Nora and Nick always had houseguests, and so did the Spielbergs. On the weekend of the Fourth, everyone would congregate on the beach, build a fire, sing songs. The Spielbergs had a movie star or two as guests, occasionally Gwyneth Paltrow, and maybe Nora would have Meg Ryan or Tom Hanks and Rita Wilson.

The Navaskys came out, Alice and Michael Arlen, too—the screenwriter and former newspaper editor Kurt Luedtke, who back then was so addicted to cigarettes that he smoked in the swimming pool—in the shower, too, he confessed.

When Nora wrote about these summers, they were long gone. Some of the people were dead—Alan Pakula and Sidney Lumet, the directors; Peter Stone, the screenwriter and playwright; Joe Fox, the book editor and her former boyfriend; Judy Corman, her close friend; Lee Bailey, the ultimate host; Warner LeRoy, the restaurateur. And some had just moved away: John Irving; Winston Groom; Willie Morris, who went back to Mississippi, where he was revered and where he died in 1999; and, of course, Carl Bernstein, who seemed to go away and then come back. He now has a place in the nearby village of North Haven.

Ben Bradlee and Sally Quinn still came up in August and would end the summer with a party for Ben's birthday. One year, the TV producer Norman Lear bused in twenty or so violinists to play "Happy Birthday," but they were upstaged by one of the guests, the concert violinist Isaac Stern, who had accompanied Barbara Walters. He exuberantly grabbed a fiddle and did a solo of "Happy Birthday."

Every year Betty Bacall did the same suggestive toast to Ben. Every year, I offered a toast myself. Every year, we would cross the street afterward to Nora and Nick's for a postmortem, and every year the geese would mock our mortality. The summer was dying, and so were we all.

Why Jon Hamm?
Why Not Me?

When *Lucky Guy* opened on Broadway, April 1, 2013, Nora got a good review. The play did not. In commercial terms, it hardly mattered. With Tom Hanks as Mike McAlary, the play sold out for its entire run—it was even extended—but it is doubtful it will ever be seen again. It has its flaws, but as a memorial to Nora it brought down the house. As far as the opening night audience was concerned, *Lucky Guy* was not about Mike McAlary. It was really about Nora Ephron.

But it was not about Nora Ephron the playwright. It was about Nora Ephron the beloved writer, wit, public personality, film director, and, in the mind-jumbling that movies inevitably do, the characters in *Sleepless in Seattle* and *You've Got Mail*. Both movies starred Meg Ryan and Tom Hanks, and of course, Hanks played Mike McAlary in *Lucky Guy*. That came about not because Hanks liked the play, but because he loved Nora.

Hanks is one of the titanic figures in all Hollywood history—hugely popular, hugely successful, and somewhat mysterious as to why any of that is true. You can look at Clark Gable and understand why he was Clark Gable. The same is true for Cary Grant or Humphrey Bogart or even James Stewart, to name an actor with an everyman affect similar to Hanks's. But Hanks is remarkable only in his unremarkableness. Nora once said she turned around as Hanks and Nick were walking behind her on the street, talking, and noticed not just that no one had noticed them, but that neither in a way did she. She was struck by Hanks's total lack of distinction. On the screen he was vivid. The camera, as they say, loved him, but the people passing on the street didn't give him a second look.

The camera sees the truth. The camera exposes Hanks for what he is—smart and decent. He has been a prudent custodian of his own career. He has made very few missteps. He is not only an actor, but he functions also as a producer, director, writer, and, if it can added to this list, reader. He consumes books, many of them about World War II, not just battlefield stuff such as what went into *Saving Private Ryan* or the television series *Band of Brothers*, but such esoteric stuff as *Not I*, the memoir of the German historian Joachim Fest.

Nora, too, was a kleptomaniacal reader, taking everything from everywhere. She was on every publisher's list of tastemakers whose word-of-mouth praise for a book could make it a best seller. She read everything in either its manuscript or bound galley form, but she also ferreted out the old, the obscure—classics from another age. She put Hanks onto *The Aspirin Age*, a compendium of quirky, sometimes important stories by various writers and public figures, edited by Isabel Leighton and published in 1949. ("The Mysterious Death of Starr Faithfull" is reason enough to read the volume.)

Over the years, Nora and Tom maintained a steady correspondence, not only swapping books but scripts and ideas. She sent him David Maraniss's *They Marched into Sunlight*—as stunning a book about war as has ever been written—which Hanks optioned three times; but as often happens, nothing happened.

Hanks showed her an installment of his HBO miniseries *From the Earth to the Moon*, to see if she wanted to direct it. She did not. She, in turn, showed him various projects she was working on. One of them was the perennial *Higgins and Beech*, which Hanks liked but, like everyone else who had read the script, could not see how it could be made. She also sent him the screenplay version of what was then called *Stories About McAlary*.

This was a film that needed a star. It needed one who could bring in the crucial first weekend crowds. It needed a star who could attract other actors. It needed a star who could attract a director. The project was getting that distinct Hollywood smell of death. It had been around. Everyone had seen it. Everyone had passed. Mike McAlary. Who cared?

Tom Hanks did. He didn't care about McAlary, but he wanted Nora in his life. From his days on the set of *Sleepless in Seattle*, he had been dazzled by her.

"The thing is I wanted to be a part of her life and I wanted it until Kingdom come."

As it happened, Hanks was in London in the summer of 2011, promoting his movie *Larry Crowne*. Nora was there as well. They got together—dinner at the Wolseley. In the end, about eighteen people showed up. One of them was John Hamm, who had become a huge star in the television series *Mad Men*. Hanks asked Hamm what he was doing in town. He said he was doing a reading for Nora. A play.

"Oh, really, what play?" Hanks asked. He turned to Nora. "Hey, Nora, what play is he reading that you are doing?"

"She said, 'Oh, I'm doing that thing that I sent you a long time ago about the tabloid reporter that you thought was a jerk, Mike McAlary.'

"I said, 'Oh, is it a play now?'

"She said, 'Well, yeah.'

"I said, 'Oh, okay. Can I read it?'"

Nora sent Hanks the script, which was still substantially similar to the screenplay that he didn't much like. Still, he was both intrigued and feeling competitive. He asked how Jon Hamm had done. Nora replied that the reading was "interesting." She had learned a lot.

Hanks asked, "Is it going to be done in London?" Possibly, Nora said, but probably not. In that case, Hanks said, why not let him do a reading? If Jon Hamm could do it, why couldn't he? You could, Nora said. And soon he did.

Hanks did not cry, as Hugh Jackman had, but his reading was equally moving. The mood in the room was celebratory and for Hanks, who had never done something like that before, exhilarating. He was, if only for that afternoon, in a nondescript rehearsal room in the New York theater. On the other side of the door was Broadway. For the boy from Concord, California, the son of a hospital worker and an itinerant cook, it remained a big step.

Nora started clearing her desk for *Lucky Guy*. Her time was limited; so was her energy. She had completed the script of a project called *Lost in Austen*, an adaptation of a four-part British television series about a present-day Jane Austen fan who, by going through a certain door, enters the world of Jane Austen. Nora would also direct.

Nora was a huge Jane Austen fan. She not only mentioned the books from time to time, but in her valedictory essay in the collection *I Remember Nothing*, she lists *Pride and Prejudice* among the things she will miss. She had urged me to read the book and could never comprehend why I did not—could not, actually. (I could never get past the first three or so pages.) Nevertheless, she sent me her script for *Lost in Austen* and asked me what I thought of it. I thought, in short, that it was swell.

So did Bryan Lourd, her agent. He had been fighting to get the movie made. But suddenly, his screenwriter-cum-director backed out. The film was to be shot in England, and Nora, sicker than almost anyone knew, had to change her plans. She did not want to be away from her medical team in New York. Not realizing that her disease, sort of on schedule, was worsening, I argued against her. England has doctors, I said. England has hospitals. No, no. She wasn't going.

Lourd was stunned. "All of a sudden, one day I got a call saying you've got to get me out of this movie. It was completely out of left field." He was bewildered, and some days later he had a telephone conversation with Nora, repeatedly asking, "What am I missing?" Finally, she told him.

"I have a little problem, and this is what it is. I am going to be fine, and you are never allowed to talk to me about this again. Don't bring it up!"

Nora told Lourd that she had only one project she cared about: *Lucky Guy*. Lourd was as perplexed as everyone else about why McAlary mattered so much to her, but he did as he was told. "The play became the focus. Everything shifted to that. It was, literally daily, the play, the play, the play."

By then, the play was no longer just about McAlary or journalism or the romance of the tabloids. In retrospect many people saw it as unavoidably about a journalist who was dying of cancer by a playwright who herself was dying of cancer. It had not been that at the start, because Nora had begun the project while she was still healthy, and really, it was not that way even at the end, because the play was always about something and someone else. Still, McAlary's cancer and Nora's cancer—two writers dying of the disease we all fear—overwhelmed everything else. The play got to be about their death when all the while it was also about their lives.

In the meantime, *Lucky Guy* was not yet a play—a finished play—and Hanks had not yet committed. He had expressed interest, he had done the reading, he had mulled it over—but he had not yet said yes. That was understandable. He was not a stage actor. He had not done a play since college, but he knew theater and he knew he was not in shape for a huge role. It took stamina. It entailed a huge feat of memorization and, for Hanks, the forsaking of other projects.

Yet he was intrigued. "I thought about it, just how it was going to fit into my life," he said. He was "petrified of doing any stage work," and that fear was a good sign. A challenge awaited, an antidote to apathy and staleness. The contract was before him. Hanks was reaching for yes. He was a man who honored his fear. He paid it obeisance. It enticed him. The play was about journalism and New York and the world of New York tabloid journalism in the urban mosh pit of the 1980s. All that came together for him.

"I realized that I couldn't get it out of my head."

As Hanks knew at the time, and as was going to become more and more clear, the play was hardly a finished work. Right off the bat, it needed a director. George Wolfe was brought in. As is almost always the case, he knew people who knew people. He knew Colin Callender when Callender was at HBO, and he knew Bryan Lourd, and he had a connection of sorts with Mike Nichols since Nichols had directed *Angels in America* for HBO while Wolfe had done it on Broadway. Last, but hardly least, Wolfe has been the artistic director of New York's prestigious Public Theater. He was considered a genius.

He was also appropriately theatrical, given to moments of near hyperventilation but possessed, as all good directors are, of a kind of X-ray vision. He could see the interior of a play, the dialogue that was not there that explained the dialogue that was there. With *Lucky Guy*, he had one persistent question: "What is this play about?

"Why are you writing this play? Why did you write this play?" Pointing at the script, he would ask, "Why is this here? Why are you doing this? Why is this there? Why, why, why, why, why?"

Nora paid attention. She would take notes and, as fast as possible, make revisions—and then exhausted, get some sleep. (At one point, Wolfe threatened to quit because Nora was pushing back too vigorously. A lunch patched things up.) She was working against both the clock and what she thought were her own limitations. Like any writer, she had to wonder about what worked and what did not, about the reach of her talent. It was that quality of McAlary—his ambition roaring past his talent—that had so attracted her to this project in the first place, she told Wolfe. She felt the same way, she said. Wolfe was stunned by that admission.

"I thought it was a completely naked moment," he said. "It felt very vulnerable when she said it, and I felt it was a brave thing for her to say."

It is possible, I think, to make too much of this admission. In *Imaginary Friends* Nora had indeed come up against the limits of her talent. The play was good, well worth an evening, and its themes were extraordinarily rich, not some boy-meets-girl confection. It was about important stuff—the blacklist, McCarthyism, political and personal loyalty, petty jealousy, two women and not a woman and a man. Nora had set a high bar for herself, a bar that maybe she thought either one of her protagonists—certainly Hellman—could have reached. She had come to the limit of her talent as a playwright, and that must have vexed her. She was a brilliant and effortless essayist and a charming public personality, a director and writer of clever and popular movies, but she read and thought on a deeper level and she wanted to write there as well. *Lucky Guy* was different. In some sense, it was almost autobiographical—the *New York Post*, tabloid New York, and the screech of brazen journalists. Nevertheless, people were raising the question she herself was always asking: What's the point?

The Point?

The answer to George Wolfe's staccato question—"why, why, why?"—was once located on Mulberry Street in what was Manhattan's Little Italy—a now-gone red-sauce Italian restaurant called Paolucci's. The place was a two-minute walk from the old police headquarters at 240 Centre Street. Across from it was a humble tenement that had been cubicled for offices of the city's many police reporters. This was known as the Police Shack and it was where many a great writer started and many of them ended. Covering cops was once an exalted calling.

For Nick's sixtieth birthday, two of New York's most respected journalists, Pete Hamill and Jack Newfield, took over Paolucci's and threw a party for him. A dinner like that for Nora would have included a bevy of Hollywood types, but this was one was pure Nick—cops (some robbers), Feds and prosecutors, reporters who could crack a safe with a phone call, a private investigator or two, lawyers of the criminal bar, magazine editors who eschewed readership surveys for their own gut, and the former mayor of the City of New York, John V. Lindsay. Paolucci's had once been Nick's place. On the menu was an item called Pork Chops Pileggi.

It was a cold but bracing February night, and at the end of the evening Nora and Nick walked out onto Mulberry Street. Over their shoulder loomed the doomed World Trade Center. Before them was the nineteenth-century façades of Little Italy. I remember Nora's face that night. Nick had been regaled for his abilities, his character, his inappropriate humility, and she was taking in Lower Manhattan at its cinematic best. She was visibly delighted.

As far as I'm concerned, the party at Paolucci's answered all of Wolfe's demanding "why, why, whys." It spoke to Nora's romance about old-time newspaper journalism, harkening back to her days at the *New York Post*. It was what she meant when an exasperated Wolfe, a man of the stage and not the newsroom, asked her what in the world she found so compelling about journalism and she replied "I love it."

"Why?"

"Because I love being in the bar with the guys."

McAlary's tale was rich and its setting was rich and the characters were rich and the parallel cancers became an obvious and compelling deus ex machina—felt by the audience but absent from the play itself. But it was Nick, his world and his friends, Nick and the street reporters who were novelists or poets at heart, who not only was at the heart of the play, but made it possible.

McAlary's world for all its flamboyance, was a closed society. It was working-class, mostly Irish, almost entirely male, and, like the cops themselves, somewhat defensive. Nora was at a disadvantage here. She was famous and charming, but she was hardly working class and she was definitely of the wrong tribe. She knew the people who owned the city. She did not know the ones who made it work. Nick did. He vouched for her. Her street cred came down to this: She was Nick's wife.

One by one, Nora had approached the people who knew McAlary best. She was, of course, well known to them all and the prospect of being portrayed in what was then a proposed movie is almost irresistible. Still, what paved the way for her—what gave her entry into the insular world that had been McAlary's—was a very special credential.

"You got to understand the awe that we all had for Nick," said Eddie Hayes. "Everybody knew Nick. You'd meet him some place. . . . It was like, 'Oh, Nick Pileggi, Nick Pileggi.' He'd look sharp, and he carried himself good, and he was always polite and respectful. He dressed very, very nicely, classy. Anybody connected to him was like on the first team."

Jim Dwyer, another veteran of the New York tabs who wound up at the *Times*, had been at the hospital with McAlary the night he died. He, too, opened up to Nora out of respect and admiration for her work—and for her husband. "It's funny, I don't know Nick very well at all but everyone I've ever spoken to in my world, in the New York journalism world, they all think he's the greatest guy who ever walked the earth." With appropriate awe, Dwyer noted that even the legendary grouch Jimmy Breslin liked Nick.

Nora Ephron was a very smart, totally realistic, woman. Yet the New York she inhabited was partly a back lot in the Hollywood she had once left. She was utterly smitten with the city in all its cinematic aspects, its literary life, for sure, but also the parts that could not be seen—not the steam tunnels, subways, conduits, and such that course under the city but its film noir aspects that Nick understood and had mastered: the Mob and it characters. Say what you will about them—sociopaths or whatever—they are far more compelling than, say, the pallid types that play by the rules and commute down to Wall Street, crooks of a different kind, she might say. It was the shady types who called Nick, sometimes late at night, sometimes from the cushy gulag known as the witness protection program, that captivated her. Nick knew them. They knew Nick. Nora was a moll two or three time removed. It was close enough for her and just thrilling enough.

That world and the reporters who knew it best, the guys at the bar and above all Nick, was the "why, why, why?" of Nora's final work. *Lucky Guy* was for Nick.

Nick was the luckiest guy of all.

A Lunch Before Dying

As Nora died, she lunched. She lunched for business and just with friends. She lunched with people she had known a long time and she lunched with people she had just met. The closer she got to death the more she lived her life.

Near the end, her friends started to sense that something was amiss. Sometimes she didn't look quite right. To Gail Collins, Nora looked frail. Collins, a former *New York Times* editorial page editor turned columnist, had been interviewed by Nora because she had worked with McAlary at the New York *Daily News*. She had quickly been granted a membership in Nora's ever-widening circle of women friends, including a book club that met occasionally to take up what I thought of as "Nora books"—writers such as Virginia Woolf and Doris Lessing. Once Nora and Gail had discussed breast cancer and Nora had volunteered that she had had "some blood issues." True to form, Nora made it appear as if these "issues," while very scary, were over. She did not seem to be in any distress.

Rita Wilson sensed something was wrong. She was appearing at Joe's Pub, the café attached to the Public Theater, and on her last night there, Nora gave her a party at a nearby restaurant. It was May 9, 2012.

"Her mood was subdued," Rita recalled, but what remains italicized in her recollection is what she said following her curtain calls. She said she wanted to thank three people who were in the audience that night, one of whom was Nora. She said, "I don't know why I'm saying this, but I feel this is the last time I may ever get the opportunity to do this."

It was.

Looking back on it all now, some people recall things that Nora said that in retrospect are freighted with meaning.

She had lunch with Sally Quinn. Their relationship had become episodic. Sally was in Washington much of the year, and when she did decamp for East Hampton, it was for August and Nora and Nick were gone. Nora was putting things back in place, doing some mending. She was in Washington for the Kennedy Center Honors. She asked Sally to lunch and they went to the Ritz-Carleton. Sally wrote about it afterward. The lunch was wistful, a word Sally used. There were long pauses. Something was not being said. When they left the restaurant, they hugged good-bye.

"I wish we saw more of each other," Sally said.

"I know," Nora said. "I feel like there's a hole in my heart."

Nora had lunch with Marie Brenner. Later, they walked a bit and stopped for pastries. Marie was surprised. Nora never had dessert. And then she asked for a ride to her house. Marie was puzzled. They were only three or four blocks from Nora's East 79th Street apartment. They hailed a cab.

In December of 2011, Nora, Nick, and the boys went to Istanbul, found it not to their liking, and fled to Paris. There, Nora and Nick hooked up with the cookbook author and food show personality Ina Garten and her husband, the Yale economist Jeffrey Garten. The Gartens maintain an apartment in Paris, and Nick and Nora went there for a drink and then, along with Alex Witchel and Frank Rich, they headed to La Cigale Récamier, famous for its soufflés.

Nora had known Frank Rich since the 1960s, even before he became the movie critic for the *New York Post*. (He later was the theater critic for the *New York Times* and, after that, a political columnist whom Nora greatly admired.) Witchel, his wife, was another writer, often on food. These were foodies par excellence in the seventh heaven of Paris on a rare cloudless day.

"It was one of those magical lunches with the most wonderful people," Ina Garten recalled. "It was a bright sunny day. And Nora raised her glass and said, 'To better days.'

"And we all laughed hysterically because, of course, there wasn't a better day. This was the best day we could ever remember. And six months later we realized that she already had the dreadful news and there was nothing they could do. And I look back at that day and I think, she was the ultimate hostess."

Nora and Ina had met years before, at a birthday party for James Lapine, the stage director and writer, where they both discovered a mutual passion, not just food but a particular restaurant in Nice, famous for its truffle sandwiches. Nora had the recipe and later mailed it to Ina, who keeps it to this day.

The two saw each other only occasionally after that, but Ina was present for one of Nora's most notable meals. She served roast beef and Château d'Yquem, a celebrated sauterne with the retail value of a nice car. The pairing was eccentric, and the guests were even more puzzled when Nora started reading from the diary of Prince Felix Yusupov, the vastly rich Russian aristocrat, who had originated this meal. The wine was fabulously expensive, and the roast beef succulent and dripping with fat, and while it worked for the prince, it did not work for those of us whose Russian ancestry was not quite so exalted. (I hate sweet wine.)

Over the years others have duplicated the prince's princely meal, and they did so, probably, out of love of food or love of wine or merely to show off. But Nora did it out of love of guests, a quality Ina Garten, herself a self-taught cook, immediately sensed and appreciated. The food was not a meal, but an offering—a gift.

Nora and Ina made one last plan for a meal. Nora would supply the wine;

Ina would cook. On the designated day, Nora called to say she wasn't feeling well. They never met again.

Laurence Mark, a producer, was set to go on with *Lost in Austen* when Nora told him she was dropping the project. Like Bryan Lourd, he was shocked, but Nora explained that she only wanted to concentrate on *Lucky Guy*, which was true but not the only reason. Still, Mark did not suspect anything was seriously wrong—not even as they were making *Julie & Julia*, and Nora took him aside. "We each found ourselves standing on some platform outside the set . . . and she just said out of the blue, 'I just want you to know that I love that we're getting to make this movie together. I love that you're here and I love you.' And a kiss on the cheek. And I was like, wow, I feel exactly the same way and that is incredibly sweet and thank you.

"And then we just went on. She never wore her emotions on her sleeve. It was an odd moment and it somehow meant more to me in retrospect. I can't help thinking she had this on her mind. . . . I just want you to know that. That's all. And then we went on with the day."

Nora, of course, was saying good-bye.

We'll Always Have Paradoxes

Rita Wilson wrote an essay about Nora, It mentioned the Prince Yusupov meal and, also, Nora's love of music, especially show tunes from Broadway's golden age. What she didn't mention was that these are paradoxes. Nora had no appreciation for wine, for fine wine that is. In restaurants, she asked for something cheap, invariably a red that was light on the palate, nothing too complex, and she asked for it with all the verve and authority of a connoisseur demanding a very specific vintage. Waiters occasionally didn't get it and reacted as if their leg was being pulled, and Nora would persevere: The cheap stuff please. (In champagne, which she loved, she took it pink.)

As for music, it's true that she mentally archived the great Broadway songbook, but it is equally true that she almost never played the music—indeed, for a time, she had nothing to play music on. Hers was the only home I knew which had neither a phonograph nor a cassette deck nor a disc player—no music player of any kind. When she had asked me to help her choose the music for *Sleepless in Seattle*, and I roared over to her place in East Hampton with a dozen or so compact discs containing songs I thought she could use. A look of mystification came over her. She turned to Nick. Did they have a CD player?

Nick ransacked the house. He looked in the dining room cabinets. No player. He looked in the living room ones. Still, no player. He looked everywhere he could think of. Nothing. No player. It turned out that the woman who was even then choosing the music for her movie was living a life barren of music. Ultimately, Nick and Nora bought a boom box which must have cost considerably less than any one of their frying pans. It hardly mattered. It was almost never used.

Nora was not indifferent to the role of music in her films. She spent a great deal of time considering what music to use and which version of a particular song was best. She listened carefully in the studio, playing some songs over and over. Yet in her daily life, music seemed to play no role whatsoever. I never knew what to make of this, since I write to music and have always had music players of some sort, in every office I've ever had. This was certainly not the case with Nora; she seemed to have no use for it. (Once, when Howard Stringer, a music aficionado, invited her to attend a prized performance of Luciano Pavarotti singing *La Bohème*, she replied, thanks, but she had once heard the opera.) To add to the paradox, however, I should mention that late in life Nora had an upright piano moved into her East Side apartment and a baby grand for the living room in Beverly Hills and resumed the piano lessons she had abandoned as a kid. She played in the afternoons. It calmed her.

Another paradox: Nora was renowned for her sexual frankness, but her movies could have been shown in any church basement. In none of them did anyone take off their clothes. When it unavoidably came time for a couple to couple, she sternly directed the camera to mind its manners and look the other way. On *Julie & Julia*, when the Julie character and her husband made love, Nora filmed the scene delicately, insisting "I don't want to see any skin." Even then, most of what was filmed was cut.

Similarly, in *Lucky Numbers*, Nora tried to avoid shooting a scene in a strip club. The script called for it, but Nora balked. The writer, Adam Resnick, had to talk her into doing it. Even so, there are no strippers in the club, an odd way to make money in an odd business. Nora insisted on no nudity, and when, in the same movie, John Travolta and Lisa Kudrow have their sexual moment, the scene opens after they have concluded and both characters are more or less clothed—he in a T-shirt, she in a nightgown and under the covers. This is a long way from X.

And yet in *Higgins and Beech*, the script Nora cowrote with Alice Arlen, there's a good deal of sex, much of it under covers, mind you, or—since it takes place in Korea during the war—tents of one sort or another. In one scene the script calls for the war correspondent Keyes Beech to put "his hands on her [Marguerite Higgins's] breasts." It's tame compared to some films, but the script ripples with sexual tension relieved periodically by lovemaking and the sudden intrusion of war.

Of all of Nora's scripts, *Higgins and Beech* is the most erotic and also perhaps the most realistically romantic. Maybe because it is based on real characters, it eschewed a happy ending—merely a mutually agreed parting of the ways, his career and her career taking precedence over everlasting love.

I have no idea how much of the script was Nora's and how much was Alice's. On the very day it occurred to me to ask Alice, she died. All I know is that Nora very much wanted to get this movie made and sent the script to anyone who had the remotest chance of making it, but she had no luck.

Higgins and Beech was about newspapering, which she loved, combat correspondents, some of whom she had known in Israel, women out of their supposed place, love and sexual attraction and the rush of endorphins that comes when shells explode close, but not too close. Higgins and Beech were brave, maybe recklessly so, but their affair was as hopeless and as muddled as the Korean War itself. The war ended precisely where it started—and so did Higgins and Beech.

How to account for these paradoxes? The wine one is easy. Nora was the child of two alcoholics. She might have feared that she had inherited that awful proclivity, although I never heard her say so. Still, she had certainly witnessed the effect of too much drink, and it was not roisterous good fun, a quip followed by a hiccup—the fictional Nick and Nora of the *Thin Man* series— but a sloppy brawl. That the drunks were her parents must have been both painful and terrifying. For whatever reason, Nora was a moderate drinker, and while just about everything about food fascinated her, very little about wine did.

Music was more of a mystery, but here again I would suggest something akin to taste. I cannot envision her at a concert, or, if I do, she is twitchy and impatient, wondering not just, as I sometimes do, why she cannot also read a book or open a newspaper, but what she is doing there in the first place.

Her reserve as a director is harder to explain, unless the explanation is as simple as the number 1941. That was the year Nora was born, and it meant she was the child of an era—of several eras, actually. She came of age in the starchy and white 1950s, when married couples (in the movies anyway, which is how I know this stuff) slept in twin beds and men wore pajamas and kept a robe at the edge of the bed in the event they had to get up and walk a few paces to the bathroom. Women, of course, did the same. They in fact wore veritable ball gowns, billowy, lacy things suitable for presentation at court or, more routinely, a stroll to the bathroom.

Then came the sixties and the rediscovery of sex. It had gone underground in the forties and fifties, like some stream that disappears and then bubbles to the surface, and anyone formed by those years might mouth the mantra that sex was an ordinary part of life, but we all deeply felt that it was not—that it was extraordinary.

Nora, like me, was part of that generation, the generation that had no generation, the generation that had no name—pre–baby boomer or something like that—and the gift to our generation, aside from never taking air conditioning for granted, was appreciating the eroticism of restraint. What was not seen, what was not explicit, was more titillating than what was shown in dermatological detail. Nora was no prude—her essays show that she could write casually about casual sex—but she knew that patience is provocative and, to resort to a cliché, less is more. That was a lesson she took from the romantic comedies of the 1940s and 1950s, she once told Howard Stringer; and indeed one of her signature films, *You've Got Mail*, was explicitly based on the 1940 film *The Shop Around the Corner*, which in turn had been based on a 1937 play. In all its versions—including the musical-comedy adaptation, *She Loves Me*—the eventual lovers are at first antagonists and don't even kiss until the end of the movie. (On Broadway, that scene causes the audience to applaud—a palpable release of tension.)

Sleepless in Seattle employs the same device. Meg Ryan and Tom Hanks not only don't meet until the end of the movie, they don't even live in the same city—she in Baltimore and he in Seattle. And when they do meet, it's at the top of the Empire State Building where, as it happens, Deborah Kerr was supposed to meet Cary Grant in *An Affair to Remember*, a 1957 remake of the 1939 film *Love Affair*, where, once again, the lovers never get to make love.

If Nora had a red line concerning sex, it had to do with women who had affairs with married men. She would sometimes name this or that celebrity who was unabashedly linked to some married man and roundly denounce her a tramp. The rest of the celebrity-soaked world might not agree—no opprobrium is applied to these matters anymore—but Nora had a refreshingly admirable grip on the bottom line: There are some things one does not do. This was both moral and emotional. More than once, it had been done to her.

The 2009 movie *Julie & Julia* encapsulated Nora's ethic. *Julie & Julia* is two parallel stories, one about how the blogger Julie Powell decided to cook all 524 recipes in Julia Child's classic cookbook, *Mastering the Art of French Cooking*. The other depicts how Julia Child herself learned to master French cuisine and, with Simone Beck, came to write her cookbook. Julie, a young, married woman, is played by Amy Adams. Julia, various ages in the movie but never really young, is played by Meryl Streep.

Of the two relationships, Nora preferred Julia Child's. She was a woman in a loving relationship with a supportive man. They were childless but clearly not sexless. They engaged in nooners, aka matinees. Paul Child hurried home from his job at the American Embassy in Paris, Julia Child from classes at Le Cordon Bleu. She needed, she once wrote, only two rooms: the kitchen and the bedroom. "I would go to school in the morning, then for lunch time, I would go home and make love to my husband."

"You cannot have too much butter," Julia would say—and so would Nora.

Butter is the secret, essential ingredient in almost anything that tastes good. But it is rarely on the surface. Never even in the description. It is, in this way, like the sexual component of a romantic relationship—not blatant, not obvious, but essential, smooth and blended in.

Julie Powell's sex life, in contrast, was spelled out in even greater detail in her subsequent book, *Cleaving: A Story of Marriage, Meat, and Obsession.* At the time, the book worried Nora. In it, Julie reveals an extramarital affair. Her language is occasionally course, and Nora worried that the book would sully the image she had given a more wholesome Julie in the movie.

Nora and Julie, and indeed Nora, Julia, and Julie, were peering suspiciously at one another across a considerable generational gap, possibly one that the audience shared. Julia Child, a star of what was once called *educational* television, was a generational figure herself. She had been born in 1912, and by her own admission—noted in the movie—she did not lose her virginity until she was in her thirties and had met Paul Child in China during the war. His next posting was Paris, where they cooked, ate, had lovely dinner parties, and made love often.

"We had a happy marriage because we were together all the time," Julia wrote. "We were friends as well as husband and wife. We just had a good time."

Julie & Julia, a sweet movie, neatly encapsulates Nora. It is about food. It is about love. It is about the passion of the supposedly passionless middle-aged man and woman, love arriving not late, but right on time. It is about Paris. It is about writing and it is, in all those themes, about the life Nora made for herself with Nick.

Bon appétit!

Room 242

Sometime around early 2012, Nora's condition worsened. She was working on *Lucky Guy* and her energy was flagging. As always, we celebrated my birthday (February 6), but Mona was too weak for us to go out. In the past, we had gone to Peter Luger's, the renowned steak joint hard by the Brooklyn waterfront, and sometimes we went to Trattoria Dell'Arte for its heroic veal parmigiana and once or twice to the Four Seasons for its anything. This time we stayed home, and I don't remember what we ate, and I don't remember either if we discussed how Mona was dying or if we discussed that Nora was dying, and I don't know whether later that night the two of them emailed each other about how we had not discussed how they were both dying, and maybe we didn't.

Looking back over my calendar, I see a dinner here and there with Nick and Nora and a reading of her play and a couple of screenings with her name attached—maybe I was just going to meet her there. There were other dinners of mutual friends, and in February she went to see Mike Nichols's revival of *Death of a Salesman*, and she remained swaddled in her heavy coat throughout the performance.

Bit by bit, she disappeared from my calendar—no lunches, no dinners—although we talked on the phone, and there was, looking back on it, the occasional reference to her time being limited, but I never knew what to say in response, and so, as I was doing with Mona, I denied the undeniable. I knew she was dying, but we rarely talked about it, as if just acknowledging it could bring it on faster or make it happen at all. Familiarity with cancer breeds respect, even awe, but also a huge, furious hate. I had come to see the disease as not merely some cells running amok, but as evil. It hid in the body, lurking God knows where, ready to pounce after the clueless chemo passed it by. This is why people say they have to "fight" cancer, make war on it, all these martial words that only empower it. I wouldn't grant it the power to kill. I snubbed Nora's cancer. "Fuck the cancer," I would say to Nora. "Fuck the cancer," I would say to Mona.

Nora and I did not frequently talk about how she was feeling. We did not talk about whether she was angry, as Mona was from time to time, feeling cheated, as Mona often did, repeating the mantra "It isn't fair," which it wasn't (But what is? And so what?) We did not talk about fear or whether she had scoured the Internet seeking information about death: How does it happen?

At noon on April 20, three months or so before her death, Nora went down to the Great Hall at Cooper Union where, in 1860, Abraham Lincoln had delivered a famous pre-presidential speech. She was there for a memorial service for Christopher Hitchens. Hitch, as he was often called, was a celebrated, iconoclastic writer and public intellectual, and while I knew him, I was not aware that Nora did. (Although she knew everybody.) I arrived a bit late, and took a place toward the rear of the hall on the right. I glimpsed Nora on the other side of the auditorium, to the left and closer to the stage.

Hitchens was a brave and brazenly talented writer, but his politics were occasionally bizarre and not always to Nora's liking. He had exuberantly supported the war in Iraq and he was famously opposed to abortion, a lonely position for a writer who at one time was on the left. So it could not have been political affinity that drew Nora to Cooper Union that day, although it could well have been the power and the verve in which Hitchens powered his ideas. (He once talked me into writing a column in defense of David Irving, a Holocaust revisionist later revealed to be a crackpot Nazi apologist.) There was much to admire about Hitchens, but he was surely trailed by an asterisk or two.

What strikes me now, what didn't even occur to me then, was the real, the secret, the awful reason Nora must have so admired Hitchens—not just for how he lived but also for how he died. He went down keyboard blazing, a succession of essays in *Vanity Fair* about his cancer and his treatment. He was, as usual, courageously honest, even embracing the "war" metaphor that is so often applied and misapplied to cancer. He, too, made it into a fight, while all the while recognizing that the cancer itself was blithely unaware that it was in a battle. He was frank, too, about the hideous repercussions of chemotherapy—the loss of hair being just a clichéd example, the loss of sexual drive being a more doleful one.

Nora must have read the essays in dread. It's not possible that she did not read them. Graydon Carter, *Vanity Fair*'s editor, was a friend and if not a regular at dinner than a frequent guest, both in Manhattan and on Long Island—but friendship aside, Hitchens was impossible not to read. Everyone did.

Hitchens had gone where Nora was going. He was in fact just a bit more than sixty days ahead of her, but he had chosen a different path. He had chronicled his death, as he had to, because his condition was impossible to conceal. Nora, standing down the Hall from me, was even then concealing her condition. She was just a mere month from entering the hospital for the final time. Famous writers saluted Hitchens—Martin Amis, Salman Rushdie, Tom Stoppard, Ian McEwan—a brace of Brits once again repossessing *their* language—and Nora must have wandered in her mind to her own planned memorial service, which she had outlined just two months before.

In his final writings, Hitchens continued his lively remonstrations against religion and its fellow travelers. He would not, he insisted, abandon his religious devotion to atheism just because he was on his deathbed. Nora, I'm sure, felt the same.

Now I peer down the Great Hall and I see Nora once again. I knew then that she was stricken, but it did not compute—she looked so unlike someone who was dying. Now I feel her loneliness, not because she was in any real sense alone, but because she was, like any dying person, very much alone. When I turned to go, Nora was gone. I looked for her but to no avail. Knowing Nora, she hopped the subway, and vanished.

Nora worked. She worked hard, as hard as she could. She wanted to get the play done, but why? Why, if you do not believe in God and an afterlife, do you work as if there is one? Who are you working for? The applause, the rave of the critics, the fun of the after party, the surge of the limos—all of that. What for? Why not just lie on some beach? Why not sit by the pool in East Hampton or Beverly Hills or shoot craps in Vegas? Why even care about how you are remembered if you and your memory are gone? I remember Shakespeare. He does not.

I think Nora worked because she was a writer and writing is not just something one does, but something one is. She worked, because to stop would have been like a death that precedes death.

Is that right, Nora? I think of her as I write, imagine her head nodding or her rolling her eyes at my pretensions. I am currently reading *The Violet Hour*, Katie Roiphe's book on how certain people, mostly writers, died. I picked it up because the last chapter is about James Salter, who died in 2015 at the age of ninety. He died as he wrote, without fuss, at the gym. I knew Salter, and the reason I knew Salter was Nora. She had introduced me to Joe Fox, and Fox had been Salter's friend and editor, and so we all had some dinners and I played tennis with him, but we never talked about writing or being a fighter pilot in the Korean War or, for that matter, sex, which pervades his work, like the remarkable and graphic *A Sport and a Pastime*.

I would have discussed this all with Nora—Salter, Roiphe, Susan Sontag, who is also in the book, and Sigmund Freud, who according to Roiphe refused morphine and instead took aspirin for his intense pain because he didn't want to lose his mental acuity—if he was going to live, he would live. He died of mouth cancer, first, though, of soothing morphine injections.

Somehow, word began to leak. Her friends were connecting the dots. Nichols had gotten some calls, and so, suspecting something, he called Nora, poking around in a faux innocent way. Nora instantly confronted J.J.: Had he talked? He had not. Tom Brokaw called me. By then Nora was in the hospital. Something was wrong, he said. Nothing was wrong, I said. Brokaw and I were old pals, and I was lying to him. I was doing what Nora wanted, but I felt lousy about it, and later, when he found out the truth, he used his howitzer of a voice to berate me—and then, after his ire had been damped, to forgive me.

Christopher Lospalutto was summoned to the hospital. This was his second trip, both times to blow out Nora's hair. He was one of New York's primo hairstylists, and he worked on many celebrities and women who thought they either were or ought to be celebrities, but even among the special, Nora was somehow special. She had this way, this approach, this coy way of making demands or asking a favor—and all you wanted to do was do it. The first time she had called Chris she described herself as "a hag"

"'Hey, Chris, it's Nora. I'm feeling like a hag. I hear you're the guy to make me feel young. Can you help me out?' I sort of chuckled and I'm like, 'Nora?' Thinking in my head, 'Oh, Nora Ephron.'"

From there on, she was a regular. She would sit in the chair, reading scripts and sometimes the newspapers. Once when she asked Chris about a local political race, he confessed ignorance. There then followed a lecture. He lived in the city and was obligated to know something about its governance, its politics. He must start the day with a newspaper. It would be permissible just to skim it, but he had to know the basics.

Chris became a newspaper reader.

He challenged her once to play Words with Friends. She was sitting in the chair playing, and Chris said he wanted to play, too. She gave him her quizzical are-you-kidding-me? look and said, "I will destroy you. I'm not going to play you."

Chris broke up, laughing. "You know what. You're right. You will totally annihilate me in this game."

Chris heard all about Nora's concerns about aging, which she related in a lighthearted way. " 'Don't make me look old, don't make me look old,' she would say. Not in a vain way. It was just she realized obviously she was getting older and things were changing, but she came to me because she's like, 'I know you're the guy who's going to make me look young.' "

In the hospital, the challenge was no longer to stave off aging but to disguise the disease. She made it clear that Chris was not to tell anyone that she had been hospitalized. It was June 9, the day of the Belmont Stakes, which Nora and some others were going to watch on television. She wanted to look nice. He brushed her hair.

The second visit was different. By then, she had been through chemo. Chris brushed carefully, softly, taking clumps of hair with each stroke. Nora looked away. Soon, she was wearing caps, a sort of turban. She looked cute.

She lost her appetite, and then it came back and she craved scrambled eggs. The nurses had recommended a place, and so J.J. went there, insisting on lots of butter. The eggs were entombed in an appetite-repelling Styrofoam container, and J.J., fearing the worst, hurried to New York Hospital. Nora tasted, and put the eggs aside. Not enough butter. J.J., whom Nora cherished, felt he had failed her. It was such a small thing. It was, though, a final thing.

Shortly before Nora died, the columnist Liz Smith announced her friend's passing. Liz quickly retracted her item, but it was amazing to me then and remains so now that news of Nora's condition had not leaked. After all, by then numerous people knew—and some had known for quite some time. Besides Joyce Ashley, who saw Nora on occasion at Memorial Sloan Kettering, there was Margo Urban, the wife of the celebrated private investigator Bo Deitl. They had bumped into Nick at the hospital. Margo was suffering from lymphoma, and she shared a doctor, Stephen Nimer, with Nora. Nick asked them to keep the secret. For five years they did.

In addition to Nora's doctors and their staffs, a vast number of nurses and hospital administrators knew of Nora's condition. In an era of rancid Internet gossip sites, I kept expecting news about Nora to become public. It never did, not because she was of no interest, but rather because she was so cherished.

On the Oprah show back when she said how much she wanted to eat good bread and butter every day, she also said she would be miserable at dying. Oprah asked her if she had fears, and she said yeah. "I'm afraid of dying. That's the reality. I don't think I'm going to be very good at it. Really, I don't. I mean, there are people who are really, you know, there are people who die magnificently. I am going to—it's going to be horrible."

Room 242 began to fill with people. The days spilled into one another. Nick, Delia, Max, Jacob, Amanda, and I trailed Nora from the seventh to the fourteenth floor. Jacob, peripatetic and twitchy as a ganglion, worked off his grief by phoning the hard news to those who had to know. Max, the tattoos on his arms that Nora hated concealed by his shirt, glumly waited. Hallie came from Massachusetts and Amy from California and, a bit later, her old friend Diane Sokolow joined the vigil. Ken Auletta rushed off to India on assignment for the *New Yorker*.

Nora asked Nick to contact Louise Grunwald, her friend and the successor to Lee Bailey as her mentor as a hostess and, more pertinently, the widow of Henry Grunwald, the former editor in chief of Time Inc., later U.S. ambassador to Austria but also the son of a Viennese librettist. Henry Grunwald, who died in 2005, had prepared instructions for his memorial service, not only the speakers but the music to be played—a bit of Haydn's Sun Quartets and a sprinkling of opera, *La Bohème* and *The Marriage of Figaro*, with a rousing "Battle Hymn of the Republic" as the penultimate number. Nora had been appropriately impressed by the service. Grunwald's instructions had been placed in a file labeled "Exit."

Nora had prepared a version of her own. It, too, was labeled "Exit." It suggested the speakers she wanted at her memorial service, its length (forty-seven minutes), and suggested a venue, the auditorium of the Ethical Culture School on Central Park West. She did not want a languid memorial service with too many speakers making too many speeches mostly about themselves—Nora harshly reviewed memorial speakers who felt that the loss was mostly their own—and she asked that the event be held soon after her death, a prolonged waiting period being "creepy."

Nora's memorial service was held at Alice Tully Hall in Lincoln Center. Nora was finally wrong. The Ethical Culture School was way too small. About eight hundred people came that day for a program that Nora had largely planned. (Her "Exit" instructions even told Nick where to get the sandwiches for the smaller reception he'd give the day following her death.)

There were eleven speakers in all. Marty Short led off and then I followed and then, in probably not the right order, Delia, Max, Jacob, Meryl Streep, Mike Nichols, Rosie O'Donnell, Tom Hanks and Rita Wilson, and J.J. Sacha. A large picture of Nora hung as a backdrop. She was dressed in her customary white blouse with a high collar. She smiled and I smiled, recalling her condemnation of anyone who ducked a funeral by saying that the deceased "would understand."

"Well, I would not understand," Nora used to say. I saw her up there, taking names.

Before the program began, we eulogists gathered in a room backstage. J.J. issued last-minute instructions of some sort—it is all a blur—and then had some moments of intense anxiety in which to steady ourselves. People greeted one another, but there was not a lot of talk. Many of the eulogists were seasoned performers, but still they maintained the silence of the terrified.

It was an emotionally draining event. Most of the speakers were still coming to grips with the suddenness of Nora's death, and they were, I think, also measuring themselves against her. She was a eulogist without parallel, and the only good reason I could think of for dying was to be sent off by Nora. Meryl Streep acknowledged what we all felt. "Normally what I would have done on a day like today is call her up and get some jokes and some advice," Streep said in her eulogy. "She'd ask me who was speaking and in what order, and I'd eventually make her write the speech for me."

We were all on our own.

Tom Hanks and Rita Wilson did a skit imitating Nora and Nick, particularly Nick's ability to solve almost any problem with a large tip. Rita, as Nora, started fine, but composure slowly slipped from her. She cried. She soldiered on, playing Nora to Tom's Nick, but her grief overwhelmed her humor. She couldn't hold back the tears.

Hanks, clearly distraught, nevertheless stayed composed. When he and Rita had finished, when the program itself was completed, Hanks met with Colin Callender and George Wolfe. They told Hanks he had to do *Lucky Guy* for Nora.

"Let's do it," Hanks said.

In the lobby, mourners were being served pink champagne.

Nora used to scoff at people who spoke for the dead: This is what they would have wanted—something like that. And yet, Nora's memorial service was exactly what she would have wanted, although she couldn't have known it. But back in room 242, back where she was dying, the immensity of the mourning was not yet evident, not to her, not to us. Nora was our friend. She was the hostess, the game player, the organizer, the writer, the director—well-known, of course, but not famous. Not in that way. No. Of course not. Even she had it wrong. The Ethical Culture School. No. Not even close.

The nurses, I think, sensed the truth. They walked in and out of the room, gravely professional in their demeanor, moving silently, as if on the sterile hospital air itself. They said nothing.

The room filled and then spilled out into the hallway. Nick came and went, doing the necessary next-of-kin chores, never saying much. Mostly, he sat by the side of the bed, hands clasped on top of the sheets, slumped over in a defeat so total that pain itself would have been relief.

The numbers—platelets, reds, whites, and the like—recovered a bit and then, confusingly, went their own ways, some up, some down, some no change at all. There was reason to hope, a cruel tease, then very quickly no reason to hope at all. Nora slipped away, asleep then awake, then asleep again. Friends, relatives went in and out, sometimes talking to Nora, sometimes just peering at her. The morphine drip was applied.

I went home and attended to Mona. It was evening, time for her medications, and that night it occurred to me that there was something urgent I needed to say to Nora. In the morning, I hurried to the hospital and sat on the bed as close to her as I could get. She was asleep. I got closer. I told her that I loved her. I had told her that before, of course, but not enough, not nearly enough. Now I said it to her and then I said it again. She opened her eyes and looked at me and said, "Who is that?"

"Richard," I said, dismayed that she didn't know who I was.

She laughed. "I know that."

She laughed again and so did I.

She always made me laugh.

Acknowledgments

Writing this book was both an exercise in nostalgia and discovery. I knew Nora Ephron very well indeed but memories of her kept sneaking back into my recollection through the anecdotes of others. At the same time, her many friends had their own memories of Nora—ones I shared and ones I knew nothing about. Here, with immense gratitude, are their names: Ken Auletta, Alice Arlen, Joyce Ashley, Francie Barnard, Carl Bernstein, Bo Burlingham, Patricia Bosworth, Marie Brenner, Marcia Burick, Colin Callender, Kate Capshaw, Lisa Caputo, Jennifer Carden, Ellen Chesler, Gail Collins, Barbara Cochran, Alexander Cohen, Deborah Copaken, Avery Corman, Meghan Daum, Dianne Dreyer, Peter Davis, Barry Diller, Kristin Doidge, Jim Dwyer, Lee Eisenberg, Hallie Ephron, Ann Fleuchaus, Al Franken, Roy Furman, Sandy Gallin, Ina Garten, David Geffen, Peter Goldman, Robert Gottlieb, Dan Greenburg, Lynn Grossman, Louise Grunwald, Clyde Haberman, Tom Hanks, Pete Hamill, Eddie Hayes, Arianna Huffington, Edward Kosner, Rosalind Krauss, Aaron Latham, John Leo, Lucy Le Page, Michael Levett, Christopher Lospalluto, Bryan Lourd, Mary Ann Madden, Anthony Mancini, Laurence Mark, James McCauley, Alice MacAlary, Steve Martin, Lawrence Meyer, Anne Navasky,

Victor Navasky, Lynn Nesbit, Mike Nichols, Stephen Nimer, Jack O'Brien, Amy Pascal, Maurie Perl, Abigail Pogrebin, Stanley Pottinger, Sally Quinn, Frank Rich, David Remnick, Howard Rosenman, Ann Roth, Scott Rudin, Meg Ryan, J.J. Sacha, Diane Sawyer, Deborah Solomon, Robert Spitzler, Liz Smith, Martin Short, Lynn Sherr, Joel Schumacher, Sasha Spielberg, Steven Spielberg, Alessandra Stanley, Meryl Streep, Howard Stringer, Gay Talese, Rusty Unger, Amanda Urban, Mary Pat Walsh, Jane Wenner, Jann Wenner, Jim Wiatt, Rita Wilson, Margo Winkler, George Wolfe, Tom Wolfe and—out of order alphabetically—Walter Isaacson. He suggested I write this book.

I am indebted to Alice Crites of the *Washington Post*'s research staff for her magical ability to find just about anything ever printed and to Emily Loose for her heroic attempt to organize my chaotic manuscript. Stuart Roberts of Simon & Schuster is not only a deft editor but repeatedly had to tutor me in the ways of the S&S computer programs and he did it always with great patience and inexplicable good nature. Along the way, I had the help of Elizabeth Gay, who handled publicity; Nicole McArdle, who did the online marketing; Ruth Lee-Mui, a designer who got it just right; Martha Schwartz, production editor; and Elisa Rivlin, who read the manuscript as both a lawyer and, it turned out, a fact-checker. I thank them all.

Alice Mayhew was the editor of *All The President's Men*, Carl Bernstein and Bob Woodward's 1974 book on their Watergate reporting. That's when we met, and I was impressed with her editing then and I am even more impressed with it now that she has worked on two books of mine. She is a skilled editor, a steady guide through the vicissitudes of book writing, and enormously good fun. She is a gift.

Index

About the Author

RICHARD COHEN is a nationally syndicated columnist for *The Washington Post*, where he has covered national politics and foreign affairs since 1976. His writing has appeared in *The New Republic, The Nation, Esquire, GQ, The New York Review of Books*, and many other publications.